lonely planet

TASMANIA

Andrew Bain, Charles Rawlings-Way

Meet our writers

Andrew Bain

@bainonbike

Andrew is a travel writer who was drawn to Tasmania almost 20 years ago by the presence of so many outdoor opportunities. Any escape to the mountains – Cradle Mountain, the Southwest, the Walls of Jerusalem – is a trip to his happy place.

Charles Rawlings-Way

@crawlingsway

Charles is an ordinary swimmer but loves beaches – even just for a moody stroll on a rainy afternoon, somewhere like Verona Sands. He was born in Devon, grew up in Hobart, and is back in Hobart again after 25 years of adventures elsewhere.

LIAM PREECE/SHUTTERSTOCK

PREVIOUS SPREAD: BY VISUAL COLLECTIVE/SHUTTERSTOCK

Northwest & West Coast 190
Highlands Midlands & Cradle Country 106
East Coast 128
Hobart & Around 40
Turrakana/ Tasman Peninsula & the Southeast 80
Zeehan
Trial Harbour
Queenstown
Strahan
Cradle Mountain-Lake St Clair National Park
Leeawuleena/ Lake St Clair
Lake Burbury
Derwent Bridge
Lake King William
Macquarie Harbour
Franklin–Gordon Wild Rivers National Park
Southwest Conservation Area
Gordon River
Lake Gordon
Strathgordon
Lake Pedder
Southwest National Park
Wreck Bay
Bathurst Harbour
Hartz Mountains National Park
Southport
Maatsuyker Group
Southern Ocean
Yingina/ Great Lake
Lake Echo
Tarraleah
Bothwell
Ouse
Hamilton
Mount Field National Park
New Norfolk
Lake St Clair (2½hrs)
Huon Valley (½hr)
Huonville
Geeveston
Cygnet
Kingston
Kettering
Alonnah
Bruny Island
South Bruny National Park
Campbell Town
Ross
Lake Sorell
Lake Crescent
Oatlands
Melton Mowbray
Kempton
Richmond
Sorell
Lauderdale
Turrakana/ Tasman Peninsula
Storm Bay
Port Arthur
Tasman National Park
Lake Leake
Swansea
Bicheno
Coles Bay
Freycinet National Park
Schouten Island
Triabunna
Orford
Maria Island National Park
National Park
0 50 km
0 25 miles

Get an art fix, underground. Tee off across the Southern Ocean. Walk in the company of Australia's most spectacular mountains, or atop its highest sea cliffs. Drink world-beating whisky and wine. Chase waterfalls. Flow through the forest on a world-class mountain-bike trail. Hear growers' stories as you sample produce fresh out of the ground. Find the sort of empty beach that would be crowded almost anywhere else in the world. Shuck an oyster straight off the racks.

This is Tasmania.

TURN THE PAGE AND START PLANNING
YOUR NEXT BEST TRIP →

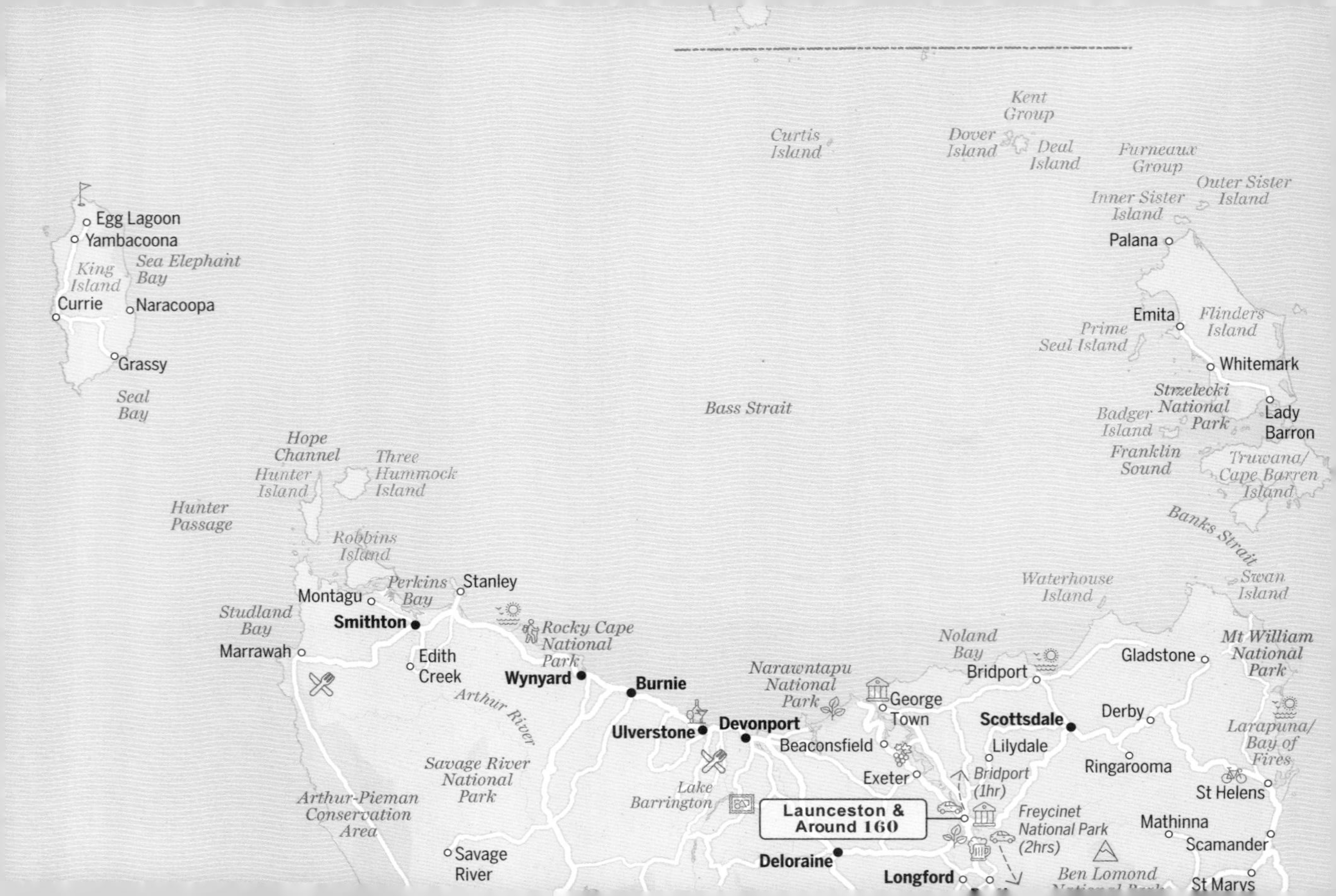

Kent Group
Curtis Island
Dover Island
Deal Island
Furneaux Group
Outer Sister Island
Inner Sister Island
Palana
Egg Lagoon
Yambacoona
King Island
Sea Elephant Bay
Currie
Naracoopa
Grassy
Seal Bay
Emita
Flinders Island
Prime Seal Island
Whitemark
Strzelecki National Park
Badger Island
Lady Barron
Bass Strait
Franklin Sound
Truwana/ Cape Barren Island
Hope Channel
Three Hummock Island
Hunter Island
Hunter Passage
Banks Strait
Robbins Island
Swan Island
Waterhouse Island
Perkins Bay
Stanley
Montagu
Studland Bay
Smithton
Rocky Cape National Park
Marrawah
Edith Creek
Noland Bay
Mt William National Park
Gladstone
Bridport
Wynyard
Burnie
Narawntapu National Park
George Town
Arthur River
Scottsdale
Derby
Ulverstone
Devonport
Larapuna/ Bay of Fires
Beaconsfield
Lilydale
Ringarooma
Savage River National Park
Exeter
Bridport (1hr)
St Helens
Lake Barrington
Arthur-Pieman Conservation Area
Launceston & Around 160
Freycinet National Park (2hrs)
Mathinna
Scamander
Savage River
Deloraine
Longford
Ben Lomond
St Marys

Above Solomons Jewels Lake, Walls of Jerusalem National Park (p113)

Acknowledgement of Country

Lonely Planet would like to acknowledge all First Nations people throughout this country, who have nurtured and maintained the land since time immemorial. This guide was written on, and is written about, the lands of many diverse nations. We recognise the unique and ongoing connection that Aboriginal peoples have to land and waters and thank them for their efforts to preserve them. We pay our respects to Elders past and present and extend this respect to any Aboriginal or Torres Strait Islander people who may be reading this guide. We also recognise the ongoing efforts of Aboriginal peoples for reconciliation, justice, and social, cultural and economic self-determination. Sovereignty was never ceded. Australia always was, and always will be, Aboriginal land.

Cultural Sensitivity Warning

Aboriginal and Torres Strait Islander readers are advised that this guide may contain names and images of people who have since passed away.

Contents

NESS VANDERBURGH FOR LONELY PLANET

Above Kanamaluka/Tamar River, Launceston (p160)

WALK THIS **WAY**

National parks cover around 40% of Tasmania, with World Heritage wilderness blanketing 20% of the state, so it's little wonder that Australia's best bushwalks live here. Tracks wind through alpine valleys, ascend to rugged summits, disappear into deep temperate rainforests, inch across clifftops, and thread along empty coastlines and beaches.

Left Larapuna/Bay of Fires (p141)
Right Three Capes Track (p96)
Below Overland Track (p113)

→ GREAT SHORT WALKS

Check out the multitude of day walks on offer with 60 Great Short Walks, compiled by the Parks and Wildlife Service.

SUMMIT ART CREATIONS/SHUTTERSTOCK

PERMIT ME

Book well ahead on the Overland and Three Capes tracks – only 34 independent hikers a day can set out on the former and 48 on the latter.

RIGHT: FILEDIMAGE/SHUTTERSTOCK, LEFT: JOHN WHITE PHOTOS/GETTY IMAGES

↑ COMFORT WALKING

Find the near-complete suite of Tasmania's guided bush-walks – most with a touch of trail opulence – at the Great Walks of Tasmania website (greatwalkstasmania.com).

Best Walking Experiences

- **Weave past some of the state's most spectacular mountains on the Overland Track.** (p113)
- **Immerse yourself in the old palawa (Tasmanian Aboriginal) ways on the First Nations–led wukalina Walk.** (p154)
- **Step out in style on the clifftop Three Capes Track, lined with plush public huts.** (p96)
- **Discover Launceston's wild heart on a stroll through Cataract Gorge.** (p173)
- **Cross through the Hazards to squidge your toes in the sands of Wineglass Bay.** (p142)

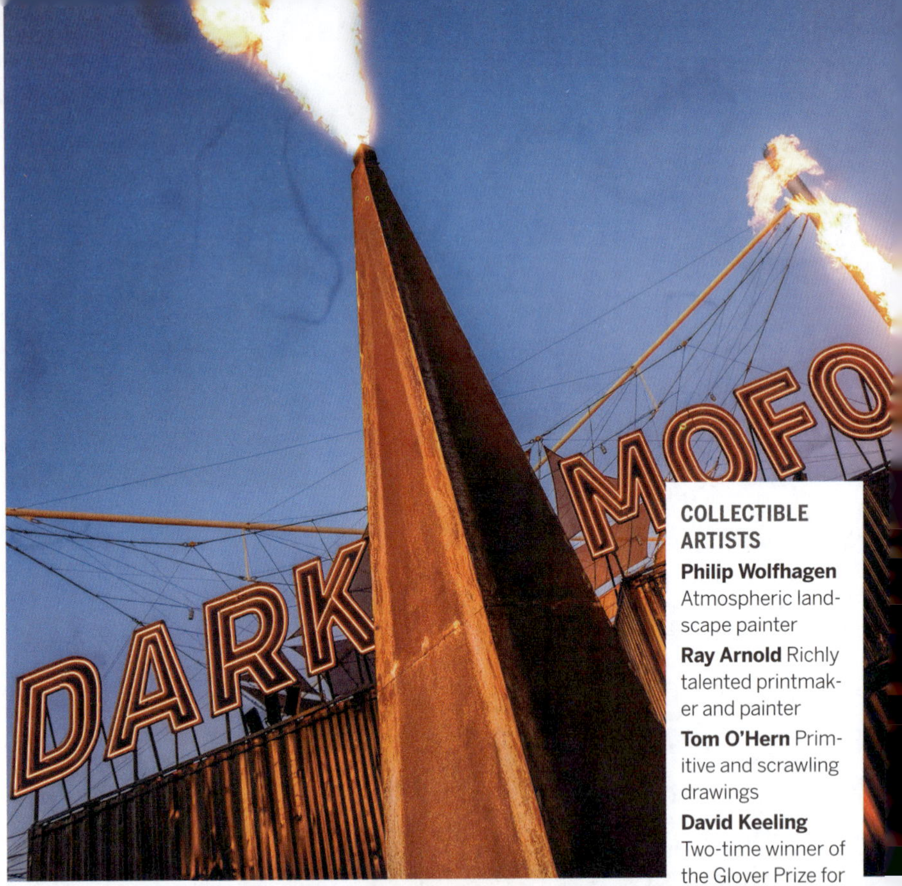

COLLECTIBLE ARTISTS

Philip Wolfhagen Atmospheric landscape painter

Ray Arnold Richly talented printmaker and painter

Tom O'Hern Primitive and scrawling drawings

David Keeling Two-time winner of the Glover Prize for landscapes

Tom Samek A distinct whimsical style that you'll see from restaurant walls to gift shops

CULTURE VULTURES

An underground art gallery designed to shock, a country town with 200-plus murals, a festival framed around a nude swim, a Dalí drawing inside a historic warehouse, an ancient culture finally enjoying a rebirth. Tasmania's art, museums and festival calendar makes it clear that this is a little island big on culture.

Left Dark Mofo festival (p65)
Right Performer, Dark Mofo
Below MONA (p52)

→ THE MONA EFFECT

It's easy to get blinded by MONA's presence, but don't ignore the equally vibrant arts scene in Tasmania's above-ground galleries.

TERMINALCRAZY/500PX/GETTY IMAGES

STREET ART

Hobart's lanes and the levee walls of Launceston's Royal Park are colourful canvases, while Sheffield is Australia's mural capital.

RIGHT: CHAMELEONSEYE/SHUTTERSTOCK, LEFT: MICHAEL R EVANS/SHUTTERSTOCK

THE PRIZE OF PRIZES

Each March, Evandale displays entrants from the Glover Prize, Australia's most prestigious landscape art award. You can even vote for the People's Choice Award.

Best Cultural Experiences

- **Head beneath the earth to be awed, angered or astonished – or all three – at MONA.** (p52)
- **Wrap up warm for Dark Mofo's eerie and unnerving shows, or strip off and get cold for its nude swim.** (p65)
- **Watch fine art emerge from mined earth at Queenstown's Unconformity festival.** (p214)
- **Find the world's largest collection of Salvador Dalí drawings at Launceston's dAda mUse.** (p167)
- **Discover walls as historic as the displays at TMAG, set around Tasmania's oldest existing public building.** (p59)

MEET THE PRODUCER

The farm gate is rarely closed in Tasmania, with producers welcoming visitors into a range of experiences and tastes. Hunt for winter truffles, pick your own summer berries and source your dinner ingredients direct from the hand that harvested them. Food miles here are often measured in metres.

Left Strawberry farmer **Right** Havilah (p188), Launceston **Below** Tasmanian truffles

→ CULINARY CITY

In 2021 Launceston became only the second city in Australia (along with Bendigo) to be crowned a UNESCO City of Gastronomy.

NESS VANDERBURGH/LONELY PLANET

TASTING TRAIL

Gather a holiday feast on a road trip along the Tasmania Tasting Trail, which features almost 40 producers between Launceston and Smithton.

RIGHT: BLOOMBERG CREATIVE PHOTOS/GETTY IMAGES. LEFT: CHAMELEONSEYE/SHUTTERSTOCK

↑ NATURAL ADVANTAGE

The key ingredients to the freshness of Tasmania's food are the rich red volcanic soils of the north and what has been officially declared the world's cleanest air.

Best Produce Experiences

▶ **Hunt with the dogs for black truffles at the Truffle Farm.** (p231)

▶ **Spin past the world's only drive-through oyster window at Get Shucked.** (p102)

▶ **Cook up your own storm with a cooking class at the Agrarian Kitchen.** (p62)

▶ **Forage for a six-course long lunch with a Farm Gate Market stallholder.** (p74)

WORLD-BEATERS

World's Best Sparkling Wine 2020 House of Arras EJ Carr Late Disgorged 2004

World's Best Single Cask Single Malt 2018 & 2019 Sullivans Cove Distillery

Single Malt Whisky of the Year 2025, London Spirits Competition Callington Mill Distillery

WINE, WHISKY & BEER

Once upon a time, Tasmanians believed there were only two drinks in the world – Cascade and Boag's – but these days the state is pumping out some of the world's best wine, whisky, cider, gin, craft beer, vodka and rum, with the awards to prove it. Cellar doors and taprooms might easily delay your travels.

Left Sullivans Cove Distillery (p47) **Right** Taylor & Smith Gin, Salamanca Market (p74) **Below** Australian beer

→ EXPERIMENTS IN SPIRIT

Tasmanian distillers are an experimental lot. Among other drops, you'll find a vodka made from sheep whey and the world's first spirit distilled from sassafras.

LIES OUWERKERK/SHUTTERSTOCK

DEDICATED TRAILS

There's a driving trail for every drop: the Tasmanian Whisky and Spirits Trail, Tasmanian Beer Trail, Tasmanian Cider Trail and four wine trails.

RIGHT: FRANKZ01/SHUTTERSTOCK, LEFT: ADAM GIBSON/SULLIVANS COVE

↑ HOPS TO IT

The secret to all that great Tasmanian craft beer? Bushy Park, northwest of Hobart, is one of the southern hemisphere's largest hops gardens.

Best Drinking Experiences

- **Tour the Tamar Valley, Tassie's top wine region.** (p182)
- **Share a single malt with a dinosaur at Evolve Spirits Bar.** (p47)
- **Stroll between craft brewers In Hobart; there are half a dozen within 2km of the CBD.** (p76)
- **Wander the grand grounds of Lark Distillery, Tasmania's OG whisky producer.** (p47)

OLGA KASHUBIN/SHUTTERSTOCK

FALLS FACTS

Tasmania's highest waterfall Montezuma Falls (104m)

East coast's highest waterfall St Columba Falls (90m)

Database of waterfalls waterfallsoftasmania.com.au

CHASING WATERFALLS

There are dozens of accessible waterfalls across Tasmania pouring out of the mountains, tipping over cliffs, brightening dark rainforests, and often requiring little more than a short walk to view. The first bit of land ever protected in the state was around a waterfall.

Best Waterfalls

- **Connect a trio of Mt Field waterfalls on the Three Falls Circuit walk.** (p51)
- **Walk or cycle along an old mining tramway to the state's highest waterfall, Montezuma Falls.** (p232)
- **Search the slopes of Kunanyi/Mt Wellington for more than half a dozen falls.** (p69)
- **Admire the perfect form of Liffey Falls, pouring down the slopes of the Great Western Tiers.** (p115)

TEE TIMES

Tasmania is home to Australia's oldest golf course, but it's a string of new links courses across the north coast and King Island that have chipped in to secure Tasmania's status among the world's great golfing destinations.

INESA HILL/SHUTTERSTOCK

→ TOP COURSES

In 2025 Golf Australia rated Cape Wickham as the top golf course in Australia. Barnbougle Dunes, Barnbougle Lost Farm and Ocean Dunes were the second, third and fifth best.

DAVID CANNON/GETTY IMAGES

Best Golf Experiences

- **Find coastal golf excellence beneath Australia's tallest lighthouse at Cape Wickham Links.** (p226)
- **Succumb to the distraction of the views at Barnbougle Dunes.** (p187)
- **Tee off into postcard scenes along King Island's frayed edge at Ocean Dunes.** (p226)
- **Discover new hazards – grazing sheep – at Ratho Farm, the oldest golf course outside of Scotland.** (p117)

★ PLAYING THE PART

Find reward at Ratho Farm by playing your round in a kilt – Ratho will shout you a beer if you do so.

Far left Horseshoe Falls (p51), Mt Field National Park **Top left** Barnbougle Dunes (p187) **Bottom left** Barnbougle Lost Farm (p187)

Length of the Franklin River 130km

Kilometres of MTB trails at Derby 125

Largest wave recorded in Australia 18.4m at Cape Sorell, near Strahan, in 2010

ADAM TAYLOR/GETTY IMAGES

ADVENTURE **ISLAND**

Ride legendary mountain-bike trails, ponder some of the world's fiercest surf waves, raft rapids past 2000-year-old trees, kayak beneath Australia's tallest sea cliffs (or simply into Hobart's docks for fish and chips), dive into Australia's largest sea-cave system and walk cultural paths along the vibrant Larapuna/Bay of Fires. It's just another day in Tasmania.

Best Adventures

- **Ride a marathon-length mountain-bike trail to a Bay of Fires beach.** (p140)
- **Raft into deep and pure wilderness on the Franklin River.** (p236)
- **Surf one of the world's best waves – and have it to yourself – on King Island.** (p227)
- **Touch geological greatness (or at least kayak near to it) on a paddle to the Totem Pole.** (p87)

SEAFOOD, EAT FOOD

Wrapped in ocean, Tasmania is unsurprisingly rich in seafood and, in recent years, seafood experiences. Whether you kayak to a floating lunch in Hobart, wade hip deep through oyster racks or take a boat trip to gather your own seafood banquet, the onc guarantee is freshness.

AUSCAPE/GETTY IMAGES

★ SALMON SPAT

Tasmanian salmon farming has been in the crosshairs since the publication of Richard Flanagan's book *Toxic* in 2021. Have a read and make up your own mind.

GARYENCHANTINGPHOTO/GETTY IMAGES

Best Seafood Experiences

▶ **Slurp down oysters atop a dune overlooking the leases at Melshell Oyster Shack.** (p134)

▶ **Tuck into old-fashioned fish and chips from a floating fish van as the sun sets on Hobart's docks.** (p77)

▶ **Celebrate the state's favourite bivalves at Bridport's Tassie Scallop Fiesta.** (p167)

▶ **Don waders and tour the oyster racks at Freycinet Marine Farm.** (p134)

← AW, SHUCKS

Want Tasmania's freshest oysters? Head straight to the source, with many oyster farms now running their own farm-gate eateries on site.

Far left Dove Lake (p114) **Top left** Oyster leases, Freycinet Marine Farm (p134) **Bottom left** Fresh oysters

↘ Blooming Bridestowe

The world's largest privately owned lavender farm is purple perfection from December through to early February.

Cygnet Folk Festival

Cygnet's annual gathering of guitars, mandolins and duelling banjos brings Woodstock-style vibes to the earthy Huon Valley town.

Cygnet

▶ p99

Christmas Day, Boxing Day, New Year's Day and Australia Day are public holidays. January sees an exodus to the beach.

Festivale

Launceston's City Park hosts this three-day chill-out-on-the-grass affair, with Tasmanian food, wine and beer, and plenty of live tunes.

Launceston

▶ p167

DECEMBER

Average daytime max: 20°C
Days of rainfall: 7

JANUARY

Tasmania in SUMMER

LEFT TO RIGHT:LAWRENCE_CHUNG/SHUTTERSTOCK, KATACARIX/SHUTTERSTOCK, CHAMELEONSEYE/GETTY IMAGES, ALEX FONDA/SHUTTERSTOCK
BACKGROUND IMAGE: JAX10289/SHUTTERSTOCK

Demand for accommodation peaks during summer school holidays, which stretch from just before Christmas to early February. Book ahead.

→ Sydney to Hobart Yacht Race

The world's most arduous open-ocean yacht race sails to its finish in Hobart around 28 December.

Hobart

▶ p65

↑ Taste of Summer

Indulge at Hobart's waterfront food festival as the Sydney to Hobart yachts nip across the finish line.

Hobart

▶ p65

Average daytime max: 22°C
Days of rainfall: 6

FEBRUARY

Average daytime max: 22°C
Days of rainfall: 5

↙ DIY Berry Season

Prepare to stain your fingers – the berry bushes are bulging at pick-your-own farms across the state.

Packing Notes

The UV runs high in Tasmania; bring plenty of sunscreen and a wide-brimmed hat.

↘ Turning of the Fagus

One of Australia's few deciduous native trees, the fagus, ignites the alpine regions with autumn colours.

Ten Days on the Island

Spreading the arts love across the state, Australia's only statewide multi-arts festival is a biennial event (odd-numbered years).

Peak travel season gets a momentary surge over Easter, which often coincides with school holidays.

↓ Autumn Tones

It's not all about natives. Find vibrant autumn colours on New Norfolk's Esplanade walk, the Royal Tasmanian Botanical Gardens and in Ross.

MARCH

APRIL

Average daytime max: 20°C
Days of rainfall: 6

Tasmania in AUTUMN

FROM LEFT: DAVID LADE/SHUTTERSTOCK, KIRSTEN COVINGTON/SHUTTERSTOCK, SEAN DAVEY/GETTY IMAGES, WRIGHT OUT THERE/SHUTTERSTOCK, LKONYA/SHUTTERSTOCK. **BACKGROUND IMAGE:** TARAS VYSHNYA/SHUTTERSTOCK

→ Perfect Paddling

Winds typically ease through autumn, making it the ideal season to kayak the coastline.

↘ Surf's Up

The big swells are starting to roll in along the east coast, King Island and the grandest place of all, Shipstern Bluff.

TrailGraze

The farm gates are propped wide open all weekend during this foodie event along the length of the Tasmania Tasting Trail.

Northwest

▸ p230

Average daytime max: 17°C
Days of rainfall: 7

MAY

Average daytime max: 15°C
Days of rainfall: 7

← Forest Fungi

Forest walks are brightened by a profusion of colourful fungi. Can you find the elusive ghost mushroom?

Packing Notes

Pack for warm days and cold days; the seasons are fast on the turn.

→ Dark Mofo

Hobart celebrates all things dark and subversive at this mid-winter festival. Fancy a nude swim with a couple of thousand friends?

📍 Hobart

▸ p65

The King's Birthday, on the second Monday in June, is the lone winter public holiday.

↙ Whisky Warmth

Whisky bars such as Evolve and The Still come into their own on cold southern nights.

📍 Hobart

▸ p46

Festival of Voices

Tune up your vocal chords for the Big Sing Bonfire, the star event at this homage to song.

📍 Hobart

▸ p65

JUNE

Average daytime max: 12°C
Days of rainfall: 7

JULY

Tasmania in WINTER

FROM LEFT: ANDREW MERRY/GETTY IMAGES, CASSIE SULLIVAN/SULLIVANS COVE, BLOOMBERG/GETTY IMAGES, BRUCE GRAHAM/SHUTTERSTOCK, FILEDIMAGE/SHUTTERSTOCK, BACKGROUND IMAGE: KEIICHIHIKI/GETTY IMAGES

→ Truffle Hunt

The truffle dogs are on the scent in winter. Join them for a truffle treasure hunt at the Truffle Farm.

▶ p231

↓ Ski Season

OK, it's not Aspen, but Tasmania's two ski fields – Ben Lomond and Mt Mawson – are into their low-key seasons.

📍 Ben Lomond & Mt Mawson

▶ p178

Bicheno Beams

Light up a winter seaside visit to Bicheno with two nightly laser light shows playing in the sky for three weeks.

📍 Bicheno

Average daytime max: 12°C
Days of rainfall: 8

AUGUST

Average daytime max: 13°C
Days of rainfall: 8

← Cradle in Snow

Tasmania's most famous mountain, Cradle Mountain, never looks better than when it's covered in snow.

📍 Cradle Mountain

Packing Notes

Down-jacket season. Beanies, thick socks, gloves and thermals complete the outfit.

Junction Arts Festival

Four days of live music, theatre, installations, street art, walking tours and dance in Launceston.

Launceston

▶ p167

The Unconformity

Rough-and-ready Queenstown's biennial celebration of the arts takes place in venues such as mine shafts and a limestone quarry.

Queenstown

▶ p214

↗ Tulip Time

Blooming good times at the Table Cape Tulip Farm when the tulips burst into colour beside a lighthouse.

Table Cape

▶ p223

Great Eastern Wine Week

Four days of clinking wine glasses with winemakers and producers at east-coast wineries. Cheers.

▶ p152

SEPTEMBER

Average daytime max: 15°C
Days of rainfall: 9

OCTOBER

Tasmania in SPRING

FROM LEFT: KATIE STEVENS PHOTOGRAPHY/SHUTTERSTOCK, ARTIE PHOTOGRAPHY (ARTIE NG)/GETTY IMAGES, ELLGEEMAC/SHUTTERSTOCK, MLHARING/GETTY IMAGES
BACKGROUND IMAGE: GLANZPUNKT/SHUTTERSTOCK

Don't mention public holidays to a Tasmanian. They have none in spring.

↗ Water World

The most impressive time of year for waterfalls across the state thanks to rain and snowmelt.

↑ Whale Watching

Humpback whales are returning past the east coast to Antarctic waters. You can even try seeing them from a kayak.

Average daytime max: 17°C
Days of rainfall: 9

NOVEMBER

Average daytime max: 19°C
Days of rainfall: 8

← Fish Frenzy

Trout season opens in August, with the best fishing starting around October.

Packing Notes

Your windproofs should be in the suitcase. The weather is warming, but the winds are blowing.

DEEP SOUTH

Trip Builder

TAKE YOUR PICK OF MUST-SEES AND HIDDEN GEMS

Tasmania's capital, Hobart, sits handily nestled in nature, making it a short trip from urban streets to dramatic coastlines and high mountains. There are convicts and towering cliffs in one direction, and the edge of wilderness and the Southern Ocean in the other.

Trip Notes

Hub town Hobart

How long Allow 2 weeks

Getting around Hire a car on arrival at Hobart Airport for the greatest freedom. Buses can get you to Huon Valley towns and Turrakana/Tasman Peninsula, but not to the attractions around them.

Tip Visitors typically base themselves in Hobart and radiate beyond on day trips, but to get a real sense of southern life, spend a few nights out of the city.

Coal River Valley

Follow an avenue of vineyards and food producers to Richmond, arguably Tasmania's prettiest town.

20mins from Hobart

Hobart

Discover a place that blurs the lines between city and nature. Even its famous art gallery is cut into the earth.

Port Arthur

Set aside a day to explore the Port Arthur Historic Site and then range beyond to caves, beaches and coastal cruises.

1½hrs from Hobart

Tasman National Park

Stand atop 300m-high cliffs, or even at sea level, to appreciate that geology is doing crazy-good things in this narrow coastal park.

1¼hrs from Hobart

Bruny Island

Walk a beach, watch wildlife or wolf down cheese, oysters and whisky...island life is pretty damn good on Bruny.

+ *1hr from Hobart*

EAST COAST
Trip Builder

TAKE YOUR PICK OF MUST-SEES AND HIDDEN GEMS

The east coast is Tasmania's sunny coast, with beaches as good as any in the country and a laid-back vibe to match. Come for Wineglass Bay, but stick around for actual wine, wildlife and other stunning beaches.

Trip Notes

Hub towns St Helens, Bicheno

How long Allow 10 days

Getting around There are Tassielink buses to east-coast towns from Hobart, but you'll need your own wheels to find those empty beaches in between.

Tip Be prepared for time-consuming detours to see some of the coast's finest features, including Freycinet Peninsula, Larapuna/Bay of Fires and Maria Island.

Mt William National Park
Visit a park where the 'mount' might be just a hill, but the wildlife is plentiful, the beaches are dazzling and Tasmanian Aboriginal culture is on full display.
2¼hrs from Launceston

Douglas-Apsley National Park
Look beyond the coast to find this gorge-gouged national park wrapped around the hills and dry forest behind Bicheno.
2hrs from Launceston

FROM TOP: KEIICHIHIKI/GETTY IMAGES, SOPHIE COSTELLO/SHUTTERSTOCK

Larapuna/Bay of Fires

Indulge in the classic beach dream of white sand, clear blue sea and granite headlands smothered in orange lichen.

2¼hrs from Launceston

St Helens

Stay in the coast's largest town, bookended by sublime beaches and fun mountain-bike trails, with good restaurants completing the picture.

2hrs from Launceston

Bicheno

Step into a town where quality surf and seafood meet equally good beaches and cafes, with the potential for whale and penguin sightings to boot.

2hrs from Launceston

Swansea

Thread along the coast into Swansea, with its Freycinet views and proximity to the region's vineyards.

1¾hrs from Hobart

Freycinet National Park

Spend time in Tasmania's oldest and perhaps best-loved national park, which protects Wineglass Bay, but so much more. Coles Bay, at its edge, is the perfect holiday town.

2¼hrs from Launceston

Maria Island National Park

Skip across the sea to this island of curious cliffs, airy peaks, copious wildlife and the World Heritage–listed Darlington convict settlement.

+ *2hrs from Hobart*

NORTH COAST
Trip Builder

TAKE YOUR PICK OF MUST-SEES AND HIDDEN GEMS

Tasmania's most heavily populated edge is also a place where the world's cleanest air blows through, with the state's most fertile soils underfoot. It's city attractions one moment, and rural, beach or mountain experiences just a few minutes later.

Trip Notes

Hub towns Launceston, Devonport, Burnie

How long Allow 10 days

Getting around If you're just town-hopping – Launceston, Devonport and Burnie – it's possible to get about by bus, but the world opens up with your own vehicle.

Tip The north coast is the easiest region in Tasmania to explore with your own vehicle, with the *Spirit of Tasmania* ferry from Geelong docking in Devonport.

Wynyard
Find brilliant colours at the Table Cape Tulip Farm, prehistory in the cliffs at Fossil Bluff, and a vibrant cafe culture in town.
50mins from Devonport

Burnie
With platypus in its waters and whisky in its veins, gritty Burnie is a perfect paradox.
35mins from Devonport

Penguin
Pause to meet local producers and to walk in the Dial Range. And, yes, there are penguins...nearby, at least.
25mins from Devonport

FROM LEFT: PAWAN KAWAN/SHUTTERSTOCK, TRABANTOS/SHUTTERSTOCK, CONY SUMORO/SHUTTERSTOCK

Narawntapu National Park
Head to the beach-lined lawns of the so-called Serengeti of Tasmania, which transform with kangaroo crowds in the evening.
1¼hrs from Launceston

Derby
Discover the mountain-bike wunderkind – an unloved tin-mining town transformed into one of the world's hottest trail networks.
1½hrs from Launceston

Devonport
Savour a small-city cocktail of maritime history, art, beaches and a welcoming distillery.
1¼hrs from Launceston

Evandale
Stroll through this pretty-as-a-postcard town, with period-piece streetscapes and the canvases of Australia's top landscape art prize.
20mins from Launceston

Launceston
Settle into Tasmania's second city, which was named a UNESCO City of Gastronomy in 2021 – eat up, explore Cataract Gorge and wander the heritage streetscapes.

WEST COAST
Trip Builder

TAKE YOUR PICK OF MUST-SEES AND HIDDEN GEMS

Things get wild out west. The ocean is fiercer, the forests are thicker, the rain is heavier, the mountains are more rugged and the rivers run freer. It's an elemental place on the edge of wilderness.

Trip Notes

Hub towns Queenstown, Strahan

How long Allow 2 weeks

Getting around There's a bus service between Strahan, Queenstown and Burnie, but the only feasible way to really get around in the west is with your own vehicle.

Tip No roads are more tortuous or treacherous than those out west. Take it slow, stop often and build in plenty of extra time for drives.

CLOCKWISE FROM LEFT: STEVE LOVEGROVE/SHUTTERSTOCK, SHUANG LI/SHUTTERSTOCK, TARAS VYSHNYA/SHUTTERSTOCK

Stanley

Climb The Nut, indulge in fresh seafood and watch the penguins march ashore in everyone's favourite fishing village.

1hr from Burnie

Rocky Cape National Park

Lace up the walking boots for coast and cave strolls in one of Tasmania's least-known national parks.

30mins from Stanley

Corinna

Cross the Pieman River by barge to find a gold-mining town turned tourist village tucked into the edge of the Takayna/Tarkine rainforest.

1½hrs from Strahan

Lake St Clair

Walk the shores of Australia's deepest lake, which feels like a portal into the mountains and west coast, or simply settle into one of Tasmania's plushest hotels.

2½hrs from Hobart

Lyell Highway

Drive west along a road that's a highway in name only – it's more a corridor through World Heritage mountains and wilderness.

3hrs from Hobart

Queenstown

Explore a town that's no beauty, but has a heart of gold (or copper), as well as a burgeoning art scene, a transformative mining history and a remarkable railway.

4hrs from Hobart

MIDLANDS & HIGHLANDS
Trip Builder

TAKE YOUR PICK OF MUST-SEES AND HIDDEN GEMS

Rural on one side, rugged on the other, Tasmania's centre holds its history dear, but it's the alpine country that is the region's prized possession. Admire the colonial heritage in Ross and Oatlands, then head for the heights around Cradle Mountain and Lake St Clair.

Trip Notes

Hub towns Campbell Town, Oatlands

How long Allow 10 days

Getting around The Midlands' towns are strung along Tasmania's main intercity bus route, but the best stuff is beyond, accessible only with your own wheels.

Tip Scenically, the Midland Hwy isn't Tasmania's most inspiring stretch of road, so be sure to dart away into the Central Highlands for copious helpings of natural beauty.

FROM LEFT: JLEFTWICH/SHUTTERSTOCK, FILEDIMAGE/SHUTTERSTOCK, ROBERT HARDING VIDEO/SHUTTERSTOCK

Yingina/Great Lake

Cast a line for trout, delve into Tassie's hydro history at Wadd-amana and settle in for dinner at a lakeside lodge.

40mins from Bothwell

Ross

Cross the most striking convict bridge of all, and wander the scattered remains of the town's Fe-male Factory probation station. The town streets glow golden in autumn.

25mins from Oatlands

Great Western Tiers

Heed the call of the mountains. Climb Quamby Bluff or Mother Cummings Peak, or simply marvel at ancient pencil pines by Pine Lake.

40mins from Yingina/Great Lake

Bothwell

Tee off on Australia's oldest golf course in a town that still suitably clings to its Scottish origins – check out the tartan road signs.

1hr from Hobart

Kempton

Veer off the highway for a nip of whisky in one of the spirit's heartlands. Pick your time right and there might even be sheep racing at the local festival.

45mins from Hobart

Oatlands

Discover a heritage town strung with Aus-tralia's largest collection of Georgian sandstone buildings, now reinvent-ing itself with a distillery and arts spaces.

1¼hrs from Hobart

7 Things to Know About TASMANIA

INSIDER TIPS TO HIT THE GROUND RUNNING

1 It Ain't That Small

Too many visitors look at Tasmania's size and think it can be lapped in ease in a week. Journeys are slow, with single-lane highways wriggling across the island's complex topography, and experiences are plentiful. At a minimum, allow two weeks for a full circuit of the island, ideally longer. Or pick a side – east or west – and focus your attention there.

▶ For road distances, see p243.

3 Out of Range

Mobile-phone coverage is poor once you leave cities and towns. The service provider with the greatest reach across the state is Telstra.

▶ More info on phone coverage can be found in each region's *Practicalities* section.

4 Public Wi-Fi

The Tasmanian government has free wi-fi hot spots in cities and towns across the state. Look for 'TasGov Free' in your wi-fi networks. There's 30 minutes of free wi-fi per device at each location.

▶ Check each region's *Practicalities* section for wi-fi information.

2 Weather

The one constant about Tasmanian weather is change. Befitting an island, weather blows in fast, and blows out just as fast, so come prepared for all conditions at all times – in 2025 there was snow on Kunanyi/Mt Wellington on Christmas Day. Rainfall fluctuations are massive: Strahan on the west coast averages 1640mm a year, while Swansea on the drier east coast averages 590mm. Rain-shadowed Hobart is surprisingly Australia's second-driest capital city, averaging 612mm a year.

▶ Plan for the weather on p18.

1 FAFOSTOCK/SHUTTERSTOCK, **2** ROBUART/SHUTTERSTOCK, **3** CATALINA ARAGÓN, **4** BYEMO/ SHUTTERSTOCK, **5** SIBERIAN ART/SHUTTERSTOCK, **7** ALFMALER/SHUTTERSTOCK

5 Blend In

Black down jackets (puffer jackets) are so ubiquitous in Tasmania that they've become known locally as 'Tasmanian tuxedos'. Wearing a beanie is also de rigueur, especially if photographing yourself for Instagram in one of the state's many outdoor baths. And can you even attempt the local fashion of wearing shorts through the winter?

6 The Green Divide

If, as the saying goes, you should never discuss politics or religion, the same can be said of conservation in Tasmania. The state has long been divided along lines of development and protection, which has seen a few landmark clashes. The unsuccessful campaign to save Lake Pedder from being dammed and flooded in 1972 led to the creation of the world's first Greens party, while the successful campaign to prevent the Franklin River from being dammed a decade later remains a pivotal event in Australian conservation. Forestry, a pulp mill, salmon farming and the prospect of a cable car on Kunanyi/Mt Wellington have continued to raise hackles, as has private development in national parks. Plans to build a luxury lodge at Lake Malbena in Walls of Jerusalem National Park have been stridently opposed. More battles loom, with other private developments in national parks, and an approved new hiking trail through the west coast's Tyndall Range.

7 Scallop Pies

If Tasmania has a state cuisine, it's the scallop pie, an unlikely combination of scallops and creamy curry sauce inside the baked crust of a pie. You'll find them in bakeries across the state, or head for the Tassie Scallop Fiesta in Bridport in August.

Read, Listen, Watch & Follow

READ

For the Term of His Natural Life (Marcus Clarke; 1874) Classic account of convict life at Port Arthur and Sarah Island.

Death of a River Guide (Richard Flanagan; 1994) Life, death and rafting on the Franklin River from Tasmania's Man Booker Prize winner.

Dusk (Robbie Arnott; 2024) Young twins set out across the harsh Central Highlands seeking a bounty on a puma.

Palawa tunapri: Knowledge of our Ancestors (Trish Hodge; 2025) Native Tasmanian plants and their traditional uses by local Aboriginal people.

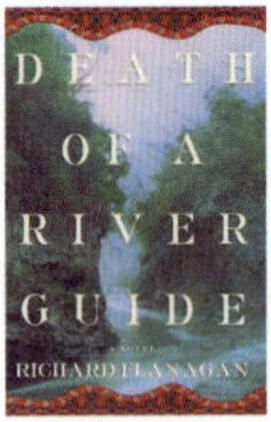

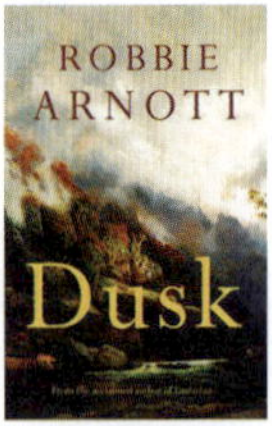

LISTEN

Mt Wellington Reverie (Augie March; 2006) Harrowing musings from the album *Moo, You Bloody Choir*.

Sometimes I Sit and Think, and Sometimes I Just Sit (Courtney Barnett; 2015) Breakthrough album from this Hobart-raised singer.

Saving the Franklin (2023) A deep dive back into the fight to save the Franklin River from being dammed in the early 1980s.

Nature Sounds Tasmania (2023) If you're here to relax, enhance the moments with these field recordings from across southern Tasmania.

The Nurse (2020; pictured) True-crime podcast account of a Launceston paediatric nurse who preyed on children, and those in power who protected him.

WATCH

The Hunter (2011) Grumpy Willem Dafoe hunts the last thylacine.

The Nightingale (2018) A female convict pursues a British officer through the Tassie wilderness, seeking revenge.

Bay of Fires (2023–25) Dark comedy ABC series featuring Marta Dusseldorp in witness protection, filmed on Tasmania's west coast.

Rosehaven (2016–21) Two friends return to their hometown, Rosehaven (Geeveston in real life), in this ABC comedy series.

The Survivors (2025; pictured) Netflix murder mystery, adapted from the Jane Harper novel and set along the shores and cliffs of Turrakana/Tasman Peninsula.

FLIXPIX/ALAMY

FOLLOW

Discover Tasmania (discovertasmania.com) Tasmania's official tourism site.

@tubsoftasmania Tasmania has a big thing for outdoor bathtubs; find them all here.

@tasmanian_shacklife Shack life is Tassie life.

Rock Monkey Adventures (rockmonkeyadventures.wordpress.com) Want to climb a mountain? It's probably been done here.

Tasmanian Times (tasmaniantimes.com) Independent news, from politics to arts.

HOBART & AROUND

CITY LIFE | FOOD | ART

RESEARCHED BY CHARLES RAWLINGS-WAY

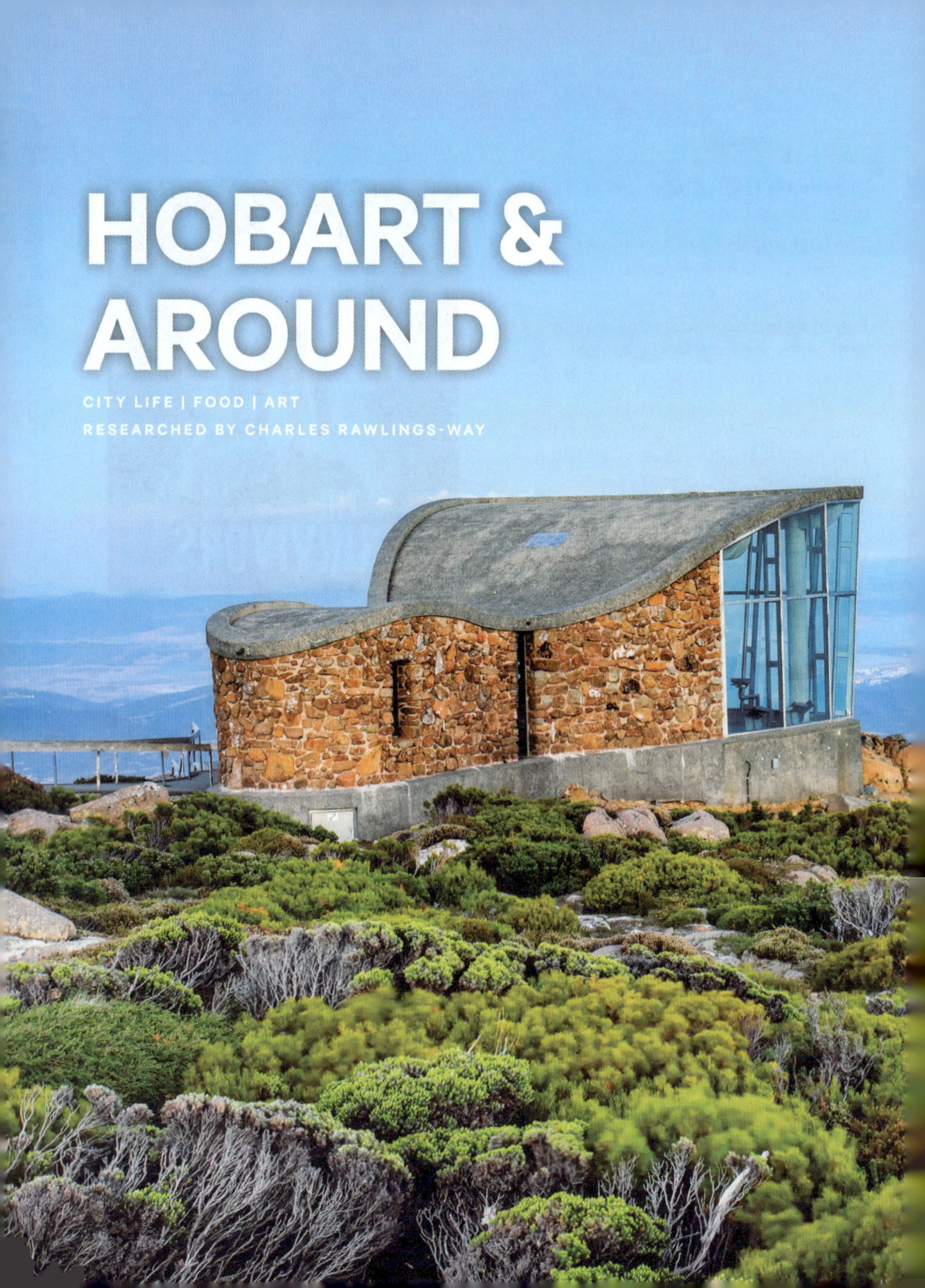

HOBART & AROUND

Trip Builder

Picture a city that's also a mountain and a river, a place where nature and culture intersect. Pinched between water and rock, Tasmania's capital is rich in history, art and eclectic festivals, with fine food, wine and whisky at its very heart.

0 10 km
0 5 miles
Hop between cellar doors in the **Coal River Valley** (p66)
20mins from Hobart
Cook up a seasonal feast at the **Agrarian Kitchen Cooking School** (p62)
30mins from Hobart
Brighton
Bridgewater
River Derwent
Richmond
New Norfolk
Forage through a bounty of produce at the **Farm Gate Market** (p74)
Coal River
Burrow into cliffs for an art fix with a difference at **MONA** (p53)
25mins from Hobart
Berriedale
Cambridge
Lindisfarne
New Town
Collins Cap
Wellington Park
Trestle Mountain
Collins Bonnet
Rosny
Hobart
Discover the peaks hidden behind **Kunanyi/Mt Wellington** (p68)
25mins from Hobart
Strip down for a nude winter swim at **Dark Mofo** (p65)
Cathedral Rock
Fern Tree
River Derwent
Sip an aged whisky with a dinosaur fossil at **Evolve Spirits Bar** (p47)
Ralphs Bay
Huonville

Practicalities

DESIGNIUM/SHUTTERSTOCK

ARRIVING

Hobart Airport Most visitors' first brush with Hobart is the airport, located in Cambridge, 19km east of the city. A taxi or rideshare into the city will cost around $50 and take about 25 minutes. SkyBus shuttle buses meet every flight and stop at six locations in the city, including by the MONA ferry and four CBD hotels. Car-rental desks proliferate in the airport terminal. Intercity coaches also service Hobart from Launceston and Devonport.

HOW MUCH FOR A

Pint of craft beer $14

Waterfront fish and chips $18

MONA entry $39

WHEN TO GO

JAN–MAR
Weather at its warmest, with sunny days and long dusky evenings

APR–MAY
Stable conditions, with cool days and cooler evenings

JUN–SEP
Crisp mornings and short days, but fire-warmed evenings across the city

OCT–DEC
Warming (and windy) conditions stir the local hibernation

GETTING AROUND

Car & motorcycle Hobart's CBD has a sometimes confusing grid of one-way streets: Macquarie, Davey, Argyle, Campbell, Murray, Harrington, Barrack and Molle streets, plus sections of Collins, Liverpool and Bathurst streets.

Walk The easiest way to explore Hobart is on two legs. Most of the wine-and-dine options are strung out between Salamanca and North Hobart (30 minutes end-to-end, tops). And there are views everywhere!

E-scooters Hobart is hilly, so e-scooters are a hit! Beam (purple scooters) is the only operator. You need to download the company's app to use a scooter. It costs $1 to unlock a scooter, and then 51c per minute thereafter.

EATING & DRINKING

Eating is one of the true pleasures of any time spent in Hobart, with local restaurateurs alert to the appeal and status of southern Tasmania's excellent produce. Plucked straight from the Southern Ocean, the seafood is masterful and plentiful along the city waterfront with its floating fish punts and seafood restaurants. Salamanca and North Hobart's Elizabeth St strip dominate the eatery offerings, though the city centre is dotted with dining rooms, such as Fico, Dier Makr and Templo, that slip onto lists of Australia's top restaurants.

Best pub grub New Sydney (p78)

Must-try whisky Lark Classic Cask 43% (p47)

TOP: EYEOFPAUL/SHUTTERSTOCK
BOTTOM: BLOOMBERG/CONTRIBUTOR/GETTY IMAGES

CONNECT & FIND YOUR WAY

Hobart is divided by the River Derwent, running north–south. The CBD is on the western shore; the airport is out east. Free wi-fi access is pretty much a given in most Hobart accommodation; you might have to ask for the password in cafes and pubs. The CBD is dotted with free government-sponsored wi-fi hot spots – see digital.tas.gov.au/free-wifi.

WHERE TO STAY

Hobart is compact enough that you can decide where you want to stay based on the accommodation's charms rather than proximity to attractions.

Neighbourhood	Pros/Cons
City centre	Central, with several big-name hotel openings in recent years. Pretty quiet at night.
Waterfront	The most scenic addresses in town have few downsides.
Battery Point & Salamanca	Historic options among cosy cafes and stores. Handy nightlife in Salamanca (equally a downside).
Berriedale	If you're here just for MONA, it has a luxury hotel of its own and a basic motel or two nearby. A long way from town.
Richmond	Historic digs, easy access to airport. An option only if you have your own wheels.

METRO GREENCARD

If you're getting about by bus – the only public transport option in Hobart – pick up a Metro Greencard (metrotas.com.au) for ease and 20% discount on fares.

MONEY

Credit cards are universally accepted (and preferred) in Hobart, even at markets. Petrol and food prices (including takeaways) are markedly higher than in mainland capital cities.

01 Southern WHISKY

DISTILLERIES | BARS | CITY LIFE

In the 1830s, a ban was placed on distilling spirits in Tasmania. It was another 160 years before Hobart surveyor Bill Lark had the law overturned, sparking a whisky revolution. Today, there are more than a dozen distilleries in Hobart alone, and a growing band of bars specialising in the spirit. You'll even find the whisky once named as the world's best single malt.

ADAM GIBSON/SULLIVANS COVE

How to

Getting around It's easiest to walk between the city-centre bars, but private transport will be needed to head to outlying distilleries such as Lark and Lawrenny. Want a designated driver? Drink Tasmania runs whisky tours around the Hobart area.

When to go Winter is prime time for a whisky warmer around a Hobart wood fire.

Tours Distillery tours range from around $32 (7K Distillery) to $70 (Sullivans Cove).

WILLIAM WEST/GETTY IMAGES

Whisky Estates

A fine whisky deserves a fine setting. In 2022 Tasmania's oldest distillery, **Lark**, moved from the city to Shene Estate at Pontville, a splendid property granted to the grandson of King George III in 1819. The Gothic stables alone are worth toasting. The paddock-to-still **Lawrenny**, which grows its own barley, is on an immaculate Derwent Valley estate granted to Tasmania's wealthiest resident in 1820.

The World's Best

Is it possible that the world's best whisky could be made in the industrial airport backblocks on the opposite side of the planet to Scotland? Yessiree. Take a tour of the slick black box in Cambridge that houses **Sullivans Cove Distillery**, and discover that, with whisky, it's never a bad idea to dream big. In 2014 Sullivans Cove won world's best single malt and in 2019 it became the world's first distillery to twice be awarded world's best single cask single malt (backing-up from a 2018 win).

Bones & Bars

Even the most aged whiskies look young at **Evolve Spirits Bar**, inside the waterfront MACq 01 hotel. Choose from more than 350 world whiskies as you sit among a Triassic treasury of fossils, including a cave-bear skeleton, a mineralised mammoth tusk and the horn of a triceratops. **The Still**, inside the former print room of the local newspaper, is run by the state's oldest distillery and is encyclopedic in its offerings, with more than 150 Tasmanian whiskies being poured.

Top left Sullivans Cove Distillery
Bottom left Lark Single Malt Whisky

Favourite Hobart Whiskies

My all-time favourite whisky, even after 30 years, is **Lark Classic Cask 43%**. It embodies all the wonderful Tasmanian elements that go into producing a single malt in a balanced way. For something with an edge, I'd reach for a **Killara Laphroaig Cask** maturation; it's simply stunning. Early in the day, I'm tempted by Spring Bay's elegant and complex **Bourbon Cask**, and to round out the day it's the third release of **Old Kempton's Solera Cask**, which has enjoyed maturing in a Spanish sherry tun with remnants of the previous two releases.

■ **Recommended by Bill Lark,** *founder of Lark Distillery*

@larkdistillery

The Unsettled Shape of Hobart

REMODELLING NATURE TO FIT A CITY

When European settlers first sailed into the River Derwent in 1803, the shape of things to come was very different – literally. The first attempt at a settlement was far from the site of the present-day city, and even when it shifted, there were renovations to be done.

Left Hunter St **Middle** Lieutenant Governor David Collins **Right** Risdon Cove

LKONYA/GETTY IMAGES

In September 1803 the *Lady Nelson* sailed into the River Derwent, with a party of 49 people aboard tasked with establishing the first settlement in what was then Van Diemen's Land. Reaching the site of present-day Hobart, the ship sailed on, not anchoring for another 8km...and on the opposite side of the river.

Settlement was made at Piyura Kitina/Risdon Cove, a small notch in the coastline beside today's Bowen Bridge. Five months later, Lieutenant Governor David Collins arrived in town aboard the overcrowded *Ocean* – 200 people, including almost 180 convicts, on a ship designed to carry 30 – and on the very day of his arrival declared the site unsuitable for settlement due to its lack of fresh water (ironically, there is now a dam and freshwater lake immediately behind the cove).

Hunter Island

The next day, Collins set sail to find an alternative site for the settlement and discovered Sullivans Cove, now the location of Hobart's waterfront. It was a vastly different landscape in 1804. The new settlers disembarked on Hunter Island, which was then a small island in the middle of the bay connected to the mainland at low tide by a sand spit.

The island became the new town's heart – the site of its port, its government stores and its gallows – and a track was built across the spit, which was turned into a causeway in 1820. Eventually, land reclamation connected the island to the mainland. The island lay across the junction of Hunter St and Franklin Wharf, where MACq 01 and the Henry Jones Art Hotel are now situated. The old shoreline

UNIVERSAL HISTORY ARCHIVE/GETTY IMAGES

ANDREW BAIN/ALAMY STOCK PHOTO

can be tangibly witnessed in a couple of ways. Brass markers inset into Hunter St trace its original line, while the main entrance to TMAG, around 70m inland from the coast, is named Watergate because it once stood by the shore.

Shape Shifting

That isn't the only part of Hobart's coastal topography Collins would no longer recognise. When he arrived, he wrote of a 'run of clear fresh water' flowing into the cove. A small beach lined the cove, and a low escarpment rose between the waterfront and what is now Hobart's city centre.

> Lieutenant Governor David Collins arrived in town aboard the overcrowded *Ocean* – 200 people, including almost 180 convicts, on a ship designed to carry 30

The waterway was the Hobart Rivulet, which is no longer in sight along the shore. Hobart's city centre was built atop the rivulet, with its outlet diverted to beneath the present Cenotaph when the Hunter Island causeway was built. You can still glimpse the rivulet flowing beneath the city through an opening in the ground at the northern end of the Elizabeth Mall.

The escarpment, too, is gone, quarried into oblivion. An unusual rise in one side of Davey St as it passes Franklin Sq is all that betrays its presence, while it's worth heading into TMAG to find and imagine the scene from the Private Secretary's Cottage (p59). One of Australia's oldest brick buildings (c 1813), it stood atop the escarpment, looking down onto the beach.

Piyura Kitina/ Risdon Cove Massacre

When the Risdon Cove settlement shifted to Hobart in February 1804, not everybody made the move. A band of settlers stayed on at Risdon Cove, in what became a tragic decision for the local Mumirimina people. On 3 May 1804, around 300 Mumirimina men, women and children were hunting kangaroo near to Risdon Cove. Soldiers fired on the party, later claiming that they killed three people, though estimates have suggested up to 60 deaths. It was the first massacre of palawa (Tasmanian Aboriginal) people by settlers.

Risdon Cove, known to palawa as Piyura Kitina, was handed back to the traditional owners in 1995.

02 Right FIELD

NATIONAL PARK | HIKING | NATURE

Mt Field National Park is nature's version of a multi-storey complex. Waterfalls pour through towering forest on the lower slopes, while the park's heights are an open wonderland of alpine tarns, flowering moorlands, rocky peaks and southern Tasmania's only (albeit unreliable) ski field. Four of Tasmania's 60 Great Short Walks are in this one national park alone.

GREG BRAVE/SHUTTERSTOCK

How to

Getting here The park is little more than an hour's drive northwest of Hobart.

When to go Autumn is prime time, when the deciduous fagus gets its golden glow. In summer, the slopes brighten with flowering scoparia and waratah.

Sleep high Book ahead for an alpine stay in the park's rustic Government Huts, sitting 1000m above sea level and originally built to house road workers in the 1940s.

CRBELLETTE/GETTY IMAGES

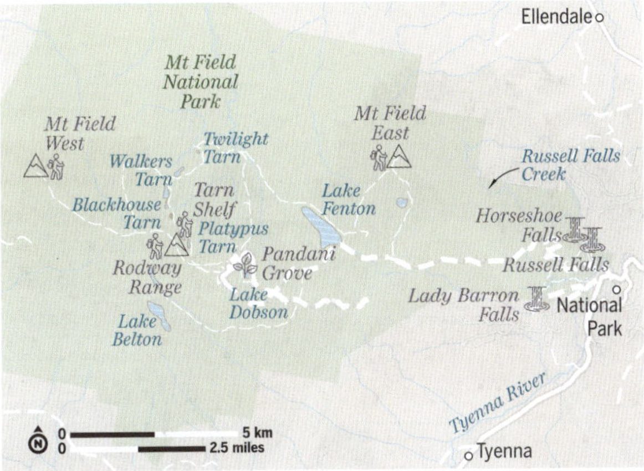

Waterfalls

Mt Field was gazetted as Tasmania's first national park (along with Freycinet National Park) in 1916 primarily because of the beauty of **Russell Falls**, which had been proclaimed their own reserve back in 1885 (and appeared on one of Australia's first postage stamps). A 700m wheelchair-accessible track leads to the falls from the back door of the visitor centre. Most visitors don't venture beyond, but climb the steps beside the falls and you'll find equally beautiful **Horseshoe Falls**. Set out from here across the slopes to **Lady Barron Falls** to complete the **Three Falls Circuit**.

Alpine Walks

Head for the heights to witness some of Mt Field's most spectacular scenes. It's a short stroll around the shores of Lake Dobson to the **Pandani Grove**, a tall stand of Tasmania's shaggy endemic pandani, the world's tallest heath plant. It's a day well spent to hike across the **Tarn Shelf**, a rung of land high in the mountains and beaded with small lakes.

Turning of the Fagus

Every autumn, sometime around Anzac Day (25 April), a motley pilgrimage begins in southern Tasmania. Known as the Turning of the Fagus, it draws worshippers to the Tarn Shelf, where it's typically showtime for the state's most brilliant blaze of autumn colour. What's remarkable about this spectacle is that it's native – the fagus is Tasmania's only native deciduous tree and one of the rare few in Australia.

Top left Russell Falls
Bottom left Pandani plants

The Park's Peaks

If you're into boulder-hopping in high places, you can't go past **Mt Field East**, **Mt Field West** and the **Rodway Range**, the three highest points in Mt Field National Park. Atop these mountains, it's not hard to imagine the glaciers that carved out this spectacular dolerite landscape some 10,000 years ago. The peaks can be walked individually, or combined in a two- to three-day circuit. The best time of year to be walking to them has to be late April, when the deciduous fagus is at its spectacular, golden best.

■ **Brendan Moodie,** *ranger in charge at Mt Field National Park @tasmaniaparks*

03 Putting the Art IN HOBART

ART | CULTURE | GALLERIES

Few cities have been so immediately and irrevocably changed by a single cultural moment as was Hobart when MONA opened in 2011. But even beyond David Walsh's subversive underground art gallery, this city has an unexpected art pedigree.

MONA/JESSE HUNNIFORD

How to

Getting here The best way to MONA is on the MONA ROMA ferry, which sails from the Brooke St Pier. Posh Pit tickets add wine and canapés to the journey.

When to go MONA is open Thursday to Monday.

Pedalling art MONA sits just 800m from Hobart's Intercity Cycleway, making it a simple pedal to the gallery – it's 12km from the city. Pick up a bike from Hobart Bike Hire.

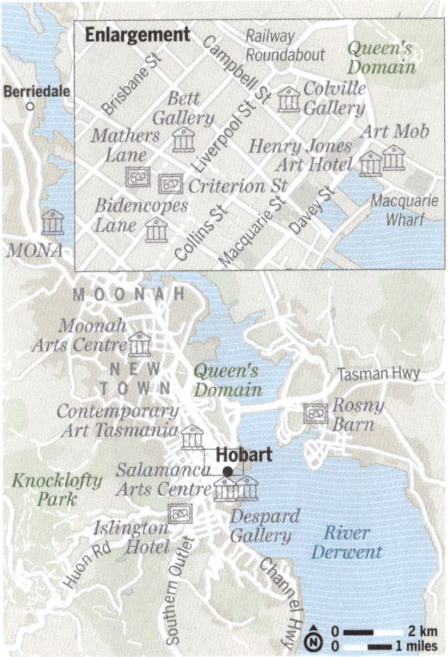

Artfully MONA

Behind all of MONA's self-styled 'wank', there is the art, which ranges from the sublime to the shocking. Australia's largest private art gallery fills three subterranean levels in a maze-like bewilderment of art and antiquities. Among it all are some signature works, such as Sidney Nolan's 1620-panel **Snake**, a painting so large it had never been publicly displayed until MONA built a room especially for it. Irreverently nearby is Wim Delvoye's **Cloaca Professional**, aka the 'poo machine', an installation that replicates the human digestive tract, complete with faeces and associated smells. There's a wall of 152 anatomically correct **porcelain vulvas** moulded from real subjects, while the very cathartic **MONA Confessional** offers the chance to broadcast your sins anonymously to random listeners far above.

SUE BURTON PHOTOGRAPHY/SHUTTERSTOCK

Top left MONA **Bottom left** MONA's garden

MONA Experiences

In true MONA style, the gallery has turned experiences into an art form of their own. Step into James Turrell's **Unseen Seen + Weight of Darkness**, a white orb jutting over the water in the Pharos extension, choosing the 'hard' or 'soft' setting for an art acid trip without the comedown. Turrell's aboveground archi-light installation **Amarna**, active at sunrise and sunset, is also worth sticking around for. The **MONA Like a Rockstar** package gives you all the fancy bits – dinner in the superb **Faro Bar + Restaurant**, a tipple in the **Void Bar** 17m underground, and the ferry Posh Pit. Eating and drinking here is all part of the experience; beyond Faro don't miss the outdoor **Heavy Metal Kitchen** (burgers, grilled meats); **Moorilla Wine Bar** (share plates and drinks in the sun); and **The Source** (five-star lunch).

Hobart Street Art

Venturing into Hobart's many lanes, you'll find a somewhat hidden but vibrant street-art scene. **Bidencopes Lane**, a favourite hangout for taggers, reveals myriad artists' work, including the distinctive work of local hero Tom O'Hern. Just around the corner in **Mathers Lane**, O'Hern strikes again with *Terraform*, a 4.5m-by-11m mural he describes as 'a foresty thing'. Stormie Mills' *Lost Giant* towers grimly over latte sippers in **Criterion Street**, while the back alleys of Elizabeth Mall reveal an endangered spotted handfish lurking opposite Jae Mills' 3.5m-high figures in antique chairs, which are a nod to the long-gone Purdy's Mart emporium.

By Emma Bett, *codirector of Bett Gallery @bettgallery*

Far left *Lost Giant* by Stormie Mills **Left** MONA and the MONA ROMA ferry wharf (p53) **Below** Salamanca Arts Centre

Art Overnight

The art experience doesn't have to finish at day's end, with a pair of Hobart hotels all but qualifying as art galleries. The **Henry Jones Art Hotel** was Australia's first art hotel, and displays up to 400 works (most for sale) by Tasmanian artists, around the hotel and rooms. Daily tours of the collection (4pm) are free to guests and $35 for nonguests. The stylish **Islington Hotel** in South Hobart has a private art collection that includes works from Henri Matisse, David Hockney and Brett Whiteley, a Pablo Picasso etching and a screen print from Andy Warhol.

Gallery Days

Hobart's love affair with art long preceded MONA. The city is rich in vibrant local spaces, such as **Rosny Barn**, the **Salamanca Arts Centre**, **Moonah Arts Centre** and **Contemporary Art Tasmania** (CAT), presenting arts-based exhibitions and experimental performances. Well-established commercial galleries are plentiful. **Bett Gallery** is one of Australia's foremost contemporary galleries. Waterfront **Despard Gallery** and **Colville Gallery** feature regular exhibitions and art auctions, while **Art Mob** specialises in Aboriginal art from across Australia. Take in an opening night or find exhibition programs through gallery websites.

04 Battery Point BACKSTREETS

ARCHITECTURE | HISTORY | CITY LIFE

Named for the battery of guns that once graced its point, Hobart's oldest suburb is an inviting web of streets trimmed with colonial-era homes and worker cottages that are now the best residential addresses in town. A walk here is a window into Hobart's evolution.

LKONYA/SHUTTERSTOCK

Trip notes

Getting here Battery Point is a 15-minute walk from the city centre.

Open doors Want a peek behind a facade or two? Open House Hobart (openhousehobart.org), held in November, sees some of Hobart's most interesting buildings open their doors to the public.

Grazing stops Cutting through the heart of Battery Point, Hampden Rd is lined with eateries, including a couple of Hobart institutions: the Jackman & McRoss bakery (p78) and **Da Angelo** Italian restaurant.

Battery Point Sculpture Trail

Continue the Battery Point exploration by walking the 2km Battery Point Sculpture Trail. Dotted with nine numerical sculptures, it tells a story in numbers about facets of local history, from the number of ships that left its slipyards in the 19th century, to the year of birth of local gadabout Errol Flynn.

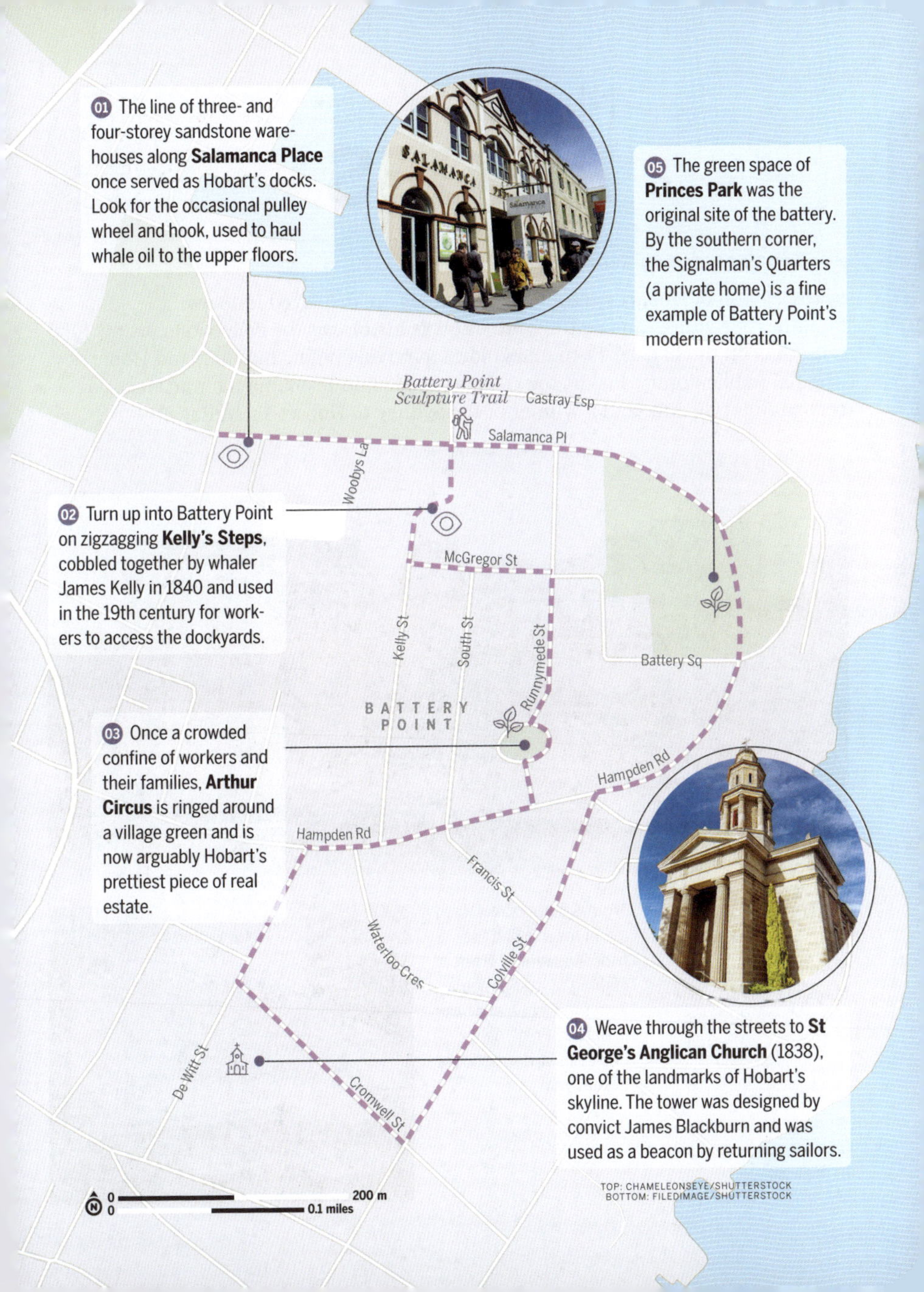

01 The line of three- and four-storey sandstone warehouses along **Salamanca Place** once served as Hobart's docks. Look for the occasional pulley wheel and hook, used to haul whale oil to the upper floors.

05 The green space of **Princes Park** was the original site of the battery. By the southern corner, the Signalman's Quarters (a private home) is a fine example of Battery Point's modern restoration.

02 Turn up into Battery Point on zigzagging **Kelly's Steps**, cobbled together by whaler James Kelly in 1840 and used in the 19th century for workers to access the dockyards.

03 Once a crowded confine of workers and their families, **Arthur Circus** is ringed around a village green and is now arguably Hobart's prettiest piece of real estate.

04 Weave through the streets to **St George's Anglican Church** (1838), one of the landmarks of Hobart's skyline. The tower was designed by convict James Blackburn and was used as a beacon by returning sailors.

TOP: CHAMELEONSEYE/SHUTTERSTOCK
BOTTOM: FILEDIMAGE/SHUTTERSTOCK

05 Museum PIECES

MUSEUMS | CULTURE | ARCHITECTURE

Not all of Hobart's great museum pieces are displayed indoors – the buildings' structures and settings are often as historic as the collections inside. Key museums fill the likes of Tasmania's oldest surviving public building and Hobart's original public library. Inside, the collections include Tasmania tiger artefacts, a replica Antarctic hut, and a winner of the Sydney to Hobart Yacht Race.

TRABANTOS/SHUTTERSTOCK

How to

Getting here TMAG, the Maritime Museum and Mawson's Hut Replica Museum are clustered by Hobart's waterfront, making them easy to access on foot.

When to go The museums are open every day of the week.

Trout & time travel Head out of town to find the fishy **Museum of Trout Fishing** at the Salmon Ponds in Plenty; and back in Battery Point, delve into colonial domestic life at **Narryna**.

TRABANTOS/SHUTTERSTOCK

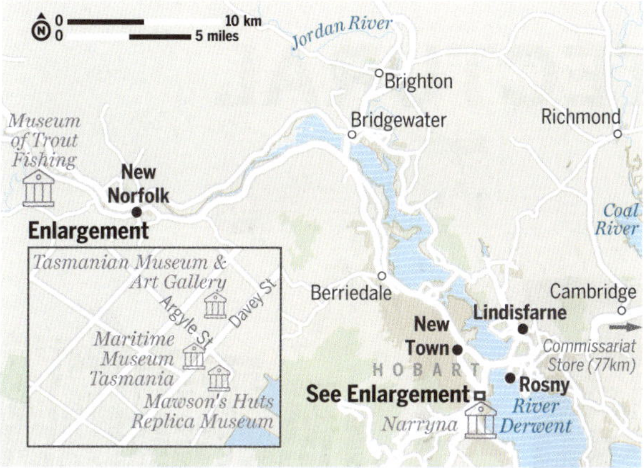

Top left Tasmanian Museum and Art Gallery (TMAG) **Bottom left** Mawson's Huts Replica Museum

History in Stone

Australia's second-oldest museum, the **Tasmanian Museum and Art Gallery**, known to all as simply TMAG, is a case of history inside history. As you enter the museum grounds, the building immediately to your right (housing the cafe) is Tasmania's oldest surviving public building, the **Commissariat Store** (1808–10). Wrapped inside the complex, accessed from the Link Foyer, is the **Private Secretary's Cottage** (c 1813), which is one of Australia's oldest brick buildings.

Tigers & Canoes

TMAG has an ever-changing roster of exhibitions, but also some compelling permanent displays. The **Bond Store Gallery** covers Tasmania's colonial era in a manner that might itself have stepped straight from a 19th-century museum. Track the sad plight of the **Tasmanian tiger** and head to the **ningina tunapri** Tasmanian Aboriginal cultural gallery, with displays on shell stringing, kelp basket-making and the revival of canoe building.

Antarctic Digs

Among Hobart's plentiful other museums, seek out dockside **Mawson's Huts Replica Museum**, a faithful recreation of the hut in which the Australasian Antarctic Expedition lived on the ice from 1911 to 1914. The ice axe, sledge and keyboard are originals. The **Maritime Museum Tasmania** is inside Hobart's first public library. Moored across the road is a key piece of its collection, *Westward,* the only Tasmanian yacht to twice win the Sydney to Hobart Yacht Race, and now being restored by the museum.

Key TMAG Displays

Thylacine film Poignant footage of the last known thylacine, aka Tasmanian tiger, pacing its enclosure around 1936.

tuylini (stringybark canoe) In 2007 a group of Tasmanian Aboriginal men revived the tradition of canoe building to construct this canoe – the first in nearly 170 years.

The Governor's wombat Fiercer than any living wombat, this specimen mimics the misleading, upright position given to the first wombat to be taxidermied in England in the early 1800s.

The Conciliation by Benjamin Duterrau It may be Australia's first history painting, but what message does it send?

■ **Recommended by Jane Stewart,** *principal curator at TMAG @tasmuseum*

ARCHITECTURAL
Hobart

01 MONA
So much here takes place underground, away from the eye, but even the Corten and concrete exterior, with its newer pyramidal Pharos extension, is commanding.

02 Silos Apartments
Standing tall at the end of Salamanca Place, this 11-storey building has been transformed from what it still resembles – grain silos – into apartments.

03 Menzies Institute Building
The facade divides opinion, but the fluid lattice lines represent the contours of the land and are a louvre system to passively shade the windows.

04 Shot Tower
Built to make gun shot, the chimney-like structure – one of only three shot towers in Australia – was, for four years in the 1870s, Australia's tallest building.

05 Hobart Synagogue
Australia's oldest synagogue, built in rare Egyptian Revival style, has early links to the convict said to have inspired the character Fagin in *Oliver Twist*.

06

07

09

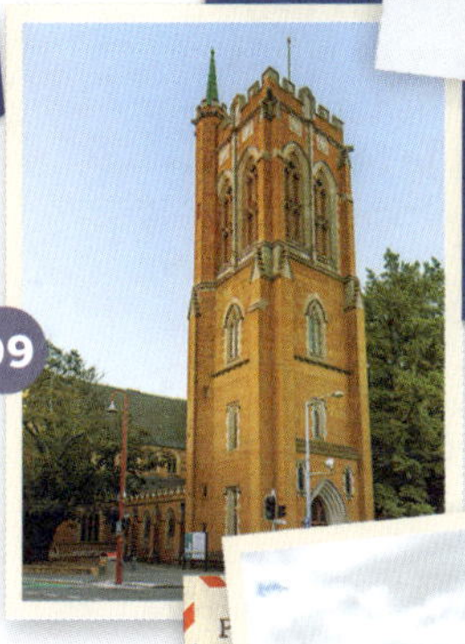

08

10

06 Wrest Point
When built in 1973, this cylindrical Sandy Bay building was Australia's first legal casino. It remains Hobart's tallest building (64m).

07 Cascade Brewery
The striking, stepped sandstone facade, standing in repose before Kunanyi/Mt Wellington, was said to have been designed in a jail cell by brewery founder Peter Degraves.

08 General Post Office
One of Hobart's landmark buildings, modelled on London's Big Ben, though it took a public subscription to raise the money to build the tower in 1906.

09 St David's Cathedral
Leading British architect George Frederick Bodley's finest Australian work, and the seat of the Bishop of Tasmania.

10 Henry Jones IXL Jam Factory
The warehouses along waterfront Hunter St are Hobart's oldest. The IXL jam factory filled much of the space, and is today a hotel filled with 19th-century industrial design and features.

01 MONA/JESSE HUNNFORD, ARCHITECT: NONDA KATSALIDIS, **02** DESIGNIUM/SHUTTERSTOCK, ARCHITECT: HBV, **03** SLOVEGROVE/GETTY IMAGES, ARCHITECT: LYONS, **04** KYLE TOWNS/SHUTTERSTOCK, **05** CHAMELEONSEYE/SHUTTERSTOCK, **06** SLOW WALKER/SHUTTERSTOCK, **07** DARYL ARIAWAN/SHUTTERSTOCK, **08** BENNY MARTY/SHUTTERSTOCK, **09** TRABANTOS/SHUTTERSTOCK, **10** VIPERSNIPER/GETTY IMAGES

06 Putting the New in NEW NORFOLK

FOOD | ANTIQUES | DRINK

Around 35km upstream from Hobart, New Norfolk is Tasmania's third-oldest town (settled in 1807), but it's no longer content to be a period piece. For so long a workaday town, it's been transformed by a string of recent openings. Old New Norfolk is now a centre of fine dining, quality antiques and home to Tasmania's first rum distillery.

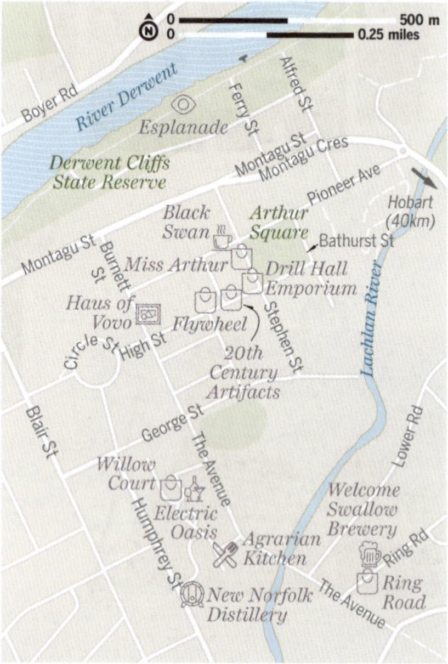

How to

Getting here Follow the Brooker Hwy out of Hobart, swinging onto the A10 beyond the Bridgewater Bridge. Suburban Metro buses service the town from Hobart.

When to go Autumn brings a golden glow to the town's riverbanks, as celebrated at the Derwent Valley Autumn Festival.

Olden days Behind the new, there's still the old. New Norfolk has Tasmania's oldest Anglican church and the **Bush Inn** claims to be Australia's oldest continuously licensed hotel.

Asylum Fare

After 14 years in outlying Lachlan, the **Agrarian Kitchen** restaurant shifted into New Norfolk a few years ago, planting a 4000-sq-metre walled kitchen garden inside the grounds of Willow Court (formerly Australia's longest-running mental asylum) and resuming its celebrated cooking classes. The restaurant itself occupies one of the asylum's wards and regularly appears on lists of Australia's best restaurants. Supplement the Agrarian fare with a visit to **Black Swan**, a wee coffee nook filled with a range of books on art, cooking, gardening and architecture.

Rum Rebellion

Tasmania's first rum distillery (this century, that is), **New Norfolk Distillery** has also set up shop in Willow Court. It's open daily for tours and tastings (book for larger groups); or swing by Friday to Sunday afternoons for drinks and tunes at the sci-fi-

WALLIX/GETTY IMAGES

themed cocktail bar **Electric Oasis**. Nearby is the **Welcome Swallow Brewery**, pumping out lovingly crafted beers; the taproom is open Friday to Sunday. Good burgers too.

What's Old is New

Passion for the old and interesting will be well sated with a visit to one (or several) of New Norfolk's antique establishments (there are at least a dozen). **Drill Hall Emporium**'s sumptuous collection of vintage wares, sourced locally and abroad, demands time to explore. **Willow Court** and **Ring Road** antique centres, together with **20th Century Artifacts**, present an eclectic mix of fine furniture through to memorabilia and curious collectables.

New Norfolk Favourites

Miss Arthur A beautiful goods store that supports high-quality local and overseas brands that are perfect for your home.

Haus of Vovo A 2021 addition to the New Norfolk art scene, with local exhibitions.

Flywheel The perfect place for custom letterpress business cards, wedding invitations and all things stationery.

Leap and Wander Studio A great way to spend a weekend morning – learning the art of ceramics, and making your own.

Esplanade The perfect place to get some fresh air is the riverfront Esplanade. It's beautiful on sunny and misty days.

Recommended by Severine Demanet, *co-owner of the Agrarian Kitchen and Agrarian Eatery @agrariankitchen*

Above New Norfolk

07 Winter FESTIVALS

FESTIVALS | CULTURE | WHISKY

There was a time, not long ago, when Hobart all but closed the shutters through winter, patiently holing up and waiting for some warmth to return. Today, in contrast, the city celebrates its dark side, predominantly through a roster of festivals that harness the long nights as an excuse to belt out a tune, tuck into whisky or take a nude swim.

XAVIER HOENNER/SHUTTERSTOCK

How to

Getting here The major winter festivals take place in locations spread across the city, typically within easy walking distance of the CBD.

Festival dates Dark Mofo is tied to the winter solstice (21 June), while the Festival of Voices takes place in July. The top comes off Tasmanian Whisky Week in August.

Tickets Dark Mofo shows can sell out in minutes, so keep an eye on the website for ticket-release dates.

ANDREW MERRY/GETTY IMAGES

YOLANDA ALEMANY/SHUTTERSTOCK

Far left Dark Mofo Left Mulled wine
Bottom left Dark Mofo's Winter Feast

Take the Plunge

As dawn breaks over the shortest day of the year, up to 3000 swimmers disrobe on Long Beach at Sandy Bay, sprinting (and squealing) naked (but for their shower caps) into the sea. Hobart's favourite winter ritual, the **Nude Solstice Swim**, is the centrepiece of Dark Mofo, the city's two-week celebration of darkness. Make a quick splash in the sea, perhaps a few swimming strokes, and then it's back to the beach and off to the rest of your day.

Dark & Delicious

Nude swims aren't **Dark Mofo**'s only deep dive into subversion. Revelling in the long hours of darkness, the festival brings MONA's distinctive irreverence to the party, with polarising themes and shows that invite controversy – from crosses hung upside down around the city, to actors performing in the bloody entrails of a slaughtered bull (woah). The nightly **Winter Feast** is a warming gathering of local producers, fire-roasted food and mulled beverages, filling Macquarie Wharf No 2 with candlelight and indulgent winter-beating vibes.

Whisky & Song

When Dark Mofo slinks off into the darkness, other festivals fill the winter void. The **Festival of Voices**, held across two weeks, illuminates the nights with song – everything from choral to cabaret, gospel to sea shanties. The **Big Sing Bonfire** signature event sees thousands singing around a raging outdoor fire. Just as warming is **Tasmanian Whisky Week**, pairing the state's distillers and drinkers in venues across the city.

Festive Summers

Of course, Hobart is pretty good at celebrating summer too! The **Taste of Summer** festival runs between Christmas and the first week of January, celebrating fine Tasmanian food, drink and music. Shoot for a table in the sun. Simultaneously, the **Sydney to Hobart Yacht Race** blows into town. Sails materialise in the River Derwent and the waterfront bars heave with sunburned sailors and sailor-fans. Don't miss a beer at the effervescent Race Village hub near Constitution Dock. You can also head over the bridge to Rosny for cool jazz, emerging talent and casual vibes at the **Clarence Jazz Festival**.

08 Coal River Valley ESCAPES

WINE | FOOD | HISTORY

No wine region in Australia is so near to a capital city as the Coal River Valley – drive from Hobart and you'll hit the first cellar door in just 15 minutes (the city's rush hour permitting). Vineyards queue orderly along Richmond Rd, making for straightforward access, and they're easily matched with a selection of gourmet producers, restaurants and the heritage charms of pretty Richmond.

How to

Getting here The Coal River Valley is squeezed between the city and the airport; turn off the Tasman Hwy at Cambridge.

Designated drivers Tour companies running valley tours include Ageing Barrel Tours, Drink Tasmania, Boutique Wine Tours Australia and Coal River Wine Hopper.

Alternative alcohol Not into wine? Don't miss a whisky tasting at **Sullivans Cove Distillery** at Cambridge, or a cold beer at the historic **Richmond Arms Hotel** on the main street.

Red & White Coal

There are more than a dozen vineyards strung through the valley and around Richmond's edges, with the bulk clustered along the road between Cambridge and Richmond. Begin at popular **Frogmore Creek**, with a smart restaurant and tastings, and continue on to **Puddleduck**, **Coal Valley Vineyard**, **Nocton** and **Domaine A** (the area's oldest winery) before settling in for a weekend wood-fired pizza and a glass or three at **Pooley Wines**, inside an 1830s convict-built homestead.

Paired Produce

What's wine without cheese or chocolate? Stop in at the **Wicked Cheese Company** to grab some of the signature triple cream brie or a whisky cheddar. There are handmade chocolates (and more cheese) at **Coal River Farm** – stick around for a 'high

BELL-DAVEY PHOTOGRAPHY/SHUTTERSTOCK

Bridging History

Tasmania's rivers are bridged by some gorgeous old convict-built structures: Campbell Town's **Red Bridge** spanning the Elizabeth River is Australia's oldest brick bridge (1838); while the carving-adorned **Ross Bridge** on the Macquarie River is Australia's third-oldest bridge (1836). But **Richmond Bridge** (1823) takes top billing as Australia's oldest still-functioning bridge. It's a massive honey-yellow sandstone edifice that doesn't look like it's going anywhere anytime soon. The golden stone, manicured lawns and upbeat ducks are picture-perfect...although, in typical Tasmanian style, Richmond Bridge has a dark history too: it's purportedly haunted by the 'Flagellator of Richmond', George Grover, murdered here in 1832.

cheese' sitting, getting a sample of four cheeses paired with a Tassie tipple. Tasmanian summers are about pick-your-own berry farms, and **Littlewood Berry Farm** is one of the best in the south.

Ye Olde Richmond

Tasmania's poster child for colonial elegance, Richmond drips history. Straddling the Coal River, convict-built **Richmond Bridge** is Australia's oldest road bridge (1823), watched over by **St John the Evangelist Church**, Australia's oldest Catholic church (1836), and **St Luke's Anglican Church** (1834), Australia's oldest Anglican church. **Richmond Gaol**'s convicts probably failed to appreciate that they were inhabiting what would become Australia's oldest prison (1825).

Above Tasmanian raspberries

09 Explore the MOUNTAIN

NATURE | HIKING | VIEWS

Rising directly above Hobart, Kunanyi/Mt Wellington (1271m) is the city's natural playground, setting the mood for its every day and season. Referred to locally as 'the mountain', it's laced with trails, providing a wealth of walking and mountain-biking opportunities.

BOY_ANUPONG/GETTY IMAGES

How to

Getting here The Kunanyi/Mt Wellington Explorer Bus runs between Hobart's waterfront and the summit, with four stops along the mountain on the way.

When to go This is an evergreen, year-round mountain. Clear winter days bring a unique clarity to the view, and snowy days on the slopes quickly become the biggest show in town.

Mapping the mount Download walking and mountain-biking maps from wellingtonpark.org.au/downloads.

FILEDIMAGE/SHUTTERSTOCK

Summit Views

The highest point anywhere near Hobart is the tower-topped tip of Kunanyi/Mt Wellington, with a view that stretches over the city's rooftops to much of southern Tasmania. You can drive all the way to the summit, but the more immersive approach is on foot, ascending from **the Springs**, midway up the slopes, on either the **Ice House Track** or the combined **Pinnacle/Zig Zag Tracks** – it's a 9km loop if you head up one and down the other. Not challenging enough? Run to the summit in the annual **Point to Pinnacle**, held in November. It's billed as the world's toughest half-marathon.

DARREN TIERNEY/SHUTTERSTOCK

Waterfalls & Tarns

The slopes of Kunanyi/Mt Wellington appear dry at a glance, but this is a mountain covered in waterfalls and occasionally (and

Setting the Table

When British explorers sighted Kunanyi/Mt Wellington in the 1790s, they named it Table Mountain after its similar Cape Town counterpart (even though Hobart's mighty mountain is 185m taller). The name was changed to Mt Wellington in 1832; the palawa name 'Kunanyi' was officially added in 2014.

Above left View of Hobart from Kunanyi/Mt Wellington **Above** Myrtle Gully Falls (p70) **Left** Kunanyi/Mt Wellington behind Hobart

spectacularly) an ephemeral lake. Walking trails lead to **Strickland Falls**, **O'Gradys Falls**, **Silver Falls**, **Myrtle Gully Falls**, **New Town Falls** and **Wellington Falls**, the largest and most spectacular of Kunanyi's waterfalls. There's even a waterfall colloquially named **Secret Falls**, the location of which was once jealously guarded by those in the know, though it has become more common knowledge in recent years. Ask around!

After heavy rain or snowmelt, a curious lake named **Disappearing Tarn** often magically appears among the boulders of the Potato Fields on the mountain's southern slopes. When the tarn does appear, which is infrequent, it draws a stream of hikers, all seemingly intent on swimming in its surreal blue waters.

Hidden Peaks

It's a common misconception that Kunanyi/Mt Wellington is a single peak – you need only look over its shoulder to find an array of

Mountain Walks

Pinnacle From the ruins of the old Springs Hotel, the Ice House Track climbs steeply through wet forest then gets *really* rocky before clearing the treeline with nothing to see but views!

Wellington Falls From the Springs, the Milles Track passes the historic mountain water supply and undulates past Disappearing Tarn to the Potato Fields, the most amazing boulder field I've ever seen.

Lost World In and out from Big Bend to this wild jumble of rocks and cliffs. Some scrambling required.

Sphinx Rock Look out over southeast Tassie from the heart of Kunanyi, and get the best views of the Organ Pipes. Get a glimpse of Country. Contemplate the old people.

■ **Recommended by Ben Masterman,** *Wellington Park ranger*

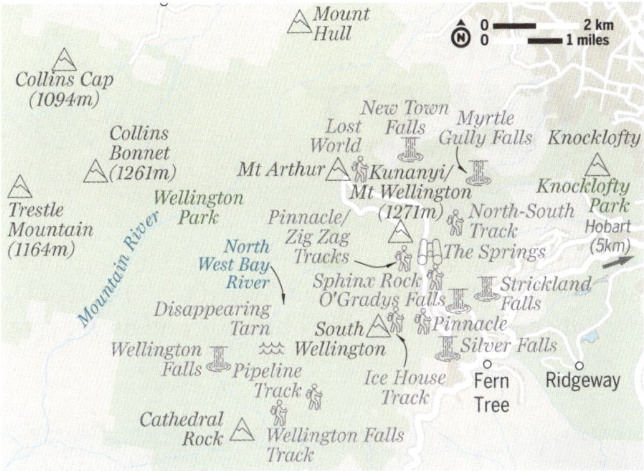

Left View of Hobart from Kunanyi/Mt Wellington **Below** North-South Track

other little-considered summits. From Collinsvale, the Myrtle Forest Track heads towards the plateau, with trails branching away to **Collins Cap** (1094m), **Collins Bonnet** (1261m) and **Trestle Mountain** (1164m), aka Sleeping Beauty. See the latter peak's profile from the Huon Valley and the reason for the name becomes clear.

At the mountain's southern end, the incisor-like **Cathedral Rock** stands tall above North West Bay River, providing a perfect grandstand view over the rest of Kunanyi/Mt Wellington.

On Two Wheels

While a master plan to build a network of mountain-bike trails across the mountain marinates, riders happily content themselves on the 11km **North-South Track**, descending from the Springs to **Glenorchy Mountain Bike Park**. Locals in the know are usually found on the trails above the Cascade Brewery in South Hobart, and there's gentle pedalling along the wide **Pipeline Track** from Fern Tree.

Hardy road cyclists grind up Pinnacle Rd to the summit – a 20km climb from the city – but you can also just do the downhill bit on a guided descent with **Tasmanian Mountain Bike Adventures**, from the summit to the city waterfront.

FROM LEFT: ZETTER/GETTY IMAGES, FILEDIMAGE/GETTY IMAGES

10 Roam the RIVULET

NATURE | HISTORY | BEER

Experience Hobart naturally along its original water source, the chuckling Hobart Rivulet. On this leafy creek-side walk (6km return) you'll pass a UNESCO World Heritage–listed convict site and Australia's oldest brewery, and maybe spot an urban platypus.

STEPHENFARNWORTH/SHUTTERSTOCK

Trip notes

Getting around Don't feel like walking back into town? The hop-on/hop-off Red Decker bus loops past Cascade Brewery on its 90-minute city circuit.

When to go This is an all-season experience. Expect a faster-flowing rivulet in winter, when Kunanyi snowmelt chills South Hobart to the bone.

Fuel up For a mid-wander coffee shot, detour up Anglesea St to Macquarie St and into **Ginger Brown**, one of Hobart's best cafes.

Bushfire Brewing

Cascade's towering (and not un-spooky) facade dates from 1927, but almost didn't make it past 1967, when devastating bushfires blazed through South Hobart and all but destroyed the brewery. Thirsty Hobartians rallied and rebuilt Cascade: amazingly, the beloved brewery was pumping out beer again within three months.

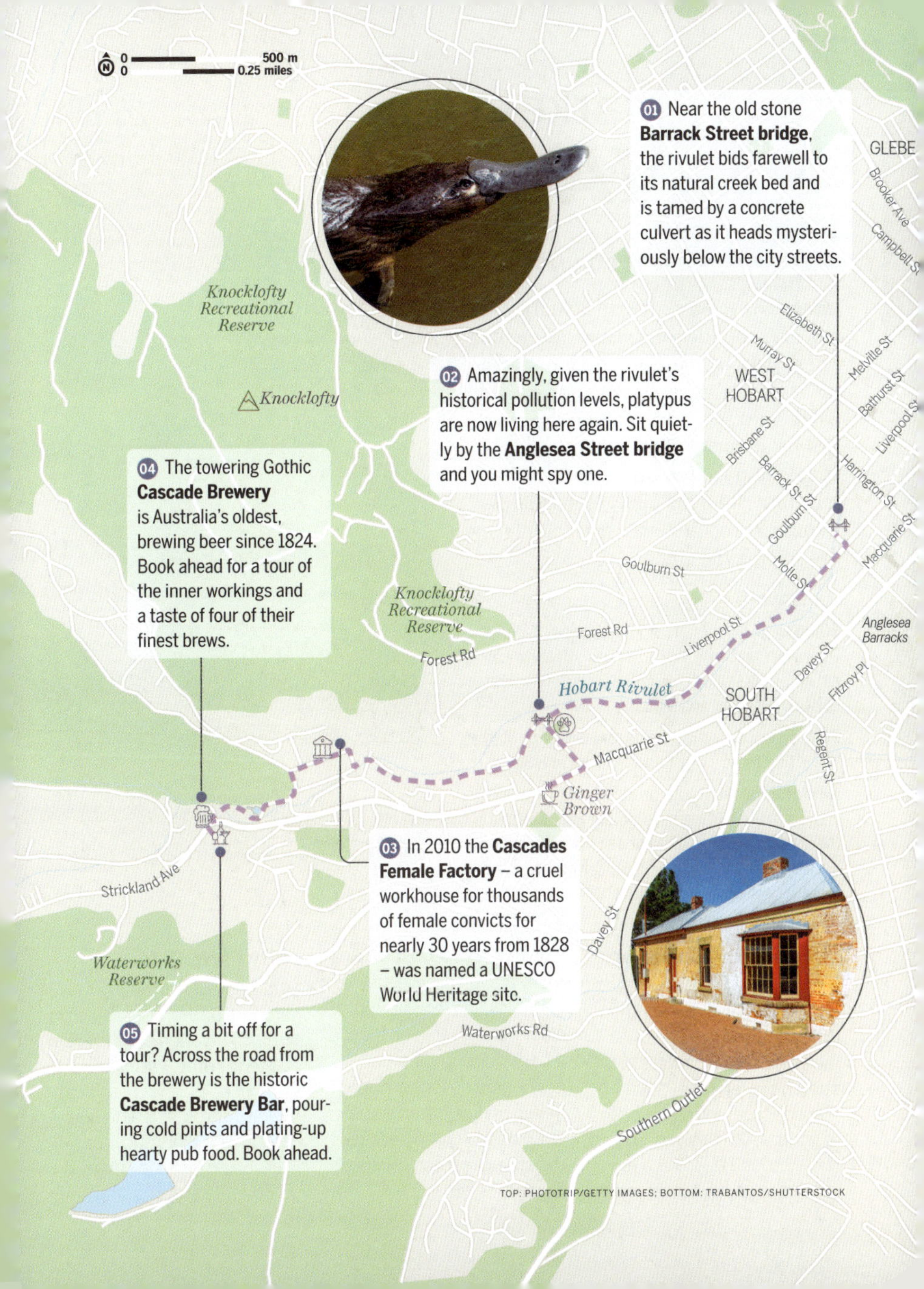

01 Near the old stone **Barrack Street bridge**, the rivulet bids farewell to its natural creek bed and is tamed by a concrete culvert as it heads mysteriously below the city streets.

02 Amazingly, given the rivulet's historical pollution levels, platypus are now living here again. Sit quietly by the **Anglesea Street bridge** and you might spy one.

03 In 2010 the **Cascades Female Factory** – a cruel workhouse for thousands of female convicts for nearly 30 years from 1828 – was named a UNESCO World Heritage site.

04 The towering Gothic **Cascade Brewery** is Australia's oldest, brewing beer since 1824. Book ahead for a tour of the inner workings and a taste of four of their finest brews.

05 Timing a bit off for a tour? Across the road from the brewery is the historic **Cascade Brewery Bar**, pouring cold pints and plating-up hearty pub food. Book ahead.

TOP: PHOTOTRIP/GETTY IMAGES; BOTTOM: TRABANTOS/SHUTTERSTOCK

11 Market VALUE

MARKETS | SHOPPING | CITY LIFE

For years, Salamanca Market was Hobart's number one visitor attraction. These days it shares top honours with MONA – and at more than 50 years old, Salamanca still attracts 800,000-plus people annually. 'The market', as it's simply known, remains a Saturday-morning ritual for many Hobartians – though a crop of newer market offerings are spicing the city up.

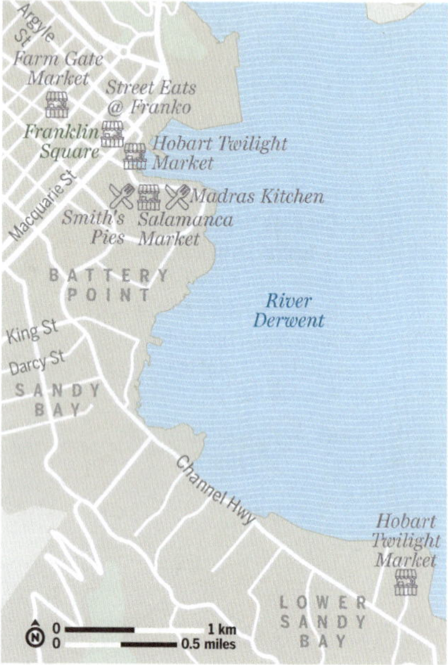

How to

When to go Street Eats @ Franko pops up between December and April, while the Long Beach incarnation of the Hobart Twilight Market only operates between October and March.

Early risers Beat the crowds at Salamanca Market by getting there early; things kick off at 8.30am.

Get foraging Want your produce even fresher? Join Farm Gate Market stallholder Mic Giuliani (siroccosouth.com.au) on one of his seasonal wild asparagus or mushroom foraging tours, rustling together a six-course long lunch.

Saturdays at Salamanca

For visitors to Hobart, Saturdays have long meant the **Salamanca Market**, when more than 200 market stalls stretch the length of Salamanca Place, selling a world of goods from this one island. If you haven't been for a few years, things have changed – there's less tourist tat and more artisan excellence, from ceramics and wood crafts to ciders and chilli beer, most of it handmade and home-grown. You no longer come here because it's on some tick list; you come because the shopping (and the food) is good.

City Farm Gate

When Sunday morning rolls around, Bathurst St closes to traffic and opens to the **Farm Gate Market**. 'Farmy' runs to simple rules: if you can't eat, drink or grow it, it ain't here, and only the producer can sell it. The farm bell rings at 8.30am to start trading, but

JODIE GRIGGS/CONTRIBUTOR/GETTY IMAGES

Salamanca Stalls

With my husband, Christo, I've been selling our handmade jewellery designs – Tasmanian gemstones found and cut by us – at Salamanca Market since 2005. When I get a break, I'll run up to grab my veggies from the organic stall, then quickly check the antiques and bric-a-brac stalls for treasures. For lunch, I'll grab Indian at **Madras Kitchen** or a **Smith's Pies** curried scallop pie, topping it off with a **Gillespie's Ginger Beer**. If I'm looking for a gift, **Buttongrass** (stall 193) sells great handmade soaps, and I love the leather bags at **Henk Berg Leather** (stall 215) and the ceramic wonders from **Sallee Warner** (stall 33).

■ **Mel Lees,** *owner of Rare and Beautiful @therareand beautiful*

the Farmy Grub Hub, with food trucks set into a streetside courtyard, fills bellies from 8am.

More Markets

Street Eats @ Franko is a fun Friday-night food and drink market – think food vans circled like wagons – in Franklin Sq in the CBD. The **Hobart Twilight Market** (hobarttwilight market.com.au) offers food, music and design at two locations on select Fridays: Long Beach (Sandy Bay, south of the city) and the central Brooke St Pier. Check the website for dates. Skip town for the Saturday **New Norfolk Market**, which consumes High St.

Above Salamanca Market

Listings

BEST OF THE REST

Craft Beer

Hobart Brewing Co

Head to the Red Shed on Macquarie Point to find a taproom and beer garden pouring core and seasonal brews. Hosts the Hobart Blues, Brews and Barbecues festival each March.

T-Bone Brewing

Malting grains from the brewer's own family farm (and distillery), this North Hobart brewery has an intimate brewpub bar. Try the winter-warming peanut butter porter.

Captain Bligh's

Hobart's oldest craft brewery still makes a Colonial Ale brewed according to colonial-era regulations. On the third Friday night of the month, the loading dock of its city-centre premises becomes a tasting bar.

Deep South

From its Pale Pedra to its prosciutto and pear pizzas, Deep South's taproom in an Argyle St warehouse doubles as a fine restaurant.

Shambles

Mop up the suds with buffalo wings, fried lentils and popcorn chicken, find the concrete table-tennis table out back, and head off into the night with one of Shambles' takeaway growlers.

Tasmanian-Made

Smitten

Merino has progressed beyond trail wear, as evidenced by this family-run Battery Point business, with apparel that ranges from high-altitude to high-fashion.

Spacebar Gallery

Artist-run gallery in a Salamanca alcove, showcasing quality designs and work from local jewellers, ceramic and textile artists, and other emerging and established makers.

Kudelka Shop

Home to works by mildly anarchic local cartoonist, the late Jon Kudelka: everything from gift cards and tea towels to T-shirts and often-seen 'Tasmania is awful. Never come here' bumper stickers.

City Wineries

Glaetzer-Dixon Family Winemakers

This inner-city urban winery, from a Jimmy Watson Trophy–winning winemaker, suitably feels more like a suave wine bar than a cellar door. Book ahead for a tasting.

Moorilla

The cellar door for southern Tasmania's oldest vineyard is in a very contemporary glass room at MONA, overlooking the gallery lawns with John Olsen's painting *The Source* on the ceiling above.

Noshing in Noho

Pancho Villa $$

Filling a former bank with Day of the Dead decor is this excellent Mexican restaurant and tequila bar. Find the secret door to the courtyard Voodoo Bar.

Born in Brunswick $$

The white Scandi design might entice you in, but you should really come here for the creative brunch offerings. Think butter chicken scrambled eggs and tom yum fried-chicken burgers.

Kalbi $$

Korean classics done well. The Korean Army stew pays rare homage to SPAM, while the 'The Set' is a shared pick through the menu's best items: bibimbap, Korean fried chicken and lettuce wraps.

Room for a Pony $$

Make room for wood-fired pizzas and heated tables outside, beer and nachos inside, and a Bloody Mary in either location. A former windscreen-installation joint turned all-comers cafe/bar.

Green Spaces

Royal Tasmanian Botanical Gardens

Australia's second-oldest botanical gardens sprawl over 14 hectares of native and exotic green goodness. Top of class goes to the Sub Antarctic Plant House, filled with flora from Macquarie Island. Rug up.

St David's Park

This formal park at the CBD's edge was Hobart's original cemetery – check out the memorial wall of headstones. It was once slated to become the city zoo.

Princes Park

Atop Battery Point's namesake gun emplacement, with daisy-studded lawns, River Derwent views and a fabulous playground. Grab some takeaways from Salamanca Place for picnic-rug perfection.

Food Gems on the Periphery

Local Pizza $$

This revered pizza parlour in unfashionable Berriedale is all about communal tables and hand-stretched dough, à la Napoli. MONA isn't too far away.

Lost Freight $

Marooned on the slopes of Kunanyi/Mt Wellington, this shipping-container cafe dispenses warming coffee (welcome at this altitude) and excellent baked accompaniments.

KIRSTEN COVINGTON/SHUTTERSTOCK

Japanese gardens, Royal Tasmanian Botanical Gardens

Salty Dog Hotel $$

Beachside hotel in Kingston Beach serving better-than-most pub food, with a raucous beer garden that's the drinking place to be in summer. Live music Sunday afternoons.

Super Seafood

Flippers $$

Grab waterside fish and chips from this fish-shaped floating caravan at Constitution Dock. Dessert is 10 steps away at the neighbouring Van Diemens Land Creamery mooring.

Fish Frenzy $$

Family-friendly fish feeds, inside and outside Elizabeth St Pier on the waterfront. Grab a table in the sun and splash the vinegar around freely. Seagulls loiter with intent.

Mures $$

A dockside regular. Upstairs is high-end; downstairs has oysters, ice-cream cones to go (promenade past the local yachts and fishing boats) and the best seafood chowder in town. Opens early.

Blue Eye $$$

Seafood linguine, char-grilled octopus, sashimi, garlic-butter abalone...all sluiced down with Tasmanian wines and beers. Long lunch? A Salamanca stalwart.

Premium Dining

Templo $$$

With only 20 seats, most of them around a communal table, and only three or four Italian-inspired mains to choose from, it's an exercise in selectivity and sharing at this tucked-away city treasure.

Fico $$$

This award-winner in the city puts magical spins on local produce, from risotto with mountain pepperberries to sea urchin tortellini. It's the nine-course set menu or nothing.

Dier Makr $$$

Nothing this good should come from a kitchen this bare-bones. It's all innovation in the degustation-only Dier Makr. Finish the evening in the front-of-house Lucinda wine bar.

Faro $$$

Suspend belief – this is MONA, after all – in this gallery restaurant wrapped around the mind-altering immersive artwork *Unseen Seen*. The food is Spanish-inspired.

Peppina $$$

Within the sassy Tasman hotel, peppy Peppina plates up divine modern Italian (try the *paccheri* pork-and-fennel sausage pasta). Super-chef Massimo Mele is at the helm.

Perfect Pubs

Winston $$

It's all craft beer, mac 'n' cheese and wings (go near the Atomic sauce at your peril) at this brilliant US-style pub at the far end of the North Hobart dining strip.

Preachers $$

Praise be that someone thinks an outdoor beer garden works in Hobart. If the patio heaters aren't enough to take off the chill, take your craft beer or wine into the bus or onto the retro sofa inside.

Shamrock Hotel $$

One of a dying breed of of old-school downtown boozers with hefty meals (chips and gravy with most things), all-comer vibes and zero posturing. Change is overrated.

New Sydney $$

Every city has its classic boozer, and in Hobart it's the New Sydney. The twist is in the taps – 15 of them, pouring craft beer. Winter gets the fire cranking.

City Criminals

Hobart Penitentiary

The gallows still work in this hellish city-centre penitentiary, with courtrooms and tunnels. Its solitary cells are built immediately beneath the chapel...so the convicts could still benefit from the sermons, of course.

Sporty Spice

Tasmania JackJumpers

The high-bouncing Tasmania JackJumpers won the National Basketball League championship in just their third season (2024). Catch a home game at MyState Bank Arena in the northern suburbs.

Tasmanian Cricket Museum

If the word 'Boony' makes you nostalgic, pop into this excellent Ninja Stadium museum charting Tasmanian cricket from Charles Eady's world-record 566-run innings to more recent local favourites.

Breakfast Bonanza

Jackman & McRoss $

This enduring Battery Point bakery is as Hobartian as the mountain. Come for breakfast, coffee or the most interesting pies in town

– think braised goat and lentil or scallop and wakame.

Hamlet $$

Tastes good, does good. Behind the quality fare at this cafe beside the Hobart Rivulet is a social enterprise providing work skills to the unemployed and people with disabilities.

Retro Cafe $

Masterful breakfasts, salads and burgers; laughing staff, jazz and the whirr of the coffee machine. Still the best cafe in Salamanca after at least three decades.

Villino Coffee Roasters $

Half the cafes in Hobart use Villino's beans, so track them to their Criterion St source, whether in its cafe or at Ecru, its hole-in-the-wall coffee bar 20m down the street.

Pigeon Whole Bakers $

If you've eaten good bread in Hobart, it's probably come from Pigeon Whole, which seemingly stocks every decent place in town. Pick up a loaf or grab a coffee and pastry.

Stagg Midtown $

Creative streetscaping has transformed this Stagg into a leafy people-watching space to enjoy great coffee and a fresh-baked muffin with seasonal produce.

Cultural Capital

Theatre Royal

Australia's oldest working theatre (treading the boards since 1837) runs hour-long tours and has a busy schedule of all things thespian, lyrical and funny. City centre.

State Cinema

Hobart's arthouse offering has an attached bookshop, cafe and bar, and the city's only rooftop cinema – albeit a summer-only affair at this latitude. North Hobart.

Federation Concert Hall

Find the big brass building seemingly welded to the Hotel Grand Chancellor on the waterfront and you've found the home of the Tasmanian Symphony Orchestra.

Republic Bar & Cafe

Just want some banging tunes? The raucous Republic is Hobart's top music pub, with live gigs most weeks and a buzzy beer garden out the back. North Hobart mainstay.

City Views

Rosny Hill Lookout

Capping its own little peninsula on Hobart's eastern shore, this hilltop lookout peers straight across the river to the city and Kunanyi/Mt Wellington.

Sphinx Rock

An easy 2.7km-return walk leads from the Springs (midway up the slopes of Kunanyi/Mt Wellington) to a sandstone escarpment with views through the trees onto the city.

Mt Nelson Signal Station

Atop the elevated bush suburb of Mt Nelson, an old semaphore station peers over South Arm and Betsey Island to distant Turrakana/Tasman Peninsula.

Trail Gear

Mountain Creek Outdoors

Hobart is an outdoorsy town, and this cluttered, locally owned store – typically the first port of call for gear-hunting locals – stocks pretty much everything you could want on the trail.

Find Your Feet

Owned by former world orienteering champion Hanny Allston, with a high-end range of quality outdoors gear. Top brands and a top store.

TURRAKANA/ TASMAN PENINSULA & THE SOUTHEAST

NATURE | FOOD | ADVENTURE

RESEARCHED BY CHARLES RAWLINGS-WAY

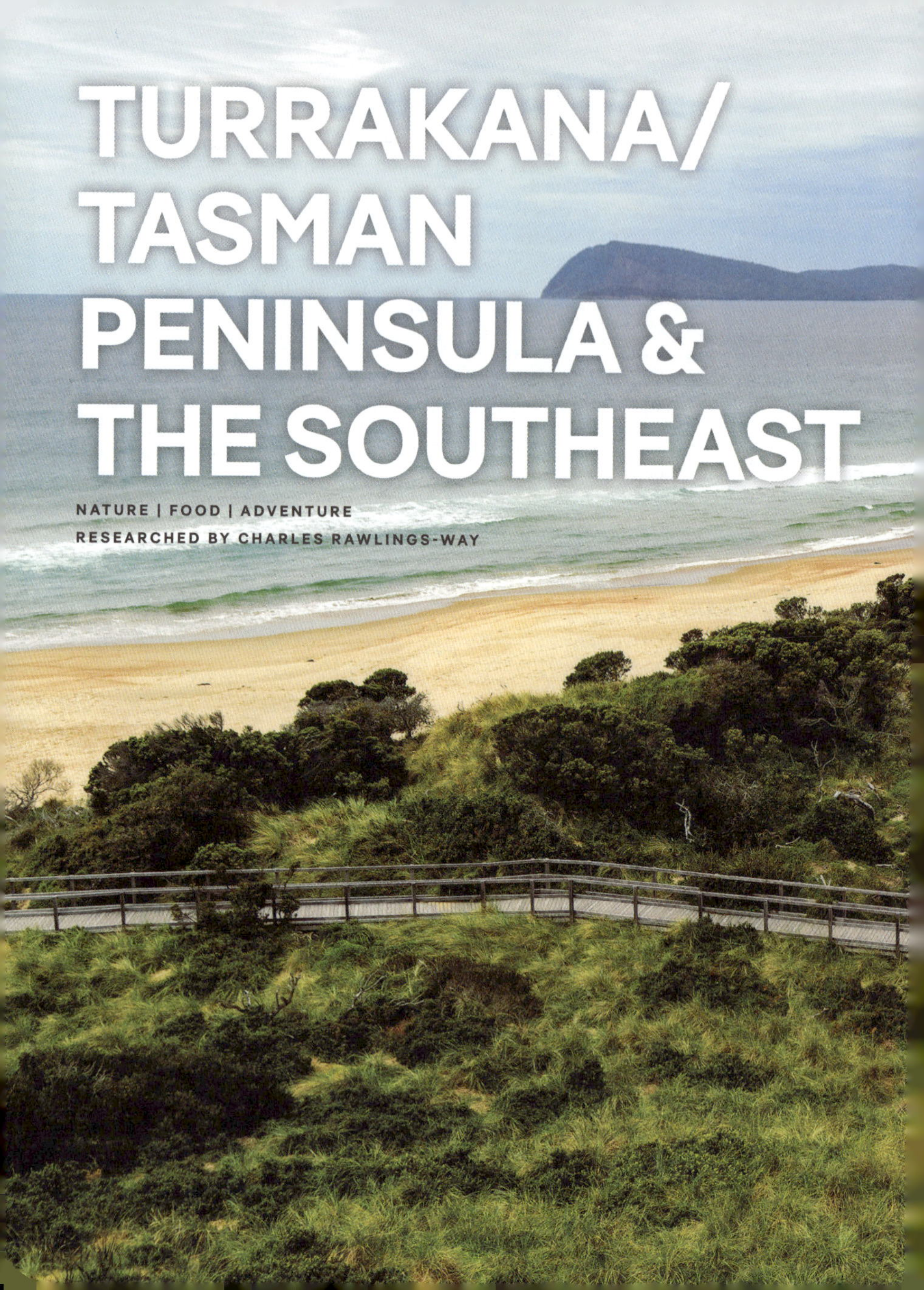

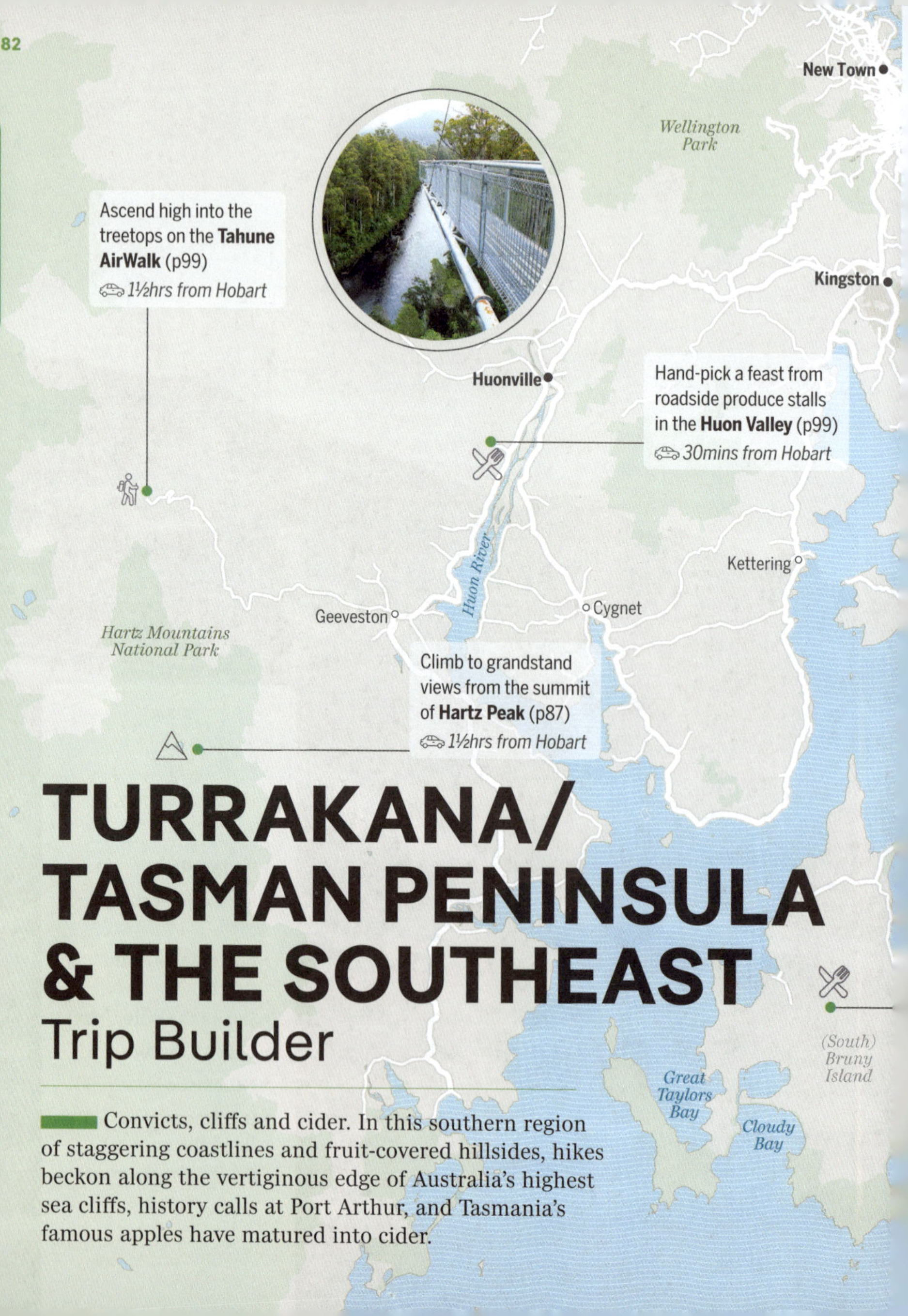

TURRAKANA/ TASMAN PENINSULA & THE SOUTHEAST

Trip Builder

Convicts, cliffs and cider. In this southern region of staggering coastlines and fruit-covered hillsides, hikes beckon along the vertiginous edge of Australia's highest sea cliffs, history calls at Port Arthur, and Tasmania's famous apples have matured into cider.

FROM LEFT: ROBERT SZYMANSKI/SHUTTERSTOCK, ACROPOLYPSEPHOTOGRAPHY/SHUTTERSTOCK, JANETTEASCHE/GETTY IMAGES. PREVIOUS SPREAD: FLORENTINA GEORGESCU PHOTOGRAPHY/GETTY IMAGES

Practicalities

BLUE PLANET STUDIO/SHUTTERSTOCK

ARRIVING

Hobart Airport Hobart is the logical point of entry into the southeast. All the main players have car-rental desks at the airport, which is on the main road towards Turrakana/Tasman Peninsula: head for Sorell and follow the signs. But to get to the Huon Valley and Bruny Island, you'll need to pass through Hobart and head south – the Southern Outlet (A6) is the quickest way out of town.

HOW MUCH FOR A

Port Arthur entry $53

Bruny Island return ferry $56

Three Capes Track walk $625

WHEN TO GO

JAN–MAR
Long sunny days stir beach life

APR–MAY
Stable weather conditions and light winds make coastal life grand

JUN–SEP
Chilly starts, but warm your bones with some Huon Valley mulled cider

OCT–DEC
Warming conditions, though often windy along the coast

GETTING AROUND

Bus Tassielink buses (tassielink.com.au) run from Hobart to Turrakana/Tasman Peninsula, stopping at Dunalley, Teralina/Eaglehawk Neck, Port Arthur and Nubeena. Tassielink also services the south, heading through the Huon Valley to Geeveston and Dover.

Car From Hobart, the Huon Hwy (A6) heads south through the Huon Valley, Dover and Southport to finish at Cockle Creek inside Southwest National Park – as far south as you can drive in Australia. For Turrakana/Tasman Peninsula, the Arthur Hwy (A9) journeys east past the airport and through Sorell to Dunalley, Teralina/Eaglehawk Neck and Port Arthur.

Ferry Bruny Island ferries (sealinkbrunyisland.com.au) depart from Kettering; there are multiple daily sailings for the 20-minute crossing.

EATING & DRINKING

Bruny Island and the Huon Valley are shining stars in Tasmania's foodie firmament. The Huon has long been inseparable from apples, but it's just as rich now in seafood, farm feasts and apple cider. Bruny Island's main road is a progressive supper – cheese, oysters, craft beer, honey, whisky, chocolate, wine – even if its evening dining options are limited. Turrakana/Tasman Peninsula is less noted for its food, but it's still dotted with a few quality options.

Best long lunch Bangor Vineyard Shed (p105)

Must-try spirit Hartshorn Distillery vodka (p100)

TOP: ASHLEY WHITWORTH/SHUTTERSTOCK
BOTTOM: MICHAEL R EVANS/SHUTTERSTOCK

CONNECT & FIND YOUR WAY

Wi-fi Phone and data signal can be patchy around Bruny Island and in the creases of Turrakana/Tasman Peninsula. There's free government wi-fi in the towns of Huonville, Cygnet, Dover and Nubeena, and at the Port Arthur Historic Site.

WHERE TO STAY

Accommodation across this region tends to be dotted through the countryside and coast rather than in towns. Self-catering is a good way to go.

Town	Pros/Cons
Port Arthur	Easy access to the Historic Site and peninsula destinations. No town life.
Teralina/Eaglehawk Neck	Holiday homes along a beaut beach. Slim dining options.
Adventure Bay	Island life in Bruny's main settlement. Dining options are scant.
Geeveston	Central to the southeast, Hartz Mountains and Tahune AirWalk. Good eating, but little holiday vibe.
Dover	Seaside stays about as far south as you can get. Cold water chills the seaside feels.
Cygnet	Artsy, relaxed vibe – good escape, but an extra drive to go anywhere.

BRUNY PETROL

Keep an eye on your fuel levels when touring around Bruny Island. The kilometres add up and the only petrol station is in Adventure Bay.

MONEY

ATMs are few and far between on Bruny Island and Turrakana/Tasman Peninsula: bring cash and credit cards. Outside the big-ticket items – Port Arthur, Tahune AirWalk – attractions are predominantly natural, keeping costs down.

12 Perfect PARKS

NATIONAL PARKS | NATURE | HIKING

National parks run like a frame around the natural brilliance of Turrakana/Tasman Peninsula and the southeast. It's the kind of place where you can climb to an alpine summit in the morning, and be camping on an empty island beach that night. Beaches, cliffs, mountains and caves are all on the agenda.

POSNOV/GETTY IMAGES

How to

Getting around The national parks are typically strung-out reserves, with multiple entry points. You'll need your own wheels to get the best from them.

When to go There's a welcome wildness in the coastal national parks during winter, but the Hartz Mountains and swim spots in the coastal parks are at their best in summer.

Passes A parks pass (passes.parks.tas.gov.au) is needed to enter the national parks. Holiday passes cover you for two months.

BENNY MARTY/SHUTTERSTOCK

The Alpine Park

Hartz Mountains National Park is the soft intro to Tasmania's vast Wilderness World Heritage Area. Strolls lead to Waratah Lookout, Arve Falls and Lake Osborne, one of a string of lakes across the base of the Devils Backbone ridge, but the big draw here is the park's highest point, **Hartz Peak** (1254m), which stares deep into the remote southwest. Pick a fine day and Federation Peak, which Sir Edmund Hillary branded 'Australia's only real mountain', soars into view.

The Island Park

South Bruny National Park runs in a narrow band around Bruny Island's southern edges. Dip into the park at **Cloudy Bay**, where Southern Ocean surf thunders ashore onto a 3km-long beach; at the edge of Adventure Bay, the island's main holiday town; and at **Cape Bruny**, where Australia's second-oldest lighthouse (1836) stands tall. It's the only lighthouse in southern Tasmania open for tours.

The Rock-Star Park

Headlined by Australia's highest sea cliffs, which reach 300m near Cape Pillar, **Tasman National Park** is the full geological magic show. Drop into the **Tessellated Pavement** to find a geometrically perfect rock shelf, and nearby **Tasmans Arch** to see what results when the ocean is in a sculpting mood. Sea pillars abound, most spectacularly at the 65m-high Totem Pole and 110m Candlestick, side-by-side dolerite pillars famed globally among rock climbers. There are good views of them from the tip of **Cape Hauy**.

Top left View from Hartz Peak, Hartz Mountains National Park **Bottom left** Cape Bruny lighthouse

What Lurks Beneath

Not all of the far south's natural treasures are above the ground. Delve beneath the surface at **Hastings Caves State Reserve**, where rangers lead tours through Newdegate Cave, Australia's largest dolomite show cave. Expect the full roster of subterranean formations – stalactites, stalagmites, shawls, draping flowstones and gravity-defying helictites. It's a constant 9°C in the cave, but a dip in the 28°C waters of the **thermal pool** behind the visitor centre will soon warm the digits. Nearby, little-visited **Mystery Creek Cave**, where a teacher and two students were killed in a flash flood in 1990, is home to one of Australia's best glow-worm displays.

13

Escape to PORT ARTHUR

HISTORY | CONVICTS | GARDENS

Few prisons have ever had the teasing beauty of Port Arthur Historic Site, where the natural magnificence of the sea, islands, coast and bush was like a mirage to tormented and tortured convicts. Today, this mix of beauty and brutality is still very evident at the World Heritage–listed site.

KARENFOLEYPHOTOGRAPHY/SHUTTERSTOCK

How to

Getting here Port Arthur is a 90-minute drive from Hobart. Pennicott Wilderness Journeys runs a daily bus service from Hobart to the site.

Spread out Tickets to the Historic Site give you entry for two consecutive days – break things up and stick around for a couple of days.

Remarkable sight It's a 6km detour from Port Arthur to **Remarkable Cave**, a tunnel bored through the cliffs, with views through the 'cave' out across the Southern Ocean.

WILLOWTREEHOUSE/SHUTTERSTOCK

Convict Town

The broken heart of the Port Arthur Historic Site is its convict settlement. The most striking structure is the **Penitentiary**, which you can wander freely through. It began life as a flour mill and granary, operated at times by convicts on treadmills. When converted into a penitentiary, it contained 136 separate cells. More chilling than this crumbled behemoth is the **Separate Prison**, where convicts were locked in isolation cells for 23 hours a day and prevented from speaking – mental punishment to go with the existing physical punishments. The individual booths in the chapel are testament to the inhumane isolation of this prison wing.

Free Town

Side by side with the convict structures was the free town of Port Arthur, once the third- or

LKONYA/GETTY IMAGES

The Human Tramway

Pause at the Taranna jetty, 10km from Port Arthur, and ponder the fact that this was once the terminus of a human-powered tramway, with convicts pushing 'trams' filled with freight and passengers along wooden rails over the hills from Port Arthur. It was Australia's first railway.

Top left Penitentiary **Above** Port Arthur Law Courts **Left** Government Gardens (p90)

fourth-largest settlement in Tasmania. The town's beauty offset the prison's brutality, with formal gardens and rows of cottages giving homesick settlers a far-flung feeling of home. The ornamental **Government Gardens** are a recreation of the original gardens, where officers and free settlers could wander, away from the disheartening sight of convicts. Behind the gardens is the shell of the **Church**, built in 1838 and unconsecrated (so multi-denominational services could be held). The decorative work was largely done by boys imprisoned at nearby Point Puer. Step into the **Civil Officers' Row**, arranged in a line along the site's western side, to see how Port Arthur's other half lived.

Ghosts & Graves

Entry tickets to the historic site include an introductory walking tour and a short harbour cruise, but a handful of other tours delve deeper into Port Arthur nuances. Tiny **Isle**

Port Arthur's Haunted Sites

The Port Arthur Historic Site is claimed as one of Australia's most haunted places, and we receive regular reports of strange activity. The **Parsonage** has held the title of most haunted building in the country. Reverend Eastman died upstairs here, and we get stories of footsteps, yelling and a real sense of unease. The **Separate Prison** has a cell where a convict took his own life; people have passed out here. There's also the **Basement**, where it's suspected people were dissected. I've had fainting here too.

■ **By Meahd Farnaby**, *ghost tour guide at the Port Arthur Historic Site @portarthuraussie*

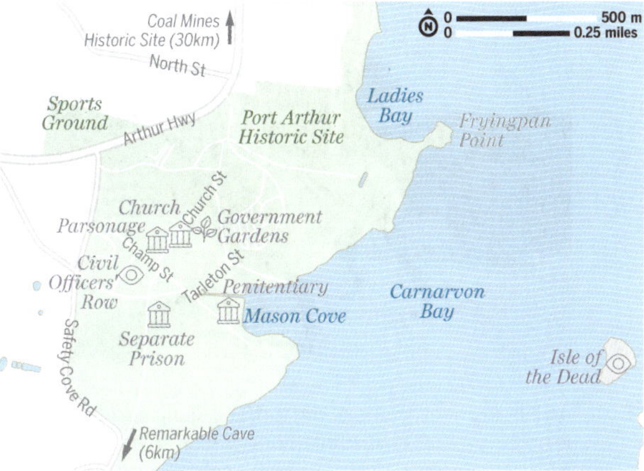

Left Separate Prison (p89)
Below Coal Mines Historic Site

of the Dead, visited on one of the site's tours, was the burial place of more than 1000 convicts, military officers and family members – convicts in unmarked graves on the island's lower slopes, the free settlers in higher marked graves. Among the convicts buried here was Henry Savery, the author of Australia's first novel. The **Premium Tour** is an extended walking tour of the site, while the **Escape from Port Arthur Tour** is all about ripping yarns of attempted (and mostly failed) escapes. The evening **Ghost Tour** delves into Port Arthur's more spirited side.

Tasmania's First Mine

Across the peninsula from Port Arthur is its little-known companion piece, the **Coal Mines Historic Site** (also part of the Australian Convict Sites World Heritage listing). Set up in 1833 to punish the worst of the convicts – solitary cells were set deep in the mine shafts – it was Tasmania's first operational mine, housing up to 600 convicts, with around 60,000 tonnes of coal extracted. A 2km walk (one of Tasmania's 60 Great Short Walks) weaves through the evocative ruins – the coal seam and some of the earliest diggings are visible on the rocky beach below the ruins.

FAR LEFT: THPSTOCK/SHUTTERSTOCK, NEAR LEFT: BENNYMARTY/GETTY IMAGES

Australia's Alcatraz

ONE NARROW DETAIL PREVENTED CONVICTS FROM ESCAPING PORT ARTHUR

Freedom teased at Port Arthur. The surrounding bush promised cover, and it might have appeared a simple task to break out, but this remote convict settlement had one ingenious bit of escape-proofing, and it was provided by nature: the Teralina/Eaglehawk Neck isthmus.

Left Bronze statue by Ruth Waterhouse and Curtis Hore representing the Dog Line at Eaglehawk Neck **Middle and right** Eaglehawk Neck and Tasman's Arch from the Werner Company 'Federated Australia' collection, unknown artist

TRAVELSCAPE IMAGES/ALAMY

As if being sent to one of the furthest-flung corners of an island in one of the furthest-flung places on the planet from Britain wasn't demoralising enough, nature and human nature conspired to make Port Arthur almost escape-proof. Turrakana/Tasman Peninsula clings to the Tasmanian mainland by a literal thread – the Teralina/Eaglehawk Neck isthmus, which, at its narrowest, is little more than 100m wide. To prevent convicts from escaping, all authorities had to do was guard this filament of land and stop the convicts from taking to the water.

Barking Mad

Preventing escape via the water was largely achieved through the age-old tactic of fear, with convicts told that the local waters were infested with sharks (only a white lie, really). Which just left the isthmus. In 1831, following a number of escape attempts in the first year of the penal settlement's existence at Port Arthur, sentries were posted at Teralina/Eaglehawk Neck, though they were ineffective because the noise of the surrounding ocean masked the sound of any convicts trying to slip through. That's when an officer came up with the idea of stringing a line of savage dogs across the isthmus.

The so-called Dog Line involved up to 18 dogs tethered across the sandy isthmus, with wooden barrels as kennels and spaced so that their snouts almost touched when they reached the end of their chains. Other dogs were placed on platforms in the sea, to detect any escapees trying to swim past the isthmus. Shells were also spread across the narrow neck of land. Any approaching convict

PRINT COLLECTOR/GETTY IMAGES

PRINT COLLECTOR/GETTY IMAGES

would have to crunch over the shells – no dog was going to miss the sound or the stench of an unwashed convict.

Today, a bronze statue of a tethered dog on Teralina/Eaglehawk Neck marks the site of the Dog Line.

Escape Attempts

Desperate times call for desperate measures, and bolts for freedom were still occasionally made. Most famously, bushranger Martin Cash managed to twice slip through the Teralina/Eaglehawk Neck dog fortress. The first time he succeeded in swimming across Eaglehawk Bay, the narrow bay on the isthmus' western side, though he was soon recaptured and returned to Port Arthur. In 1842, with two other convicts, he again swam past the Neck to freedom – note the attempt by water again, which is testament to the deterrent effect of the dogs.

An officer came up with the idea of stringing a line of savage dogs across the isthmus.

The most entertaining escape attempt belonged to George 'Billy' Hunt. The Scotsman, who was transported to Australia for stealing a handkerchief, wrapped himself in the skin of a kangaroo and endeavoured to hop across the isthmus. It all came undone because the rationed and hungry guards saw a potential meal hopping past, rather than a convict in disguise. When they raised their guns to shoot the 'roo, Hunt threw off the hide and surrendered.

Cashing In

When Martin Cash escaped from Port Arthur on Boxing Day in 1842, he set out on a crime spree that lasted for eight months, immortalising himself as one of Australia's most notorious bushrangers. His rampage only ended when he headed to Hobart in August 1843, vowing to kill his cheating girlfriend and her new beau. Confronted by a constable, he shot and killed the policeman and was sentenced to death. A last-minute reprieve saw him sent to Norfolk Island instead. He later became a constable at Hobart's Cascades Female Factory and overseer at the Royal Tasmanian Botanical Gardens.

14 Out on the WATER

WATER SPORTS | ADVENTURE | NATURE

Tasmania's southeast has almost as much coastline as land, with the cliff-wrapped Turrakana/Tasman Peninsula and Bruny Island, and the veined waterways of the far south, beckoning to be explored from water level. Sit back on a fast-paced cruise along wild shores, kayak beneath 300m-high cliffs, and dive to discover the Tassie treasures that linger beneath the ocean's surface.

SUMMIT ART CREATIONS/SHUTTERSTOCK

How to

Getting here Bruny Island Cruises depart from either Hobart or at the launch site at Adventure Bay. Tasman Island Cruises depart from Port Arthur – drive yourself or catch the Pennicott Wilderness Journeys bus. Turrakana/Tasman Peninsula kayaking trips depart from Hobart or Fortescue Bay.

When to go Kayaking trips typically operate between October and April; boat cruises run year-round.

Cold clarity Divers will find the water warmest in summer, but the clarity is best in winter.

ARTIE PHOTOGRAPHY/GETTY IMAGES

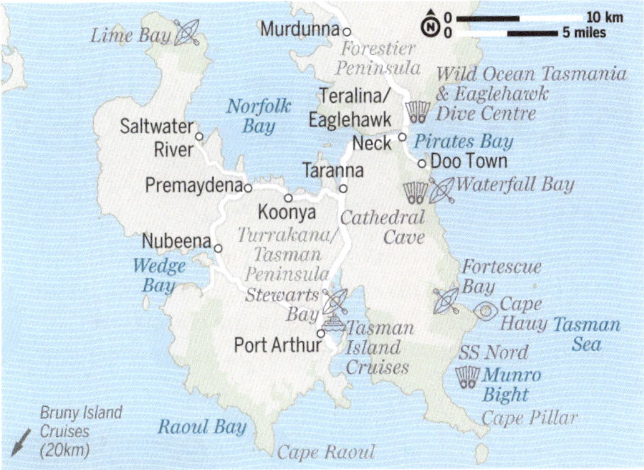

Cliffside Cruises

The Turrakana/Tasman Peninsula and Bruny Island coastlines are pieced together like a Jenga puzzle of dolerite columns, slender sea stacks and deep caves. **Tasman Island Cruises** speed beneath Australia's tallest sea cliffs to Tasman Island; **Bruny Island Cruises** round Fluted Cape to the fringe of the Southern Ocean; and eco-attuned **Wild Ocean Tasmania** heads around the cliffs near Teralina/Eaglehawk Neck to spy seabirds, Australian fur seals, and occasionally orcas and whales.

Paddle Power

Turrakana/Tasman Peninsula's cliffs look even larger from down at sea level. The **Roaring 40s Kayaking** day tour paddles out of Fortescue Bay to the cliffs (and seals) at Cape Hauy, while **Southern Sea Ventures** runs four-day kayaking trips along the Turrakana coast and a five-day Bruny Island paddle. In season (May, June, October and November) the focus of the trips turns to migrating whales. **Esperance Adventures** has a range of guided day paddles in the far south, including along the dark, tannin-stained Huon and Lune rivers.

Deep Dive

Even with the loss of Turrakana/Tasman Peninsula's magnificent giant kelp forests – hello, climate change – the area has some fantastic dives. **Cathedral Cave** at Waterfall Bay is a portal into Australia's largest sea-cave system, while the **SS Nord**, which sank off the peninsula in 1915, offers good wreck diving. Colourful weedy seadragons are another feature of peninsula dives. **Eaglehawk Dive Centre** is your go-to.

Top left Turrakana/Tasman Peninsula cruise **Bottom left** Bruny Island

Turrakana/Tasman Peninsula Coastal Sites

Fortescue Bay From this perfect quartzite beach, it's an exciting and humbling paddle out to Cape Hauy, feeling the ocean swell, visiting fur seals and seeing the iconic Totem Pole and Candlestick formations.

Waterfall Bay As the high waterfall here pours into the sea, the only way to get up close is by kayaking – into, through and around the bay's incredible formations – when the ocean allows it.

Lime Bay Filled with history, and with stunning shallow paddling when the sun is out.

Stewarts Bay A great place to be on the water, with a view to nearby Cape Pillar and Tasman Island.

Recommended by Tory Stewart, *Roaring 40s Kayaking guide @roaring40skayaking*

15 Caped CRUSADE

HIKING | NATURE | NATIONAL PARK

Tasmanian bushwalking took a twist when the 48km Three Capes Track opened in 2015, tracing the lofty clifftops of Turrakana/Tasman Peninsula. With long stretches of boardwalk and the swishest hiking huts in the country, it begged the question of all other long-distance trails: why do it rough when you can walk in Three Capes style?

POSNOV/GETTY IMAGES

How to

Getting here The walk sets out from the Port Arthur Historic Site. Pennicott Wilderness Journeys, which operates the track's boat transfer, also runs a dedicated bus service from Hobart to Port Arthur.

Best season Summer brings long, warm days – between Christmas and New Year, you might even see the Sydney to Hobart yachts passing beneath the cliffs.

Bookings It's essential to book (threecapestrack.com.au), with only 48 people permitted to set out each day.

THOMAS DEVENISH/SHUTTERSTOCK

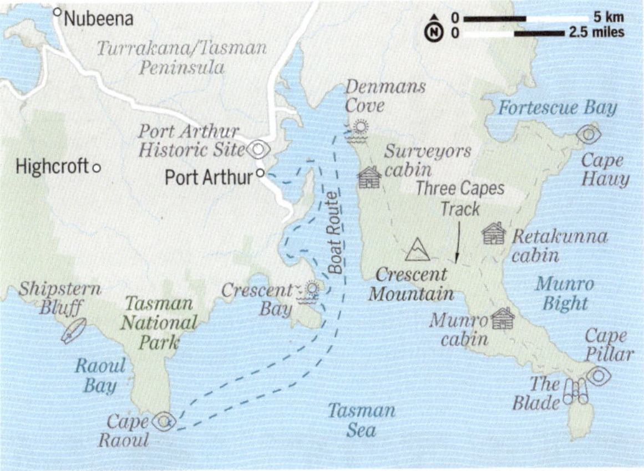

Boots & Boats

The first steps on the Three Capes Track aren't onto land. They're onto a boat, with the walk beginning with a boat-transfer-cum-cruise from the Port Arthur Historic Site. The 75-minute transfer explores the Port Arthur coastline, viewing the **Crescent Bay** dunes, **Cape Raoul** (the first cape), peeping into sea caves and providing an advance look at the Arthurs Peak section of the track. You'll step onto dry land at **Denmans Cove** – after you slip off your boots and wade ashore.

Epic Cliffs

The Three Capes' raison d'être is its cliffs, which, around **Cape Pillar**, tower 300m above the ocean, making them Australia's highest sea cliffs. On day three of the walk – the Three Capes' signature day – the track edges along the clifftops to Cape Pillar and **The Blade**, a knife-edge column of dolerite with a heady view over Tasman Island and the Southern Ocean far below.

Cool Cabins

The track is strung with three plush public cabins: **Surveyors**, **Munro** and **Retakunna**. Each one is fitted with mattresses, cooking equipment, deck chairs, yoga mats, reference books, USB charging stations and million-dollar views. Munro even has two outdoor showers. Challenged to surpass this swanky set-up, the private, luxury operator along the track, the **Three Capes Lodge Walk**, popped a day spa into one of its two huts.

Top left Tasman Island and The Blade
Bottom left View from Cape Raoul lookout

The Missing Cape

Count the capes along the Three Capes Track and you'll only get to two: Cape Pillar and Cape Hauy. The original plans for the track included neighbouring Cape Raoul, but the logistics didn't add up. Instead, you get to see Cape Raoul from the boat at the start of your journey. The southernmost point of Turrakana/Tasman Peninsula, Cape Raoul is also arguably the most spectacular of the capes, with its tip stepping down into the sea in a line of slender dolerite columns. It's also fringed by **Shipstern Bluff**, a legendary big-wave surf spot.

16 Hedonistic HUON

FOOD | CIDER | FESTIVITIES

The Huon Valley was the original apple in Tasmania's eye, the region on which the brand of the Apple Isle was founded. Though still covered in orchards, time and tastes have moved on, and today the region is squeezing out world-class cider, alongside fine wine and produce, all in the shadow of some of the world's tallest trees.

FILEDIMAGE/SHUTTERSTOCK

How to

Getting here Tassielink buses from Hobart stop at Grove, Huonville, Cygnet, Franklin, Geeveston and Dover, but you'll need a vehicle to get to places beyond and between.

When to go Harvest season for apples and stone fruit is across summer.

Cash & carry Carry some coins and small notes if you plan to pick up produce from roadside stalls. Most operate on cash-only honesty-box systems.

SOUTHERN STUDIOS/ALAMY

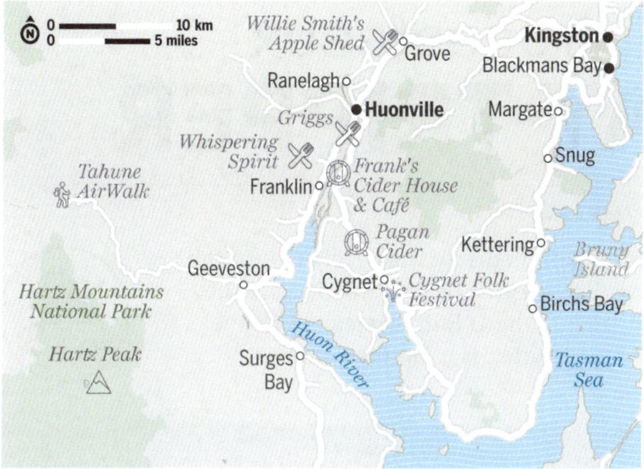

Time for a Cider

The Huon's apples are just as likely to make their way into cider as fruit aisles these days. Call into **Willie Smith's Apple Shed** at Grove, a former apple barn turned bar, restaurant, apple distillery and cider cellar door – check out the display of almost 400 apple varieties. **Frank's Cider House & Café**, inside a little old 1870s weatherboard church in Franklin, and the piety-defusing **Pagan Cider** near Cygnet are also good for tastings.

Roadside Stalls

An enduring tradition throughout the Huon Valley is simple roadside produce stalls, which become numerous during the summer harvest. The roads between Huonville and Cygnet and between Franklin and Geeveston are prime territory. A couple of stalwarts near Franklin to seek out include **Griggs**, selling its unique Rubigold apple variety; and **Whispering Spirit**, where the produce shares billing with handmade ice cream in local flavours such as mountain pepperberry and lemon myrtle.

Tree Change

The Arve Valley near Geeveston is the home of giant *Eucalyptus regnans* trees, aka mountain ash. One tree here, Centurion, has been measured at 100.5m in height, making it one of the tallest flowering plants on Earth. Drive through the Arve on your way to the **Tahune AirWalk**, where an elevated metal walkway ascends 30m into the forest canopy. A cantilevered platform overhanging the Huon River adds a little spice to the walk.

Top left Tahune AirWalk
Bottom left Willie Smith's cider

Get Folked

The second weekend in January sees the small, arts-and-craftsy Huon Valley town of Cygnet resound to the sounds of acoustic guitars, mandolins and duelling banjos. The three-day **Cygnet Folk Festival** (cygnetfolkfestival.org) is heavily community-driven – an earthy celebration of folk, roots and world music, poetry, dance and performing arts, all sluiced down with fabulous Huon Valley food, wine and endless cider. Little Cygnet is inundated with visitors from far and wide, most choosing to camp to maximise the Woodstock-era vibes. It's all kinds of wholesome, inclusive, rainbow-tinged and family-friendly fun. Book your tickets in advance.

17 D'Entrecasteaux DAY-TRIPPER

FOOD | WINE | QUIET COASTLINES

You can race along the main highway from Hobart into the Huon Valley if you like – but why rush? The slow road along the super-scenic Channel Hwy, tracing the D'Entrecasteaux Channel from Kingston to Huonville via Cygnet, is a fabulous day out.

POSNOV/GETTY IMAGES

How to

Getting around Public Metro buses will get you some of the way down the Channel, some of the time – but you'll be much better off exploring with your own wheels.

When to go This drive is as atmospheric on a windy winter Wednesday as it is on a sunny summer Saturday.

Combine walks Finish your day trip with dinner and a beer at the **Lost Captain** by the Huon River in Huonville.

French Connections

French explorers Bruni d'Entrecasteaux, Jean-Michel Huon de Kermadec and Nicolas Baudin charted much of this convoluted coastline in the 1790s and early 1800s. Bruny Island, the D'Entrecasteaux Channel, Huonville, Huon River and Kermandie are part of their local legacy. Cygnet's first European name was Port de Cygnes (Port of Swans).

01 First stop is Margate: pull over to check out the shops and cafes in the marooned **Margate Train** – actually the *Tasman Ltd*, Tasmania's last passenger train, that stopped rolling in 1978.

02 The road meanders between hills and water to pretty Woodbridge, famous for its school where students grow their own vegetables, and the flashy-but-still-earthy **Peppermint Bay Hotel**. Coffee time.

03 At Birchs Bay, **Grandvewe** offers sheep's-cheese tastings and spirits from its sister distillery **Hartshorn**. Fancy a sheep's whey vodka? It was voted 'World's Best Varietal Vodka' in 2018.

04 The Channel Hwy weaves into Flowerpot: pull into **Mewstone Wines** for a tasting with views. Run by the Hughes brothers, this former cherry orchard now produces pinot noir, chardonnay and riesling.

05 Soporific **Verona Sands** beach is good for a moody stroll on a rainy Channel afternoon – before the road, originally heading south, veers north into folky/foodie Cygnet. Cafe time!

TOP: PEPPERMINT BAY HOTEL, BOTTOM: JANELLE LUGGE/SHUTTERSTOCK

18 Bruny ESCAPES

NATURE | FOOD | WALKS

Bruny is the island every city wishes it had within a 30-minute drive of the CBD. Wrapped in beaches, cliffs and surf, and magically held together by the narrowest of sand isthmuses, it's a place devoted to nature and nurture in equal measures, with its coastal walks matched in quality only by the freshness of the island produce.

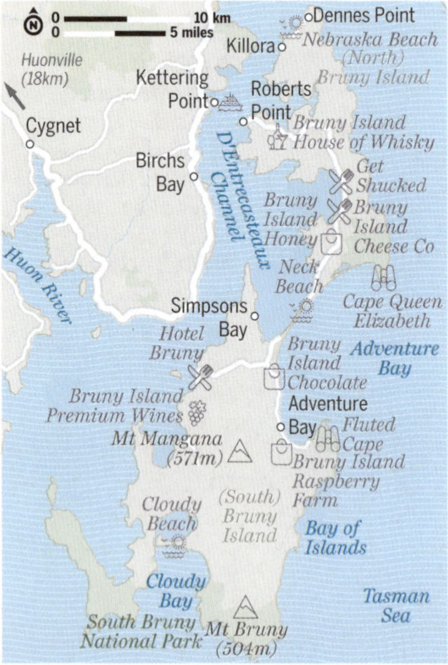

How to

Getting here The island ferry (sealinkbrunyisland .com.au) departs multiple times a day from Kettering.

When to go Long queues for the ferry aren't uncommon during school holidays. To avoid them, November, early December, February and March are good times to visit.

Happy housemates Stick around at night to watch little penguins coming ashore at the Neck, where the birds have the rare habit of sharing their burrows with migratory muttonbirds (September to April).

Bruny Bites

By day, Bruny Island is a veritable providore (by night it's a dining desert, with **Hotel Bruny** likely to be the only dinner option – try the house-made cider), demanding at least a few hours of idle grazing time. Pair cheese and craft beer under the gum trees at **Bruny Island Cheese Co**, slurp oysters at **Get Shucked** (complete with a drive-through oyster window), sip a smooth spirit at **Bruny Island House of Whisky** and a fine drop at **Bruny Island Premium Wines**, Australia's southernmost winery. **Bruny Island Honey**, **Bruny Island Raspberry Farm** and **Bruny Island Chocolate** sweeten the deal.

Walk This Way

Bruny's coast is as exceptional as it is varied. Walk to **Cape Queen Elizabeth** at low tide and it's possible to squeeze

ESTIVILLML/GETTY IMAGES

Bruny Beaches

Some of my favourite Bruny beaches are known by many people, but are large enough to make you think you're alone.

For a lazy swim, I love the crystal-white sands and blue water of **Nebraska Beach** – out to the mooring buoys and back. **Neck Beach** is long and usually deserted, with a nice surf break when the banks are working. **Adventure Bay** leaves you spoilt for choice – it's great for families. Further south, **Cloudy Bay** ticks all the boxes: the best surf and a long stretch of beach to explore.

The great secrets, though, are to be found by boat or kayak. Tiny little sandy coves reminiscent of the Greek islands emerge everywhere at low tide.

Recommended by Lee Macefield, *owner of Get Shucked oyster farm @get_shucked_oysters*

through gaps in the cliffs to find an arch of rock curling out of the Moorina Bay sand. The **Fluted Cape** walk passes through the remains of a whaling station before climbing atop some of Australia's highest cliffs – this is also the walk on which you might sight one of Bruny's rare white wallabies. Inland, an ascent through rainforest leads to the island's highest point, 571m **Mt Mangana**. The messy summit might appear to have no views, but all is revealed if you find the trail to the right, heading to an open boulder field.

Above Nebraska Beach

Listings

BEST OF THE REST

Caffeine Cravings

Cubed Espresso Bar $

Good coffee with an even better view from this solar-powered retro caravan parked beside Pirates Bay Lookout at Teralina/Eaglehawk Neck, with seats, cushions and rugs laid out beside the road.

Reba Sear $

Coffee with something extra at this funky little Huonville cafe – in this case, gifts of homewares and the likes of design and architecture books.

Pickers Pantry Orchard Cafe $

Sit out in the pear orchard for your coffee and toastie at this White Beach farm cafe on Turrakana/Tasman Peninsula, tacked onto the end of packing sheds. Check out the attached art gallery.

Porthole Cafe $

Coffee, cakes, tarts (lots of GF and vegan), milkshakes, and all-day toasties and fries. Outdoor tables on Cygnet's main street, overlooking the lush paddocks out back.

Rocket@TheEndOfTheRoad $

Wacked-out water tank at the end of the Huon Hwy in Southport, the last reasonably sized settlement heading south, selling excellent coffee and muffins. Seasonal hours.

Southern Feeds

Masaaki's Sushi $

Widely hailed as Australia's best sushi, dished up from Geeveston's former Anglican church. Come early (it opens at midday Friday to Sunday) because it's open until it's sold out (which happens quickly).

Cinnamon & Cherry $

Roll into Franklin for this excellent cafe serving Turkish baked eggs and punchy coffee, with the Huon River sliding by silently just across the road.

Old Bank of Geeveston $$

A curious but successful combo of classy Mod Oz fare and gardening store. Winner of Tassie's best wine list in 2021, but also excellent for a morning coffee on the outdoor deck.

Botega Crippa $

Superb freshly made pasta arranged in neat swirls, plus jars of homemade ragu and ready-to-eat focaccia slabs and pizza slices. On Huonville's main drag.

Red Velvet Lounge $$

Cygnet's favourite coffee-and-cake hangout also does progressive pizzas, pasta, salads and pies, inside its artful main-street shopfront (love the old ceilings). Live music on Fridays.

Summer Kitchen Bakery $

It's not unusual to find Summer's baked goods selling across Hobart – they're that good. They're best enjoyed in situ, in the side courtyard at this simple bakery.

Peninsula Pickings

The Lanterns $

Surprising Dunalley cafe, with the peninsula's best coffee, cheese-and-chive scones and beaut baguettes. The wall of providore goodies is positively urbane.

Doo-Lishus $

It's just a caravan in a car park (at the Blowhole in Doo Town) and yet it's held by many to serve up Tasmania's best fish and chips.

Cannery $$

Don't muck around – order a seafood platter and head for the deck at this Dunalley gem, down by the canal (yes, in 1942 this was a fish cannery).

On the Bay $$$

The peninsula's best restaurant is inside Stewarts Bay Lodge, with bush-wrapped, waterfront dining filled with Tasmanian flavours.

Devil of a Time

Tasmanian Devil Unzoo

A new take on zoos – unfenced (but for the enclosed Tasmanian devils), with animals free to come and go as they choose. Join a Devil Tracker tour to help out with local devil research.

Pitching in Parks

Fortescue Bay, Tasman National Park

A perpetual family-favourite camping ground, sprawled beneath tall eucalypts behind Fortescue's white sands.

Cloudy Corner, South Bruny National Park

Walk or 4WD along the hard-packed Cloudy Bay beach to this bush camping ground tucked behind the strand's far end. The wild surf dulls to a murmur in this corner, providing good warm-weather swimming.

Cockle Creek, Southwest National Park

You can drive no further south in Australia than this strung-out camping ground, facing onto protected Recherche Bay. Walk the 8km to South Cape Bay to see Australia's southernmost point.

Boats Afloat

Wooden Boat Centre

Keeping alive the ancient art of wooden-boat building, this revered Franklin centre runs guided tours of its works-in-progress, or you can sign on to build yourself something that floats.

Farmhouse Feasting

Farmhouse Kitchen $$$

Giuliana White shares her passion for the flavours of her Puglian homeland in these Italian cooking classes, held at her beautiful farmhouse near Cygnet.

Wine Times

Bangor Vineyard Shed

This vineyard on a farm dripping with Tasmanian history has a restaurant and tasting room looking over the vines and the sea to Dunalley.

Kate Hill Wines

Step into a heritage-listed 1880s Huon Valley cottage surrounded by vines for a personal tasting experience. There are wines for adults, and toys and kites for the kids.

Home Hill Wines

In Ranelagh, this stylish, rammed-earth winery attracts architecture and wine fans alike for superb pinot noir, chardonnay and dessert wines. There's an upmarket restaurant too.

Distilling Moments

McHenry Distillery

Tucked into bush 350 vertical metres up the slopes from Port Arthur, this isolated distillery has gin and whisky tasting paddles, a brewery, and runs gin-making workshops.

Bakehouse Distillery

Call in to Australia's southernmost distillery, in far-south Dover, to sample the world's first sassafras spirit. Call in advance to make sure they're open.

HIGHLANDS, MIDLANDS & CRADLE COUNTRY

OUTDOORS | HISTORY | ADVENTURE

RESEARCHED BY CHARLES RAWLINGS-WAY

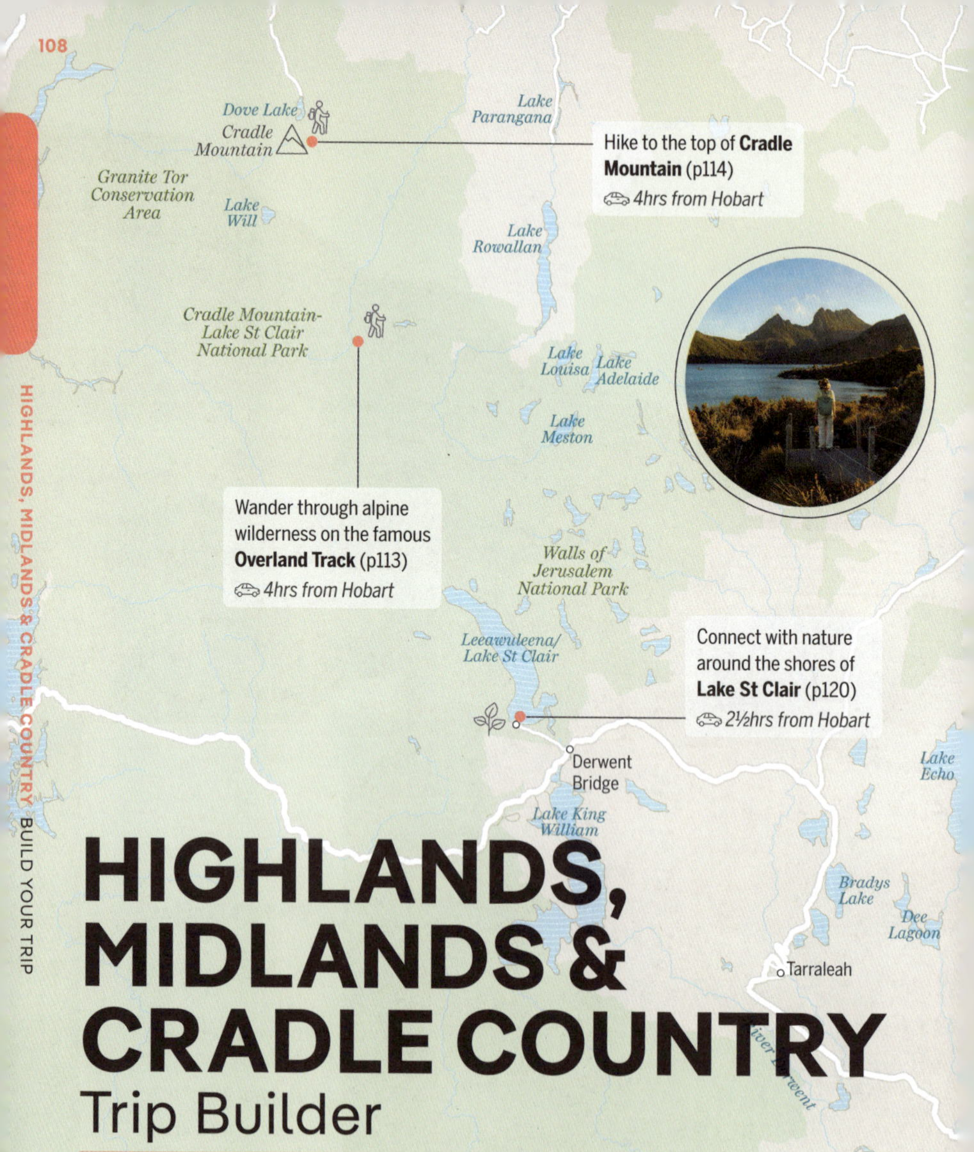

HIGHLANDS, MIDLANDS & CRADLE COUNTRY

Trip Builder

Rural, rustic and rugged: this is the heartland of Tasmania and you can feel it everywhere. From the historic towns of the Midlands to the trout-filled Highlands' lakes and World Heritage-listed wilderness of Cradle Country, you are immersed.

FROM LEFT: OLEH_SLOBODENIUK/GETTY IMAGES, TRABANTOS/SHUTTERSTOCK, RATHO FARM. PREVIOUS SPREAD: POSNOV/GETTY IMAGES

Practicalities

WILLIAM WEST/AFP VIA GETTY IMAGES

ARRIVING

Airports Flights from mainland Australian airports depart regularly for Hobart and Launceston. Pick up a hire car at either location; a car gives the best access to the region, which sits in between the two airports. Cradle Mountain is closer to Launceston; Oatlands is closer to Hobart.

Ferry Bring your car across Bass Strait on the *Spirit of Tasmania*, sailing between Geelong and Devonport daily. Sail overnight and you'll awaken ready to tackle the day.

HOW MUCH FOR A

Parma at the pub $32

Bottle of Tasmanian whisky $150+

Daily Parks Pass $48 per car

WHEN TO GO

DEC–FEB
Summer is a beautiful time for bushwalks, swimming and outdoor dining

MAR–MAY
Brisk autumn days with the sun shining across the alpine trails

JUN–AUG
Never a better time than winter for a Tasmanian whisky and open fire

SEP–NOV
Spring is green, gorgeous and bloomin' beautiful

GETTING AROUND

Car A visit to this part of Tasmania is definitely easier if you drive. The Midlands Hwy is the main north–south arterial road between Hobart and Launceston: you'll probably be driving along it for most of the destinations here – at least for the start of your journey.

Off-road travel Leaving the highway, you'll quickly find yourself off the beaten track: the roads are smaller, winding and sometimes unsealed. Travel safely and slowly.

Bus You will be able to catch buses from the main towns and there are smaller tour-bus options and connections. Check out regional bus services and book your seat where you can.

EATING & DRINKING

Local produce is the mainstay of the region, which is farming country at heart. The area is known for lamb, poultry and trout, as well as cheeses, nuts and vegetables. The push to cook and sell local produce gives visitors access to a growing gastronomy of fresh flavours in local stores and restaurants.

Tasmania produces an impressive range of booze: the region is known for spirits, especially gin and whisky.

Best cellar door Callington Mill Distillery (p124)

Must-try local dish Wallaby patties at Great Lake Hotel (p123)

TOP: WILLOWTREEHOUSE/SHUTTERSTOCK
BOTTOM: STEVE LOVEGROVE/SHUTTERSTOCK

CONNECT & FIND YOUR WAY

Wi-fi Most of the region is well covered, but be prepared for some pretty patchy wi-fi and mobile reception as you travel to the more remote destinations. If you are heading off the beaten track, it might be better to save directions offline.

WHERE TO STAY

Tasmania's Highlands and Midlands are rural and remote: there are no cities in the area, but plenty of small towns and destinations with plenty of accommodation.

Town/region	Pros/Cons
Cradle Mountain	Amazing scenery, with lodges, hotels and B&Bs. Gets crowded.
Oatlands	Free lakeside camping and a scattering of heritage B&Bs. Quiet at night.
Bothwell	Rural, relaxing countryside with a few B&Bs and hotels. Remote.
Great Lake	Dotted with shacks, many available for short stays. Dead after dark.
Ross	Historic, tidy town with historic accommodation. Good overnighter.
Kempton	Stay in camping grounds or even a converted church. Bit of a 'drive-through' vibe.

WATCH OUT FOR WILDLIFE

Tasmanian wildlife seems drawn magnetically to the roads. Avoid driving at dawn and dusk, when the local critters are most active.

MONEY

Because of the area's remoteness, ATMs are few and far between: carry some cash and/or rely on your credit card. Petrol is an unavoidable cost; fill up in the larger towns for the lowest prices.

19 Walker's PARADISE

WILDERNESS | WATERFALLS | WILDLIFE

Walks here clamour over each other as the most iconic, most beautiful, most photographed, most popular... From seasoned and experienced walkers to those who want a gentle meander in nature, this truly is a walker's paradise.

THE ETERNITY PHOTOGRAPHY/GETTY IMAGES

How to

Getting here You can get buses (or even a ferry) to the start and end of these walks, but for day walks it's best to drive yourself.

When to go Even summer can feel like winter in these parts. All but the hardiest walkers should avoid the depths of winter.

Be prepared This region is remote. Check weather warnings, pack for four seasons, carry enough water and do your research.

KEVIN WELLS PHOTOGRAPHY/SHUTTERSTOCK

Overnight Walks

The **Overland Track**, six days and 65km of one-way dazzling wilderness in a UNESCO World Heritage area, is deservedly known as Australia's premier alpine walk. Beginning at Cradle Mountain and ending at Leeawuleena/ Lake St Clair, there are no shops, no roads, no supplies on this trek; you'll reach the end of the trail enlightened (or just lightened, which may feel like the same thing).

Walls of Jerusalem National Park also borders on a spiritual experience: the three-day 23km circuit (with multiple variations) starts with a 3km walk up the Walls – climbing 600m until it feels like you have reached the heavens. Amenities are limited, so you will be carrying your life on your back as you ascend; pack sparingly but wisely – and definitely read all the advice you can find. Here, up top, you

URBANCOWBOY/SHUTTERSTOCK

Guided Walks

From the luxury guided Overland Track tour with sumptuous food, wine and accommodation every night to following professional walking guides, you can explore the region with the benefit of local expertise. If you haven't done much walking or aren't familiar with Tasmanian conditions, this is for you!

Far left Dove Lake (p114) and Cradle Mountain **Above** Hiker, Walls of Jerusalem National Park **Left** Ridge with Cradle Mountain in background

will find dolerite peaks, ancient pencil pine groves, rich cultural heritage and plenty of wildlife.

Taking it a Day at a Time

There are numerous day and half-day walks here – too many to mention and way too many to choose from – of varying grades and lengths, but here are a few favourites to consider. There are many and varied walks around iconic Cradle Mountain, from **Dove Lake** (two- to three-hour loop, with some lovely diversions along the way) to the more challenging **Cradle Summit** (eight hours return). You'll easily find a walk that suits your time, mood and motivation – and the weather! Snow is not uncommon here: a white fluffy flurry is a delight to walk in; sideways streaming sleet not so much...

The **Western Tiers** is the lesser-known cousin to destinations like Cradle and the Walls, but its appeal is rich variety and it

Wall in the Wilderness

Derwent Bridge is a small Tasmanian town in the midst of walking country, with little more than a takeaway store and 'The Wall'. Since 2005 sculptor Greg Duncan has been slowly carving a timber wall 3m high and over 100m in length. For a break between walks, why not stop in and admire this feat of patience and quiet respect for the history, hardship and perseverance of the people of the Central Highlands? This is a unique and dramatic piece of sculptural art in the middle of nowhere.

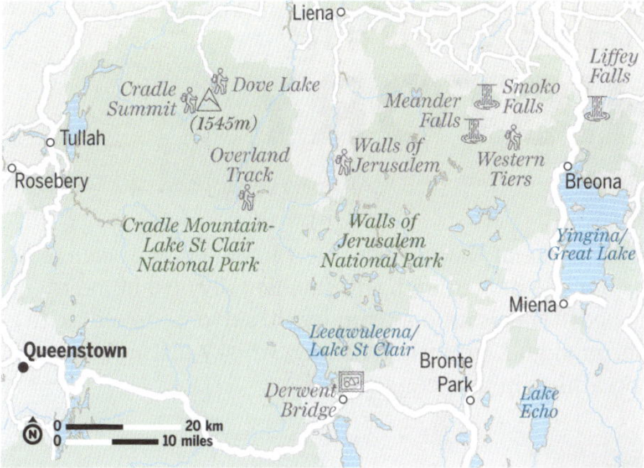

should not be underestimated. Some walks in the area include **Mother Cummings** (five to six hours), **Quamby Bluff** (four to five hours), or the easy and wheelchair-friendly 20-minute **Pine Lake** walk.

Walks with Waterfalls

Ah, the magic of falling water in the wilderness! **Meander Falls** is a five- to six-hour challenging out and back walk that follows the Meander River to a 130m fall that dramatically cascades over the Great Western Tiers. You will see iconic Tasmanian trees like King Billy pine, celery top pine and myrtle as you pass through this part of the Tasmanian Wilderness World Heritage Area.

Alternatively, for a shorter walk in the same area, **Liffey Falls** is a truly stunning waterfall that is just a 45-minute walk from the picnic ground. You can also choose your own waterfall adventure if you head along the Mother Cummings walk – you will come across the picturesque **Smoko Falls** after an hour and that may be as far as you want to go. Sit down, pop your feet in the water and have a bite to eat.

Left Overland Track (p113)
Below Wildflowers

FAR LEFT: ANDREW MERRY/GETTY IMAGES
NEAR LEFT: CATHERINE SUTHERLAND/LONELY PLANET

20 Make Golfing HISTORY

SPORTS | HISTORY | WHISKY

Historic Bothwell is the home of Ratho Farm – a colonial-era golf course boasting the oldest 18 holes outside of Scotland. (It's incidentally also home to the country's oldest chook shed!) This is an opportunity to actively connect with the history of the region: through golf, exploring, fishing, whisky tasting in a historic building and just breathing in that country air.

RATHO FARM

How to

Getting here Ratho Farm is a scenic one-hour drive north of Hobart and an hour and 45 minutes from Launceston.

When to go A crisp autumn morning of golf in southern Tasmania is an experience like no other, but any sunny day year-round is a good time for a round!

History of golf If you can't get enough golf, check out the **Australasian Golf Museum** in Bothwell village.

RATHO FARM

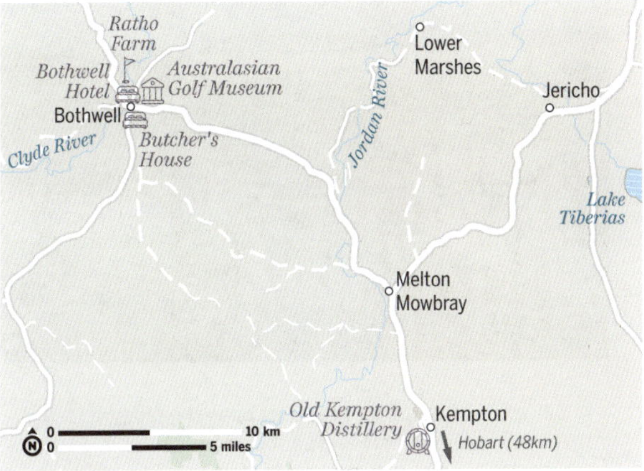

Play a Round

Ratho Farm golf course was rolled out of the Bothwell dust in 1822 by Scottish settlers. It's an eccentric 18-hole prospect: watch out for sheep, hedges, square putting greens, hay bales and fences (local rules: if you hit a fence, you can replay the shot without penalty), and test out some old hickory clubs – all surrounded by picturesque rural countryside on the doorstep of the Central Highlands.

A Quick Snifter?

Don't mind if you do. Just 20 minutes down the road is the **Old Kempton Distillery**, where a visit to the cellar door offers single malt whisky, Tasmanian liqueurs and a range of gins. Relax, sip and maybe grab a little something to take away for the end of the day. While you're there, take a turn around this 1820s colonial town and admire the sandstone architecture.

Rest Your Bones

After a long day of breathing fresh country air, return to stay at Ratho in one of the rustic old farm buildings that have been lovingly restored into boutique rooms with all the mod cons. Locally, **Butcher's House** is a quaint B&B cottage replete with blazing fire, sumptuous bath and none of the modern distractions; **Bothwell Hotel** is an 1836 inn run by the Ratho crew, with comfortable en-suite rooms right in the village.

Top left Ratho Farm golf course **Bottom left** Cow and golfer, Ratho Farm

The Father of Tasmania

About 27km southeast of Bothwell, **Kempton**, one of the state's earliest settlements, was founded in 1838. Originally known as Green Ponds, it was renamed after resident and notorious rabble-rouser **Anthony Fenn Kemp**. Kemp was a charismatic dude: one-half egotistical bankrupt with scant moral fibre, one-half progressive patriot who was critical in Tasmania's evolution from convict dump to independent colony. Fleeing debts in England, he became a dedicated pastoralist, merchant and political sabre-rattler. Never far from controversy, he made as many friends as enemies, and left behind more than a dozen children, earning him the nickname the 'Father of Tasmania'.

TRABANTOS/SHUTTERSTOCK

Colonial Midlands

A RURAL REGION WITH A BIG HISTORY

Campbell Town and neighbouring Ross provide the connection between the north and the south of the state: a place for weary travellers to stop, rest and enjoy as they travel through the sweeping rural countryside. They also house a rich and fascinating colonial history.

Left Red Bridge, Campbell Town **Centre** Ross post office **Right** Ross Bridge

Since 1821 **Campbell Town** has been the pit stop on the road between Hobart and Launceston. Campbell Town was designed as a supply centre for travellers back in the day, and remains so today – being unique in that it is one of the few historic towns that the Midlands Hwy still travels directly through.

The town of **Ross** is just under 12km (or 15 minutes' drive) south and is also known for its colonial architecture. Ross has a beautifully presented main street with cobble paths and gorgeous elms; even the currently operating Ross Village Bakery is over a century old.

The Bridges of Midlands Country

The exceptionally preserved colonial architecture in these two towns is exemplified in their bridges. The heritage-listed sandstone **Ross Bridge** is the third-oldest bridge in Australia and a simply stunning example of its kind. Crossing the Macquarie River, it was built with convict labour in 1836, and two convict stonemasons are credited for the intricate carvings along both sides of the bridge.

Nearby Campbell Town boasts Australia's oldest surviving brick arch bridge – the **Red Bridge** – on the Midland Hwy spanning the Elizabeth River. The bridge was convict-built; it was constructed from 1.25 million handmade bricks on dry land – then the river was diverted to flow under the bridge once it was finished.

Convict History

From the Red Bridge in Campbell Town, set into the footpath along High St, the **Convict Brick Trail** commemorates many of the 200,000 convicts who were trans-

TRABANTOS/SHUTTERSTOCK

ANHOIWASAKI/SHUTTERSTOCK

ported to Australia back in the day. Relatives of the convicts have provided details for the bricks – their name, age, ship and arrival date, crime, and the length of their sentence.

Just down the road are the few remains of the **Ross Female Factory Historic Site** – one of five female factories that were built in Tasmania. The Ross site was a workhouse for female convicts and their babies between 1847 and 1854. The old Overseer's Cottage now operates as a museum.

> The heritage-listed sandstone Ross Bridge is the third-oldest bridge in Australia and a simply stunning example of its kind.

Beautiful Buildings

Both towns are rich in colonial architecture: the **Foxhunters Return** (near the Red Bridge, Campbell Town) is a colonial Georgian, convict-built coaching inn. These days its extensive cellars house the **Book Cellar** and secondhand bookshop: explore the building and browse for a light holiday read.

The **Campbell Town Museum** contains the local history of the Midlands area, including a film projector built between 1930 and 1935, musical instruments, band music, photos, and uniforms from the Campbell Town Brass Band, which started in 1844.

In Ross, the main streets are a gorgeous display of historic buildings, with the town centre at the crossroads of Church and Bridge Sts. In the middle of this intersection sits a field gun from the Boer War and a war memorial. The crossroads are fondly referred to as the **Four Corners of Ross**, with each corner potentially leading your soul in one of four directions: temptation (the Ross Hotel), salvation (the Catholic church), recreation (the old town hall) or damnation (the old jail).

Transit of Venus

Find the **sundial** in Campbell Town's Valentine Park, which was designed and built in 2004 to commemorate the viewing of the transit of the planet Venus across the face of the sun in 1874. Campbell Town was the original viewing location used by scientists of the United States Naval Observatory that year – watching from the historic Grange building – and it continues to be a preferred viewing location. The transit occurs twice every 120 years; the events this century were 8 June 2004 and 5–6 June 2012, so it is due to happen again in December 2117 and December 2125.

21 Natural BLISS

RELAXATION | NATURE | WATER

Outdoor bathing, spa treatments, slow walks in nature, wellness care... Sometimes, after time spent exploring the rugged landscape of the alpine region, the best thing you can do is take a little moment to relax and pamper your grateful body. And there is no better place to do that than in the middle of Tasmania's natural wilderness.

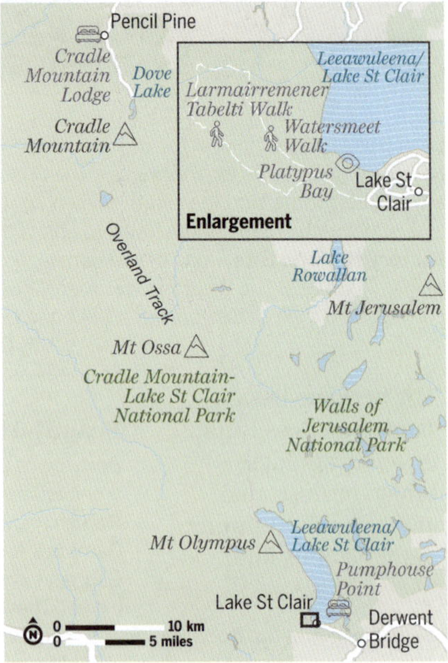

How to

Getting here Leeawuleena/Lake St Clair is 2½ hours' drive from both Hobart and Launceston. Visitors to Pumphouse Point can take a private sea plane from Hobart Airport (at quite a price!).

When to go The winter months can be a fabulous time of year to connect with nature, but October to April is safer weather-wise.

Petrol stations These are few and far between, so hit the Hungry Wombat (p126) at Derwent Bridge on your way.

Take a Retreat

Pumphouse Point at Leeawuleena/Lake St Clair is a unique adults-only retreat perched on a glacial lake and surrounded by century-old myrtle forests. And if that alone isn't enough of a drawcard, it also offers wellness retreats a couple of times each year. These retreats promote 'your own kind of wellness', which means you can pick and choose from activities that include meditation, massage, hiking, exploring on the lake...or having a lie in.

Mindful Walking

Take time and space to appreciate nature, mindfully, slowly and peacefully. No phones, no cameras and no hiking, jogging or riding...nothing strenuous. **Leeawuleena/Lake St Clair** has many options for short walks where you can truly appreciate the beauty of this region: the cultural Larmairremener Tabelti Walk, the Watersmeet Walk to the

HOLGER LEUE/GETTY IMAGES

confluence of the Cuvier and Hugel rivers, and beyond that the loop to **Platypus Bay**, where platypus are sometimes seen.

Outdoor Soak

The Retreat at Pumphouse Point, the high-end, sumptuous accommodation option, features a to-die-for outdoor bath; memories will be made when you soak in the tub as snowflakes fall. On the other end of the spectrum, a quick plunge into a natural lake is an experience like none other. Brave it when the water is cool and you will feel incredible after you warm up!

Natural Icons

Just three hours (or 200km) up the road – you will find the iconic Cradle Mountain and everything you need for a complete wellness experience: the King Billy suite at **Cradle Mountain Lodge** comes with your own private outdoor tub. You can also book in for indulgent treatments at the **Waldheim Alpine Spa**, alone or with a loved one, and find some truly inspiring opportunities for mindful walking, such as the aptly named Enchanted Walk or the beautiful Dove Lake. Take the time to treat yourself.

Above Cradle Mountain Lodge

22 Land of a Thousand LAKES

FLY-FISHING | ADVENTURE | FIRELIGHT

Tasmania's Central Highlands are rugged, raw and polarising: it can be a harsh and frigid landscape where you can't hide from the elements. But it is powerful, and so close to elemental nature that you can't help but be affected by it. For fishing, exploring and relaxing near an open fire, this is the place.

How to

Getting here/around This area is off the beaten track and you'll need to drive here. Once you're here, cycling, walking and boating are the way to go.

When to go Winter brings a cover of snow; at other times of year the rugged landscape shines through. Beware: Liawenee is officially the coldest place in Tasmania (it hit -14.2°C here in 2020).

Trout season The trout-fishing season generally runs from early October until early May.

Angler's Delight

Trout were introduced to Tasmania in 1864, and here in the Central Highlands, fly-fishers literally have a thousand fish-filled lakes to choose from. Arthurs Lake, Lake August and Bronte Lagoon all have their fans – but mammoth 114-sq-metre **Yingina/Great Lake** reigns supreme as Australia's largest freshwater lake. Guided fly-fishing trips on these pristine lakes and rivers are second to none; find local guides through Thousand Lakes Lodge, Great Lake Hotel, Rainbow Lodge or privately.

More to Life Than Fishing?

If you're staying at **Thousand Lakes Lodge**, take advantage of their e-bikes to explore myriad side roads and tracks – or pick your way between rocks along creeks and rivers on a self-guided walk. If you're up for a drive, check

THOUSAND LAKES LODGE

Above Thousand Lakes Lodge

A Local View of the Lakes

Take a moment to observe the vast landscapes: the way the light dances across dramatic open spaces; mountainsides of rocks tumbling like a giant has tipped a bucket of boulders. Everything feels ancient; some pencil pines at Pine Lake nature trail are 5000 years old.

Among the mass of rocks and lake wash, you may find ancient Tasmanian Aboriginal cutting tools that fit in the palm of your hand.

As you pass through the townships scattered through the Highlands, enjoy the varying characters of the quaint shacks: chat to a local to hear great tales of fishing escapades and other adventures.

By Jennifer Hillhouse, *owner of Coldwater Cabin accommodation*

@coldwatercabin

out the **Waddamana Power Station Heritage Site**, just 25 minutes from Miena. This free attraction is the start of the **Highlands Power Trail** and offers an insight into Tasmania's 20th-century industrial history.

Now You Take a Bite

The **Great Lake Hotel** serves up gourmet pub food; it makes use of local resources with a range of delicious seafood options. The mainstay wallaby patties are worth a taste! If you stay at **Thousand Lakes Lodge**, you can choose from delicious locally sourced meals, including adventure packs (snack and lunch) that you can take with you for a day of exploring.

23 Exploring OATLANDS

ARTS & CRAFTS | WETLANDS | WHISKY

Where history and creativity combine, historic Oatlands is the place to stop as you traverse the island north to south. This is a town that oozes charm and colonial connections, with over 150 sandstone buildings still standing. Its residents are actively utilising these spaces to provide innovative, artisan experiences in food, whisky, and arts and crafts.

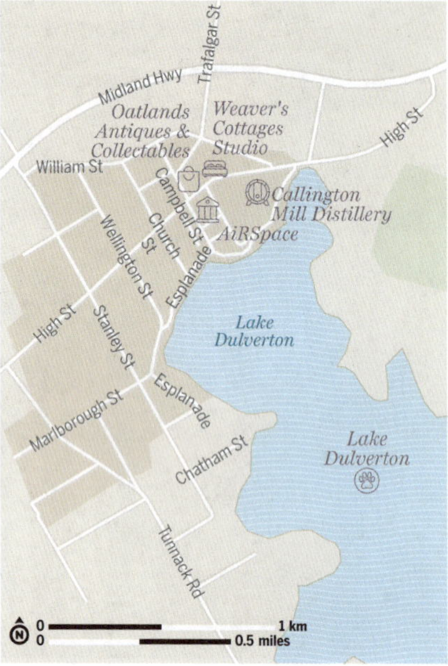

How to

Getting here Oatlands is just over an hour's drive from Hobart and about 1¼ hours from Launceston.

When to go You'll get a taste of something special all year-round, but summer is the perfect season for taking in the sights.

Winter in Oatlands It's freezing – especially over the Heritage & Bullock Festival weekend in August (but the costumes and artisans make it worthwhile!).

Midlands Arts

Weaver's Cottages Studio on High St is an absolute must. Textile artist Kat Wittman weaves beautiful rugs, scarves and clothing, but she also stocks the handmade works of over 50 local artists. Along the road is the exhibition space for the **Artist in Residence Program** – aka AiRSpace – a constantly changing and dynamic showcase. You can also uncover a few dusty treasures amid the nooks and crannies of **Oatlands Antiques & Collectables**.

Bring Your Binoculars

Duck down to duck-filled **Lake Dulverton** on the edge of town – a large lake encircling craggy Mary's Island. There's a lovely walking trail around the western shoreline, or you can cast a fly into the shallows and hook a trout. Birdwatchers will have plenty to squawk about, with frogs contributing to the natural cacophony.

Whisky Time?

Oatlands' windmill-fronted **Callington Mill Distillery**

produces world-class single malt whiskies using cutting-edge, innovative technology. Come for a guided tour (noon daily), a whisky flight, lunch in the excellent restaurant or a chance to blend your own signature whisky. Even if you don't like whisky, it's worth a wander here: the owners have spent millions restoring the 1837 windmill, stables and old cottages on the estate. There's a great kids' playground adjacent, and the glass-and-steel distillery building itself is a stunner.

The Right Time

One of the best times to explore Oatlands is in the evenings. There are no overhead power lines on High St, so when the sun goes down the streetlamps give the sandstone an eerie glow. There's a ghostly feel after dark, the air has a bite to it and the mist creeps down the quiet High St. You feel alone (lost?) in another time. Listen for the sounds of the bustling, brutal town of colonial times, explore Callington Mill, which is lit up at night and looks spectacular against the inky skies, and you can easily imagine the stories of the past.

By Kat Wittman, *local textile artist and owner of the Weaver's Cottages @theweaverscottages_oatlands*

Above Callington Mill

Listings

BEST OF THE REST

Pit-Stop Eats

Ampol Epping Forest $

This popular stop at the northern end of the Midlands Hwy features basic roadhouse fried food and petrol, and what it does have, it has in abundance. Strangely satisfying!

Hungry Wombat $

This busy little cafe and service station at Derwent Bridge offers basic but good roadside eats. You'll find a great selection of reliable and tasty food.

Mood Food Kempton $

Mood Food has been a mainstay of the southern end of the Midlands since 1973. Now the first of a chain, this is 'more than a roadhouse'!

Great Lake General Store $

Hot coffee, pies and toasties complement picnic supplies and fishing flies. At far-flung Miena, the least-small town in the Central Highlands.

Boutique Shopping

Lake Leather

Well known statewide for its quality leather goods and leather accessories, this Campbell Town shop has quality leather handbags, travel luggage and men's and women's footwear.

Weaver's Cottage Studio

Weaver's in Oatlands contains pieces from over 50 local artists; homewares, clothing, jewellery and handcrafted art that takes advantage of the resources of the region (especially the local sheep!).

Tasmanian Wool Centre

This place houses a sheep-centric museum, the Ross visitor information centre and a shop selling handmade woollen wares. Buy a beanie and head back out into the wind.

Cafe Scenes

Bunch $

The pick of the Oatlands cafes, serving pizzas, soups and deli-style sandwiches. Beer and wine; sunny footpath tables. Hard to beat.

Sweet Brew $

Top Campbell Town coffee, plus fat blueberry muffins, toasties and spinach-and-fetta *börek* (Balkan pastry). Sister cafe of the Launceston original.

Ross Village Bakery $

Delectable pies (including a version of Tasmania's famous curried scallop), loaves and out-of-this-world vanilla slices. Take a detour and enjoy the fruits of the 1860 oven.

JJ's Bakery Campbell Town $

Shiny doughnuts, quick coffee, lemon tarts, and hot pies and pasties for early-rising road warriors. A small-town country caff, just as it should be.

Sealy's Store $

A warming wood heater, proper coffee, and interesting pies and soups in an 1850 corner store in Bothwell. The best/only coffee for many miles.

Quirky Attractions

Shadows of the Past

Sixteen silhouette sculptures between Tunbridge and Kempton on the Midland

Hwy, illustrating local history: stagecoaches, bushrangers, convict chain gangs, thylacines...

Steppes Sculptures

This stone circle populated with bronze sculptures of Tasmanian native animals is near the Steppes Homestead outside Bothwell.

Oatlands History Room

A converted garage on the main street, full of old photos, bootmaking equipment, radios, lamps, farm gear and sundry knick-knacks – an amazing window into Midlands history.

Immersive Accommodation

Tarraleah $$

Tarraleah is a highland village that began its life as home to workers in the hydro-electric scheme. It's been transformed into a unique resort on the edge of the wilderness.

Elm Cottage Barn $$$

Gorgeous 1837 sandstone converted barn in Oatlands, opening onto a private garden. A secluded retreat for couples.

Bronte Lagoon Campsite $

Peaceful bush campsites in amongst the trees, right by the water's edge. Toilets are near the boat ramp. Don't forget your fishing rod.

Country Pubs

Castle Hotel $

A very rural and traditional hotel in a gorgeous old sandstone building with a menu that has all the basics, including a rather tasty chicken parmie. In Bothwell.

Great Lake Hotel $

For an upmarket pub, the hotel has a reasonably priced chicken parmigiana served with rustic fries and garden salad. Great food, service and sizes.

Cradle Mountain Lodge $$

This Cradle Mountain bar is delightfully warm and offers a generously portioned chicken parmigiana – fries and salad is the side of choice, but it also does a healthy veg option too.

Kentish Hotel $$

Oatlands' last remaining pub is hanging in there, with beer-garden burgers and an adjunct coffee shop if it's too early for a beer.

Highlander Arms $$

At Tarraleah, this pub-style restaurant does hearty evening meals (lasagne, schnitzels, steaks, burgers). Reduced winter hours – call ahead.

Huntington Tavern $$

Kempton's straight-laced country pub is the place to shovel down lamb shanks and a couple of pints of lager. Occasional live bands.

Festivals

Heritage & Bullock Festival

The annual winter festival in August in Oatlands sees locals dressed up in heritage costume, sharing their wares and parading bullocks down the main street. Great fun.

Kempton Festival

Every year the Kempton Festival Big Day Out is held in late summer and promotes rural activities, as well as local food, drinks and producers...and sheep racing!

Festival of the Fagus

Cradle Mountain Lodge holds the festival over a couple of weeks during the 'Turning of the Fagus' (April to May) deciduous event. Hosted events include walks, helicopter rides, gin masterclasses and kids' workshops.

EAST COAST

BEACHES | WINERIES | MOUNTAIN BIKING

RESEARCHED BY ANDREW BAIN

EAST COAST
Trip Builder

Outstanding natural beauty, freshly caught seafood and small family-run vineyards make the east coast an ideal destination for families, foodies and outdoor enthusiasts. Get behind the wheel to discover it all on one of Australia's best coastal road trips.

Get in the flow on the spectacular **St Helens Mountain Bike Trails** (p140)
2hrs from Launceston

Tour a cluster of welcoming wineries around seaside **Swansea** (p152)
1¾hrs from Hobart

Wander among wombats and convict relics at **Maria Island National Park** (p150)
+ 2hrs from Hobart

Drop in and drop out on the sands and slopes of **Flinders Island** (p156)

35mins from Launceston

Explore Aboriginal history and culture on the guided **wukalina Walk** (p154)

2½hrs from Launceston

Delve into the colour chart that is the beaches of **Larapuna/Bay of Fires** (p136)

2½hrs from Launceston

Tuck into a lobster roll at the **Lobster Shack** in Bicheno (p134)

2½hrs from Hobart

View the perfect curve of **Wineglass Bay** from a range of angles (p142)

2½hrs from Hobart

FROM LEFT: GREG BRAVE/SHUTTERSTOCK, CRBELLETTE/SHUTTERSTOCK, TOM JASTRAM/SHUTTERSTOCK; PREVIOUS SPREAD: DANIEL KARFIK/SHUTTERSTOCK

Practicalities

CHAMELEONSEYE/SHUTTERSTOCK

ARRIVING

Hobart Airport Serviced by direct flights from most mainland Australian cities. Car rental is available. From the airport, it's one hour and 40 minutes' drive to Swansea, and just over three hours to St Helens.

Launceston Airport In the state's north, Launceston airport is a two-hour drive from St Helens, and 1¾ hours from Swansea.

Ferry To bring your own car or campervan across, the *Spirit of Tasmania* ferry sails from Geelong to Devonport.

HOW MUCH FOR A

Ice-cream cone $6

Dozen oysters $28

One-day national park pass $48

WHEN TO GO

DEC–FEB
Warm and dry, great for beach days, walking and water sports

MAR–MAY
Mild days but cool at night; enjoy spectacular vineyard colours

JUN–AUG
Crisp, cold winter days are perfect for whale watching

SEP–NOV
Cool days, sometimes breezy, but you'll often have the beaches to yourself

GETTING AROUND

Car With towns spread along the coast, a car will help you make the most of your time in the region. Scenic views and plenty of stopping-off points make driving part of the adventure. Take it slow – the winding road will ensure that – and savour the journey.

Bus Tassielink buses operate daily from Hobart to Bicheno. Calow's Coaches runs services from Bicheno to Hobart via Swansea, St Helens to Launceston, and St Helens to Coles Bay.

Bicycle The east coast is a popular cycling destination. Hire bikes at Swansea Cycle Tours; delivery is available to Coles Bay and Bicheno (with a minimum two-day hire) for an additional fee.

EATING & DRINKING

The east coast's dining scene exemplifies the rule of not judging by appearances. Often the most delicious food can be found at an unassuming wooden shack rather than a high-end restaurant. With numerous fishing fleets along the coast, the seafood is every bit as good as you'd hope for – crayfish, abalone and oysters in particular. Locally produced wine and cheese make a perfect match, and in summer you can enjoy a bounty of fresh berries.

Best wines with a view Devil's Corner (p153)

Must-try fish and chips Freycinet Marine Farm (p134)

CONNECT & FIND YOUR WAY

Wi-fi There is limited or no mobile-phone reception at some locations on the east coast. There are a number of free wi-fi spots, with each location giving visitors access to 30 minutes of free wi-fi per device each day. A map of locations and access details can be found at digital.tas.gov.au/free-wifi.

EAST COAST FROM ABOVE

Par Avion's half-day Wineglass and Wildlife Tour is an ideal way to see the region, including a lunch stop on Maria Island, if you're only in Tassie for a few days.

WHERE TO STAY

There's an enormous variety of accommodation options on the east coast to suit every budget, from luxurious eco-resorts to rustic beach shacks and waterfront campsites.

Town	Pros/Cons
St Helens	The gateway to beautiful Larapuna/Bay of Fires and mountain-bike trails. Good amenities, great beaches.
Bicheno	Laid-back seaside town perfect for families, wildlife lovers and surfers, and handy to Freycinet.
Swansea	Quiet town with good restaurants and lovely views across to Freycinet.
Coles Bay	A grown-up shack town clustered at the edge of Freycinet National Park. Very busy in peak season.
Orford	The coast's first or last point, depending on direction of travel. A great base to explore Maria Island.
Binalong Bay	Pretty beachside community with laid-back locals and astounding natural beauty.

MONEY

All east-coast travel ambitions lead to Coles Bay, but accommodation can be costly, especially over summer. Consider basing yourself instead in Bicheno or Swansea, 30 minutes' and 45 minutes' drive away, respectively.

24 A Seafood FEAST

FRESH | LOCAL | DELICIOUS

Tasmania's seafood is celebrated for its quality and variety – no surprise for an island surrounded by cold, clear waters – and there's high export demand for premium produce such as crayfish and abalone. But as every seafood lover knows, fish always tastes better when you eat it close to the source. Head to the east coast for ocean treats with a waterfront view.

How to

When to go The east-coast crayfish season usually runs from November to April. Oysters are available year-round, but some outlets reduce their hours in winter.

Need to know If you're keen to catch your own dinner, fishing gear and boat charters are available at St Helens and Bicheno.

Know the lingo Blue-eye cod is known locally as blue-eye trevalla and is a fish favourite in Tasmania, along with local flathead.

The World is Your Oyster

Daily tours are available at **Freycinet Marine Farm**, outside of Coles Bay, where you can pop on waders, follow your guide into the waters of the Swan River estuary and harvest a few oysters straight from the rack. If you'd rather stay on dry land, the farm has its own casual restaurant where you can enjoy oysters along with mussels, scallops, fish and chips, and a glass of wine.

At Dolphin Sands, just north of Swansea, you'll find **Melshell Oyster Shack**, where the 'shack' is a retro caravan parked beside the working oyster-farm sheds. Head for the tables atop the small dunes for a view over the leases and, if you're feeling adventurous, try the at-table option of cooking your own seafood kebab.

Ocean to Plate

Overlooking the Gulch in Bicheno, **Lobster Shack** enjoys

LKONYA/SHUTTERSTOCK

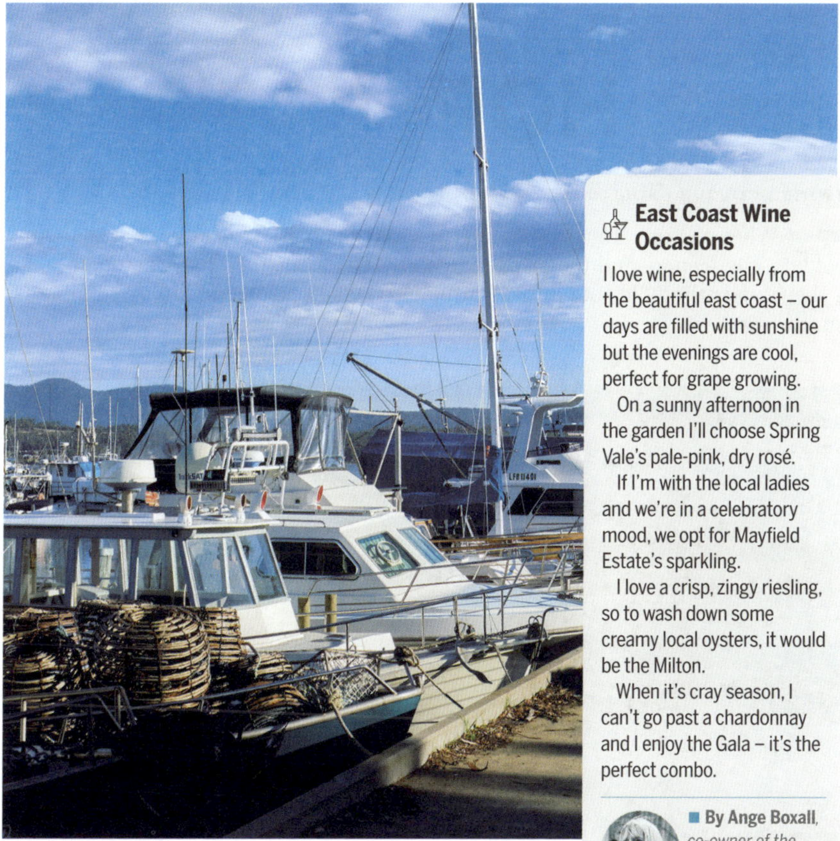

East Coast Wine Occasions

I love wine, especially from the beautiful east coast – our days are filled with sunshine but the evenings are cool, perfect for grape growing.

On a sunny afternoon in the garden I'll choose Spring Vale's pale-pink, dry rosé.

If I'm with the local ladies and we're in a celebratory mood, we opt for Mayfield Estate's sparkling.

I love a crisp, zingy riesling, so to wash down some creamy local oysters, it would be the Milton.

When it's cray season, I can't go past a chardonnay and I enjoy the Gala – it's the perfect combo.

By Ange Boxall, *co-owner of the Splendid Gin and founder of ECHO East Coast Harvest Festival @thesplendidgin @echofestival tas @angeboxall*

one of the best waterfront dining locations in Tasmania and the menu is as good as the view. Fresh abalone, prawns and oysters are all delicious, but it's hard to go past the deservedly famous lobster roll. Soft white bun, slightly spicy mayo and a generous serving of freshly steamed lobster meat. Yum.

When it's hot, fresh and made with love, nothing beats a generous portion of Tasmanian fish and chips. **Fish Van** at Triabunna serves up some of the best and can be found just a few metres from the town's fishing fleet, providing an authentically local ocean-to-plate experience.

Above Fishing boats and yachts, Triabunna

25 Beach HOP

SWIMS | COLOUR | SOLITUDE

When the sun shines on Tasmania's east coast, it's tropics be damned – the colours, the scenery and the briny scents are intoxicating. Find a secluded beach – they're plentiful – lay out a towel or blanket, take a stroll and discover Tassie's sunny side.

PETER UNGER/GETTY IMAGES

Beach Picnic

As you cruise along the coast, pause to gather supplies for a picnic on your strand of choice. In Orford, find chocolate, fudge and salted caramel popcorn at **Elly's Tasting Table**, add some berries at **Kate's Berry Farm** in Swansea and pick from the providore shelves in Swansea's **Alimento**.

Trip notes

Getting around The Great Eastern Drive stretches from Orford in the south to St Helens in the north. Public transport is limited, making a hire car your best option.

When to go Tasmania's beaches are beautiful year-round, but summer and autumn provide the warmest and most stable conditions for beach life.

Need to know Prepare yourself for the inevitable shock of the water by checking out the water temperature – cold or really cold? – at seatemperature.info.

05 Drive the no-through road to The Gardens and pick a beach, any beach along lichen-slathered **Larapuna/Bay of Fires**. There are half a dozen or so, each one as vividly colourful as the last.

04 Roll out the barrel indeed at **Beerbarrel Beach**, steps from Tasmania's easternmost point and the sandy swathe of the Peron Dunes.

03 Surf beach by day, penguin haunt by night, **Redbill Beach** also provides a stroll across a sandbar to Diamond Island at low tide.

01 Step straight off the highway onto the vineyard-backed sands of **Kelvedon Beach** – the boat shed at its southern end is arguably the most beautifully set in the state.

02 The beach by which all others are judged is **Wineglass Bay** (p142). Hike or cruise into it, or simply peer down onto its perfect curl from a hillside lookout.

ABOVE: SOUTHERN LIGHTSCAPES-AUSTRALIA/GETTY IMAGES

A Whale of a Tale

TASMANIA ONCE HUNTED WHALES, BUT TODAY IT ADMIRES THEM

Look behind Tasmania's clean and green image, into its not-so-distant past, and the scene well and truly bloodies the water. European settlement on the island was all but founded on the blubbery riches of whaling. Whaling stations dotted the colony's coastlines, and seas ran red with the blood of their hunt.

Left Pennicott Wilderness Journeys cruise, Turrakana/Tasman Peninsula
Right Humpback whale

LEISA TYLER/CONTRIBUTOR/GETTY IMAGES

The Cruel Sea

In the earliest days of European settlement, whales were a ubiquitous feature of Tasmania's seascape. In the River Derwent around Hobart, sailors noted the need to stick close to shore to avoid crashing into whales, while the town's residents are said to have complained about the noise from the whales keeping them awake at night.

Tasmania's first shore-based whaling station was established at Droughty Point on Hobart's eastern shore in 1805, just two years after the European settlement of Hobart. Soon, whaling stations spread along the shores of southern Tasmania and the east coast, including at Spring Bay, Freycinet Peninsula, Maria Island and Bicheno, chasing the wealth that could come from the whales' oil. By 1849 there were 34 whaling ships operating out of Hobart alone, and in a single decade (1828 to 1838) it's said that 3000 southern right whales were slaughtered.

By the time the whaling ceased in the 1890s – brought to its end by the fact that the southern right whale (so named because it was the 'right' whale for hunting) had been hunted almost to extinction – almost 8000 southern rights had been killed.

Recovery & Reverence

How times have changed. Today in Tasmania, whales are hallowed not hunted, and numbers have risen to the point that they are regularly sighted along the east coast and beyond during their migration seasons. Indeed, in 2010, a sighting of a whale with a newborn calf in the River Derwent led to speculation that it was the first whale to be born in the estuary since the 1820s.

MLHARING/GETTY IMAGES

Faint traces and reminders remain of the whaling industry. In Bicheno, you can climb to Whalers Lookout, where whalers once stood watch for passing whales. Relics of whaling equipment can be found on Crocketts Bay on Schouten Island, and boaties have occasionally reported spotting whale bones in the waters of Wineglass Bay – in fact, the famed Freycinet beach took its name not for its goblet shape but for the red colour of its waters when a whaling station operated at its southern end. Further afield, the remains of a whaling station can be found at Grass Point beneath Fluted Cape on Bruny Island.

> By the time the whaling ceased in the 1890s – brought to its end by the fact that the southern right whale had been hunted almost to extinction – almost 8000 southern rights had been killed.

But it's the animals themselves that are the big drawcard for locals and visitors these days. While they might be sighted at any point along the east coast and Tasman Peninsula in season, there's now the presence of an East Coast Whale Trail to bring them into focus.

Stretching from The Gardens (Larapuna/Bay of Fires) in the north to Teralina/Eaglehawk Neck in the south, the trail consists of 14 viewing locations, each one with an interpretation board adding some new detail to the whale tale, from orcas (at The Gardens) to migration patterns (at Four Mile Creek). The Shelly Point stop, south of St Helens, even has binoculars to help magnify the experience.

Migration Months

Whales pass by Tasmania's east coast twice a year, with humpback and southern right whales swimming north past the island from around May to July on their journey from Antarctic waters to northern breeding grounds.

The best time to view the animals, however, is from around September to December as they return to Antarctic waters with their calves, swimming slower and closer to shore. If you're determined to spot a whale while in Tasmania, spring (September to November) is considered prime time.

26 Pedal POWER

ADVENTURE | BIKING | ADRENALINE

St Helens is the largest town on Tasmania's east coast and its economy was once driven by tin mining. Today, it does a strong line in carbon and aluminium – mountain bikes, that is. The town boasts some of the most scenic mountain-bike trails in the state, with trails to suit riders of every ability, from families through to pros.

XAVIER HOENNER PHOTOGRAPHY/GETTY IMAGES

How to

Getting around St Helens is a two-hour drive from Launceston, and around 3½ hours from Hobart via the Great Eastern Drive.

Need to know The St Helens Mountain Bike Trails (*sthelensmtbtrails.com.au*) are spread across two locations. The Flagstaff Stacked Loops are accessed from Flagstaff Rd, 6km south of the town. The trailhead for the Bay of Fires Trail is serviced by shuttle buses from St Helens and Derby.

FILEDIMAGE/SHUTTERSTOCK

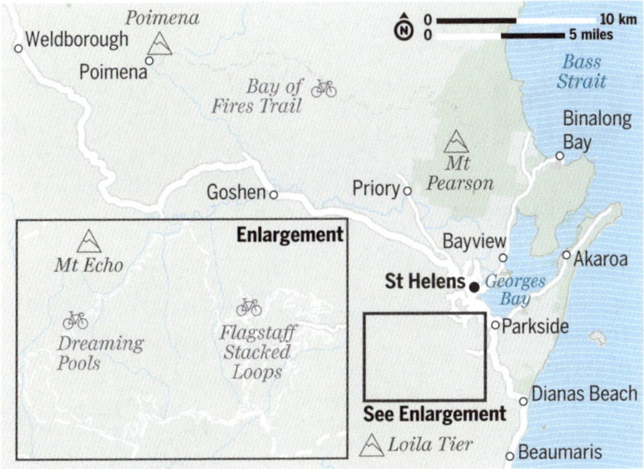

Top left Larapuna/Bay of Fires
Bottom left St Helens Mountain Bike Trails

Bay of Fires Trail

The incredible Bay of Fires Trail is St Helens' hero trail, propelling riders 42km from the top of the Blue Tier mountains to the sands of Larapuna/Bay of Fires. The trail is rated as blue – suited to intermediate riders – but you'll also need a good fitness base, with most cyclists taking at least 4½ hours to complete the wilderness trail.

Starting high in subalpine terrain, you'll be treated to spectacular views of the coastline and surrounding mountains. The initial descent is through some of Tasmania's trademark rainforest – enormous tree ferns, myrtles and giant mountain ash trees. The middle section is drier, with a long, winding climb to slow things down for a while, before a final descent down numerous ridgelines to the glimmering white sands of Swimcart Beach.

Take advantage of the shuttle services that operate from St Helens and Derby to drop you at the trailhead and then collect you from the finishing point later in the day. Make sure you're well prepared with drinking water, snacks and the right kit to patch up both you and your bike if necessary.

Flagstaff Stacked Loops

For a wider variety of trail options, the Flagstaff Stacked Loops has 10 trails suited to a range of skill levels, from family-friendly tootles to bombing descents from the Loila Tier. There's a second wilderness trail here, accessed by shuttles – the 27km **Dreaming Pools** in remote backcountry, passing waterfalls and the natural rock pools of the trail's name.

Derby's Legacy

Before St Helens, there was Derby, the forlorn tin-mining town that revolutionised Australian mountain biking when it opened the Blue Derby trail network, with more than 125km of trails, in 2015 to immediate global attention – just two years after opening, it hosted a round of the Enduro World Series. Its success inspired (and continues to inspire) other towns to follow suit. In Tasmania alone, trail networks subsequently arose in St Helens, Maydena, Queenstown, the Dial Range and Georgetown. And for all that, Derby remains arguably the finest mountain-bike destination in Australia, and among the best in the world.

27 Freycinet **FUN**

WINEGLASS BAY | BEACH WALKS | KAYAKING

Tasmania's oldest national park (with Mt Field) is also its top coastal park, sheltering one of Australia's most famous beaches, one of its most colourful mountain ranges, a wealth of wildlife and a host of other natural features. Best of all, there are myriad ways to explore Freycinet National Park.

How to

Getting here Tassielink buses connect Hobart to Bicheno, with one daily (except Sunday) bus continuing to Coles Bay, at Freycinet National Park's edge.

When to go Beach life is best in summer, but Freycinet remains (relatively) mild year-round.

Give it a pass A valid park pass is required for entry to Freycinet National Park. Purchase online *(parks.tas.gov.au)*, at the park visitor centre, or at ticket machines at the Wineglass Bay car park.

Freycinet on Foot

Almost every visitor to Freycinet comes for a peep at Wineglass Bay. You can catch a distant glimpse from the accessible **Cape Tourville** boardwalk (a 20-minute walk), while the traditional look is from the **Wineglass Bay Lookout** clipped onto the slopes of the Hazards mountains – continue down the slopes and you get the pleasure of stepping out onto the bay's sands, perhaps returning via **Hazards Beach** as part of an 11km loop. The loftiest and best view is found atop **Mt Amos**, though the climb, at times a scramble, requires sure-footedness and confidence.

Elsewhere, consider the short walk down into **Sleepy Bay**, a lingering beachcomb along the **Friendly Beaches**, or even the two- to three-day **Freycinet Peninsula Circuit**.

Water & Air

To see Wineglass Bay from the water, hop aboard a five-hour tour with **Wineglass Bay Cruises**, rounding the southern point of the peninsula and heading into the

TOM JASTRAM/SHUTTERSTOCK

One Perfect Day

A great way to begin the day at Freycinet is on our 25-minute flight over Wineglass Bay – that'll get you started and get your bearings from the air. Then you'd do the Wineglass Bay Lookout walk and see the bay yourself, and enjoy the Cape Tourville walk. Finally, you've got the nice granite rocks and the red lichen at Honeymoon Bay.

The region is also home to many excellent vineyards and eateries, where you can savour local produce, fresh seafood and spectacular views of the Hazards and surrounding coastline.

By Greg and Gabby Ross, *the owner-operators of Freycinet Air*

bay. You won't see Wineglass from a kayak, but a morning or twilight paddle with **Freycinet Adventures** will have you skimming along the base of the granite Hazards and gliding into the romance of Honeymoon Bay.

Hire a stand-up paddleboard (SUP) from **Freycinet Paddle Boards** and gently punt your way around the calm waters of Coles Bay with an eyeful of the Hazards, or take to the skies with **Freycinet Air** for a godly view of the peninsula and its famous beach.

Above Wineglass Bay viewed from Mt Amos

WILDLIFE
of the East Coast

03

01

02

06

04

05

01 Wedge-tailed eagles
Wedgies weigh up to 5kg and can reach a wingspan of 2.3m. There are around 100 breeding pairs in Tasmania.

02 Pademelons
Pademelons are small marsupials, similar to wallabies. They come out to feed at dusk and are easily spotted along the east coast.

03 Wombats
With a distinctive waddling walk and cuddly appearance, wombats are one of Australia's most loved native animals.

04 Echidnas
An echidna's spines can reach 5cm in length, but Tasmanian echidnas have more fluff than their mainland Australia counterparts to help keep them warm.

05 Little penguins
Join a guided tour with Bicheno Penguin Tours to see the smallest of all penguins, which nest in burrows among coastal rocks.

06 Cape Barren geese
These birds have quite a paint job – grey bodies, pink legs, yellow ceres – making for colourful

07

09

08

10

sightings on Maria and Flinders islands.

07 Tasmanian devils
See wild Tasmanian devils on Maria Island and on the nightly Devils in the Dark tour at East Coast Natureworld.

08 Humpback whales
The east coast lies along the migration path for whales moving from the polar region to warmer waters and back again. Spot them May to November.

09 White-bellied sea eagles
With a wingspan up to 2.2m, these graceful eagles are marginally smaller than wedge-tailed eagles. Look for their white bodies and grey wings edged in black.

10 Possums
Tasmania is home to five species of possum: common ringtail, sugar glider, brushtail possum, Eastern pygmy possum and little pygmy possum.

01 ZOE EZZY/SHUTTERSTOCK, **02** FILEDIMAGE/SHUTTERSTOCK, **03** BENNY MARTY/SHUTTERSTOCK, **04** BENNY MARTY/SHUTTERSTOCK, **05** BENNY MARTY/SHUTTERSTOCK, **06** PHOTOMASTER/SHUTTERSTOCK, **07** BENNY MARTY/SHUTTERSTOCK, **08** SASINTIPCHAI/SHUTTERSTOCK, **09** INDEPENDENT BIRDS/SHUTTERSTOCK, **10** PAGGI ELEANOR/SHUTTERSTOCK

28 Making a SPLASH

SURFING | KAYAKING | DIVING

The east coast's long, beautiful seaboard offers plenty of opportunities for fun and adventure on – and under – the water. From windswept surf beaches to cosy kayaking nooks, there's an aquatic environment to suit every interest and ability.

VISUAL COLLECTIVE/SHUTTERSTOCK

How to

Getting around Water-sport enthusiasts should consider Bicheno as their east coast base. Some of the state's best surf beaches and dive spots are right on the doorstep, and it's a short drive to popular kayaking destinations around St Helens and Freycinet Peninsula.

When to go Late summer provides the warmest and mildest surf conditions, but if you want bigger, wilder waves, you'll need to brave the winter chills and thrills.

Surf's Up

Tasmania's big-name, big-wave destinations – Shipstern Bluff, Martha Lavinia, Marrawah – might be elsewhere, but the east coast, known for small, clean waves, provides arguably the most friendly conditions for the bulk of surfers.

The highest concentration of surf waves are between Bicheno and St Helens. In Bicheno, popular **Redbill Beach** is a curving kilometre-long beach that's easy to access, with a good shore break that suits surfers of every ability. Storm conditions sometimes bring a powerful wave to the outside of **Governor Island**, attracting hard-core tow-in surfers. North along the coast, **Scamander Rivermouth** is an exposed beach break that rarely gets crowded. Check the surf from your car window as you drive over the bridge: if it's looking flat, keep driving until you reach a better spot. Other

Top left Coles Bay, Freycinet National Park (p149) **Bottom left** Surfing, Redbill Beach popular spots include **Friendly Beaches**, which has a reputation as a real swell magnet, and **Beerbarrel Beach**, known for its fine sand, turquoise water and friendly conditions.

Surf shops in St Helens, Scamander and Bicheno have equipment to buy or hire, and staff willing to share insider knowledge on the best breaks.

Deep Down

There's a great choice of east-coast dive sites, stretching from the caves and coral reef outcrops around Binalong Bay in the north, to an undersea wreck near Maria Island in the south. The 55m **Troy D** is a former coastal freighter that was scuttled off the coast of Maria Island in 2007 to form an artificial reef. It's now home to an abundance of marine biodiversity, including reef sharks, moray eels and barracuda. There's a seal colony nearby and the wreck offers full access to interior compartments, so you'll be able to explore the engine room and say hello to the resident cuttlefish.

High & Dry

If you're keen to see Tasmania's beautiful marine life without squeezing yourself into a kayak or wetsuit, book a place on **Bicheno's Glass Bottom Boat**.

Captain Maitreya Randall loves to share his passion and local knowledge with visitors on this 40-minute tour that operates three times daily. He knows the area like the back of his hand and will work hard to cram as many fishy encounters as he can into the allotted time.

The beautifully clear waters around Bicheno provide wonderful visibility – common sights include stingrays, sharks, jellyfish and seals from a nearby colony.

Water Temperatures

The water off the east coast is slightly warmer than the rest of the state due to the East Australian Current...but it's all relative. Tasmania's nearshore water temperatures range from below 10°C in winter to the low 20s in summer. Wetsuits are a necessity year-round.

DALE LORNA JACOBSEN/SHUTTERSTOCK

In Bicheno, **Governor Island Marine Reserve** is considered one of the world's best temperate-water dive locations. Sites include Hairy Wall, a 35m underwater cliff covered in sea whips, and Golden Bommies, a pair of 10m granite pinnacles aglow with yellow zoanthids. It's recommended that only experienced divers attempt this location, preferably with a local guide. Along **Waubs Bay**, Bicheno's most central beach, bottoming out at just 15m, there are half a dozen easily accessible shore dives.

Dive guides and equipment hire are available through tasdivers.com.au.

Paddle On

The east coast's sea scenes are just as beautiful above the water, and best seen from a sea kayak or SUP. The protected waters around Freycinet National Park (p142) are the prime destination, while there's equally great paddling in the calm waters of **Georges Bay**, immediately out from St Helens, with plenty of hidden coves to explore. Just south, the **Scamander River** offers more protected paddling, with good birdwatching along the way.

Kayaks and SUPs are available for hire in St Helens from Poppa's Boat Hire.

Left Kayakers, Freycinet National Park **Top right** Fishing boat, Bicheno **Bottom right** Diver at Waubs Bay

FAR LEFT: LIES OUWERKERK/SHUTTERSTOCK, NEAR LEFT: DORADALTON/GETTY IMAGES

29 Wildlife WONDERS

WILDLIFE | NATIONAL PARKS | SANCTUARY

Tasmania's east coast is sparsely populated, except when it comes to wildlife. Wallabies, Forester kangaroos, wombats, Cape Barren geese and even Tasmanian devils flourish here, roaming a string of national parks that line the coast and an island once known as Australia's Noah's Ark.

How to

Getting here Car is the best way to get between the national parks and Bicheno. Maria Island is car-free and reached by the Encounter Maria Island passenger ferry from Triabunna.

When to go It's less about seasons and more about time of day. Tasmania's native critters are at their most active around dawn and dusk.

Viewing behaviour Don't ever feed or touch wild animals, and give them a few metres of space.

Park Residents

On the lawns around the World Heritage–listed Darlington Probation Station on **Maria Island**, the one thing you're unlikely to see is emptiness. The island was used in the 1960s as a 'Noah's Ark' experiment to preserve native species, and it now bustles with animals – most notably wombats (we counted 132 one day), Forester kangaroos, Cape Barren geese and, if you're lucky, Tasmanian devils, which were released on the island in 2012 in an attempt to save the iconic species from extinction after the population was devastated by Devil Facial Tumour Disease.

Take a morning or evening drive around the 12km Forester Kangaroo Drive in **Mt William National Park**, at the foot of low Wukalina/ Mt William, and you'll find a similar suite of native animals roaming the marsupial lawns.

Marching on Bicheno

Bicheno's wildlife credentials are twofold. Each evening after dusk, little penguins puff up their courage, march-

KIM MCKEAY/SHUTTERSTOCK

Callous Maria

Wildlife is just one of Maria Island's callings in life. The island is entirely national park and Darlington Probation Station, which predated Port Arthur, is part of the Australian Convict Sites World Heritage Site. You can stay in basic bunkhouse-style accommodation inside the old convict cells (guaranteeing you a front lawn with wombats), from where you can venture out on walking trails to the likes of the whimsically patterned Painted Cliffs, the spire-topped Bishop and Clerk, and the island's highest point, 711m Mt Maria, peering directly down onto the island's paper-thin isthmus.

ing ashore and making for their burrows along the town's coast. Join a guided tour with **Bicheno Penguin Tours** to watch their tentative arrival and view life among the burrows. At **East Coast Natureworld**, 7km north of town, you can meet Tasmanian devils on a Devils in the Dark tour and, by day, meet and greet echidnas, wombats, sugar gliders and the cutest critters of all – baby devils (mid-September to March/April) – on personalised Encounter experiences.

Above Little penguin, Bicheno

30 Island WINE

CELLAR DOORS | VIEWS | DRIVING TRAIL

The east coast's mild climate makes it one of Tasmania's premier wine-growing regions, with 14 vineyards between Orford in the south and St Helens in the north making up the East Coast Wine Trail. Meet the makers and enjoy tastings as you drive through this sun-kissed wine region.

SARAWUT KONGANANTDECH/SHUTTERSTOCK
ARCHITECTS: CUMULUS STUDIO

Trip notes

Getting around Skip designated-driver duties by taking a cellar-door tour with the Long Lunch Tour Co, visiting four wineries, or even pedal between a trio of vineyards on a cycling tour with Swansea Cycle Tours.

When to go Great Eastern Wine Week is a festival of events at the region's cellar doors each October.

Need to know Visit eastcoastwinetrail.com.au for full details of the East Coast Wine Trail.

One-Stop Wine Shop

Short on time? You'll find wine from every east-coast vineyard in the one spot at the **Farm Shed** in Bicheno. There are guided tastings of wine from 24 local vineyards, as well as whisky, gin and cider, while Bicheno Brewing brews its beers on site.

PRIORY RIDGE WINES

01 Boomer Creek A small family vineyard on a working sheep-and-cattle farm. The cellar door offers wine, craft beer and platters, and enjoys a spectacular outlook to Freycinet Peninsula and Schouten Island.

02 Spring Vale Vineyard Tastings take place in a stable built by convicts in 1842, while Apéro Bistro, a French-Australian restaurant looking over the vines, opened on site in late 2025.

03 Gala Estate Vineyard Tasmania's 'Pinot Producer of the Year' in 2023, 2024 and 2025 is billed as the state's second-oldest family business. Its cellar door, inside Cranbrook's old timber post office, has plenty of rustic touches.

04 Devil's Corner The award-winning, architecturally designed lookout tower at this cellar door boasts views over Moulting Lagoon to Freycinet's Hazards mountains. Enjoy wood-fired pizza and fresh seafood with your wine.

05 Priory Ridge Wines The coast's northernmost vineyard pours generous tastings of seven wines from its cellar door inside a 1920s shearing shed. The oaky chardonnay is a delight.

31 Walk, Listen, **LEARN**

HIKING | ABORIGINAL CULTURE | WILDLIFE

The award-winning wukalina Walk is a multiday guided walk owned and operated by the Tasmanian Aboriginal community through Mt William National Park in Tasmania's far northeast. Over four days and three nights, you'll take part in cultural activities, learn about the history and language of the palawa people, enjoy bush tucker and hike along one of the state's most spectacular coastlines.

ANDREW BAIN/ALAMY STOCK PHOTO

How to

Getting around Although the walk is on the east coast, trips depart from Launceston, where they also conclude at the end of day four.

When to go wukalina Walk operates from September through to May. Find full details at wukalinawalk.com.au.

Need to know There are two main days of walking (11km and 17km) and shorter walks on the other two days. Expect to hike around 35km in total.

THE WASHINGTON POST/GETTY IMAGES

ALFOTOKUNST/SHUTTERSTOCK

wukalina Walk is a ground-breaking opportunity for the palawa/pakana (Tasmanian Aboriginal people) to tell their own story and for you, as a visitor, to see, hear and learn things you can't experience anywhere else.

Day one begins in Launceston, where you'll be welcomed over fresh scones by an Aboriginal elder and meet your guides before driving to the northeast. The walking begins on the eponymous Wukalina/Mt William, where you'll lunch atop the 216m summit looking out over the islands to the north. The walk then descends towards the coast and krakani lumi, a purpose-built standing camp of domed-ceiling huts. You'll stay here for two nights and can look forward to an evening of conversation around the fire and a cosy sleep under wallaby throws.

Day two is spent around camp, with no more than 5km of walking. The morning focus is exploring the coast, sampling bush tucker and learning about traditional food sources, medicines and animals. The afternoon is about cultural activities such as weaving and kelp basket-making, before a dinner of traditional foods such as muttonbird and wallaby.

Day three is the big one – 17km of walking as you follow the coast to the lighthouse at Eddystone Point. Most of the walking this day is on beaches – if the sun's out, they can be dazzling. This final night's accommodation is a beautifully restored lightkeeper's cottage. There are books on hand and wallaby lasagne for dinner.

Far left krakani lumi camp **Bottom left** Aboriginal elder making a basket **Left** Eddystone Point lighthouse

Tasmanian Aboriginal Experiences

Beyond wukalina Walk, there are several other ways to interact with and experience Tasmanian Aboriginal culture.

kipli takara Bush-tucker tours through Aboriginal-owned land at Piyura Kitina/Risdon Cove at Hobart's edge.

Launceston Walkabout Tours Gentle walks into Launceston's Cataract Gorge, with insights into Aboriginal culture, spirituality and tribal histories.

tunapri Patuyala A 90-minute cultural walk at Boat Harbour, including a hands-on cultural craft activity.

Kooparoona Niara Cultural Tour Take a guided walk among the artworks and healing circle of Deloraine's Kooparoona Niara Cultural Trail, as well as a visit to the culturally significant Tulampanga/Alum Cliffs.

32 Flinders KEEPERS

WALKS | BEACHES | MOUNTAINS

Flinders Island is one of Tasmania's finest natural destinations, with a population of just 900 people, blessed with powder-white sands and challenging granite peaks that rise almost directly out of the sea. Little wonder that three of Tasmania's 60 Great Short Walks are found here.

ALEX CIMBAL/SHUTTERSTOCK

Wybalenna

A church and cemetery at Wybalenna are standing memorials to one of Tasmania's most powerful and tragic historic stories. In 1834, 134 Tasmanian Aboriginal people were relocated from mainland Tasmania to this windswept spot outside of Emita to be 'civilised and Christianised'. When they were shifted to Oyster Cove 13 years later, only 47 remained alive.

Trip notes

Getting here Sharp Airlines flies to Flinders Island from Launceston and Melbourne's Essendon airfield. You can also bring a car across on the weekly (Tuesday) eight-hour car ferry from Bridport with Bass Strait Freight.

When to go Summer shines brightest on the island, promising swims at the end of, or even during, walks.

Need to know Pick up a copy of *Walks of Flinders Island* by Ken Martin to discover more island walks.

05 Palana Set out from Palana and walk as far east as your coastal legs fancy – the perfect notch of Jacksons Cove, looking every bit like a tropical idyll, awaits if you make it far enough.

04 Killiecrankie to the Dock Connect one beach to another, hiking beneath the climber-favourite cliffs of Mt Killiecrankie and past a limestone sea arch in tiny Stackys Bight.

03 Castle Rock Beach-hop north from Allports Beach to a hulking granite boulder plugged in the sands of Marshall Beach.

02 Strzelecki Peaks Ascend to the island's highest point (756m) on a steep and strenuous climb for views down onto Trousers Point and across much of the island and beyond.

01 Trousers Point Strange name, sublime scenery on this short loop walk around a granite headland furnished with white sands and lichen-drenched granite boulders.

Listings

BEST OF THE REST

Cosy Cafes

Lifebuoy Cafe $$

Sharing space with a homewares store, this ever-popular St Helens cafe specialises in all-day breakfasts, lunch and homemade cakes in a sunny indoor lounge or a bright, plant-filled courtyard.

Governörs Bicheno $

Good coffee and breakfast burgers (and Friday dinner burgers) on the edge of Bicheno's shopping strip, but you're really here for the cinnamon scrolls.

Little Bay Patisserie $

Boutique Bicheno patisserie selling fresh-baked pastries that showcase local, seasonal produce. Visit in summer for incredible cherry danishes. Also offers a small selection of knitwear, jewellery and ceramics.

Elly's Tasting Table $$

Orford cafe serving up all-day breakfast and Elly's own line of sweet treats – the salted caramel popcorn is a bit of a Tassie institution.

Ice Creamery $$

Choose from 24 ice-cream flavours (or just opt for fish and chips and the view of the Hazards mountains) at this Coles Bay sweet delight. It's a busy summer stop.

East-Coast Flavour

Géographe Restaurant $$

Bustling Coles Bay restaurant and espresso bar with beautiful views. Open for breakfast, lunch and dinner; serves wood-fired pizza and fresh local seafood. Good selection of Tassie wine.

Alimento $$

Step in past the providore to find a Spanish-accented *pintxos* menu, and a bar stocked to the brim with local drops and brews at this friendly Swansea restaurant.

Le Coq $$$

Oh là là, fine French inspiration at the salty heart of Bicheno, Francophoning the town one pork rillette and cannellini bean stew at a time.

The Social $$

Retro rules in this eclectic St Helens space furnished like your grandmother's lounge. Grab a craft beer and Balkan arancini and make for the fire-warmed beer garden or a seat by the 1960s TV and wallpaper.

The Hub – Seaside $$

Wood-fired pizza and craft beer taste even better when they come with views along the length of Larapuna/Bay of Fires from the Hub's front deck.

Crafty Beers

Bicheno Beer Co

Hidden away (head behind Blue Edge Bakery) but worth the hunt for the indoor-outdoor taproom pouring everything from golden lager to barrel-aged stout.

Iron House Brewery, Distillery & Vineyard

As the name suggests, a one-stop beer, wine and whisky producer with a waterfront cellar door and accommodation if the tastings are planned to go a little long and strong.

Easy Tiger

This clever cat combines a cinema, burger joint and bar pouring its own Thirsty Tiger beers produced by a former Boag's head brewer.

Straight from the Source

Pyengana Dairy

Enjoy a true paddock-to-plate experience as you sit and relax with a tasting board of award-winning, handcrafted cheeses at a table overlooking the cows as they let themselves in and out of the robotic milking shed.

Kate's Berry Farm

Popular berry farm at Swansea's southern edge looking over Great Oyster Bay to the peaks of Freycinet Peninsula. Fresh berries are available during picking season (November to May), and the cafe's ice creams and scones are delicious.

Lease 65, St Helens

Grab freshly shucked oysters from the shed door at this oyster farm on the shores of Georges Bay between St Helens and Binalong Bay. It's takeaway only, but it's only right that you take them to a beach to enjoy. Cash only.

Waubs Harbour Distillery

Everything but the growing of the grain is done on site at this pure whisky distillery in a former oyster hatchery at the Gulch in Bicheno. Book ahead for a distillery tour or a one-hour guided tasting.

Out & About

Cosy Corner North

If you have to pick just one Larapuna/Bay of Fires beach, it might as well be the comfortingly named Cosy Corner with its artistically jumbled granite boulders and coating of orange lichen.

St Columba Falls

An easy 15-minute walk through cool, shady rainforest near St Helens leads to one of Tasmania's highest waterfalls. Keep an eye out for enormous tree ferns by the track.

POSNOV/GETTY IMAGES

Apsley Gorge, Douglas-Apsley National Park

Rocking Rock

Right beside the more famous Bicheno Blowhole you'll find an 80-tonne hunk of granite that nature has positioned so perfectly that it moves back and forth with the movement of the tide.

Apsley Gorge

Among all those salt-encrusted beaches, fancy a freshwater swim? Delve into this gorge in Douglas-Apsley National Park for a quick dip in Apsley Waterhole, or a fun, rock-hopping hike through the gorge with myriad plunge options.

Nights in Nature

Bay of Fires Bush Retreat

Boutique bell-tent accommodation in a bush setting just a few minutes' drive from Binalong Bay. Wake up to birdsong and prepare dinner in its restaurant-worthy kitchen complete with preprepared meals from the retreat's chef owner.

Little Beach Co Glamping

Nestled in bushland at Four Mile Creek with spectacular ocean and mountain views, this is an upmarket, adults-only glamping (or hot-tub villa) experience. Enjoy the barrel sauna, and dinner in the Barn restaurant.

LAUNCESTON & AROUND

ARTS | HERITAGE | GORGE & PARKLAND

RESEARCHED BY ANDREW BAIN

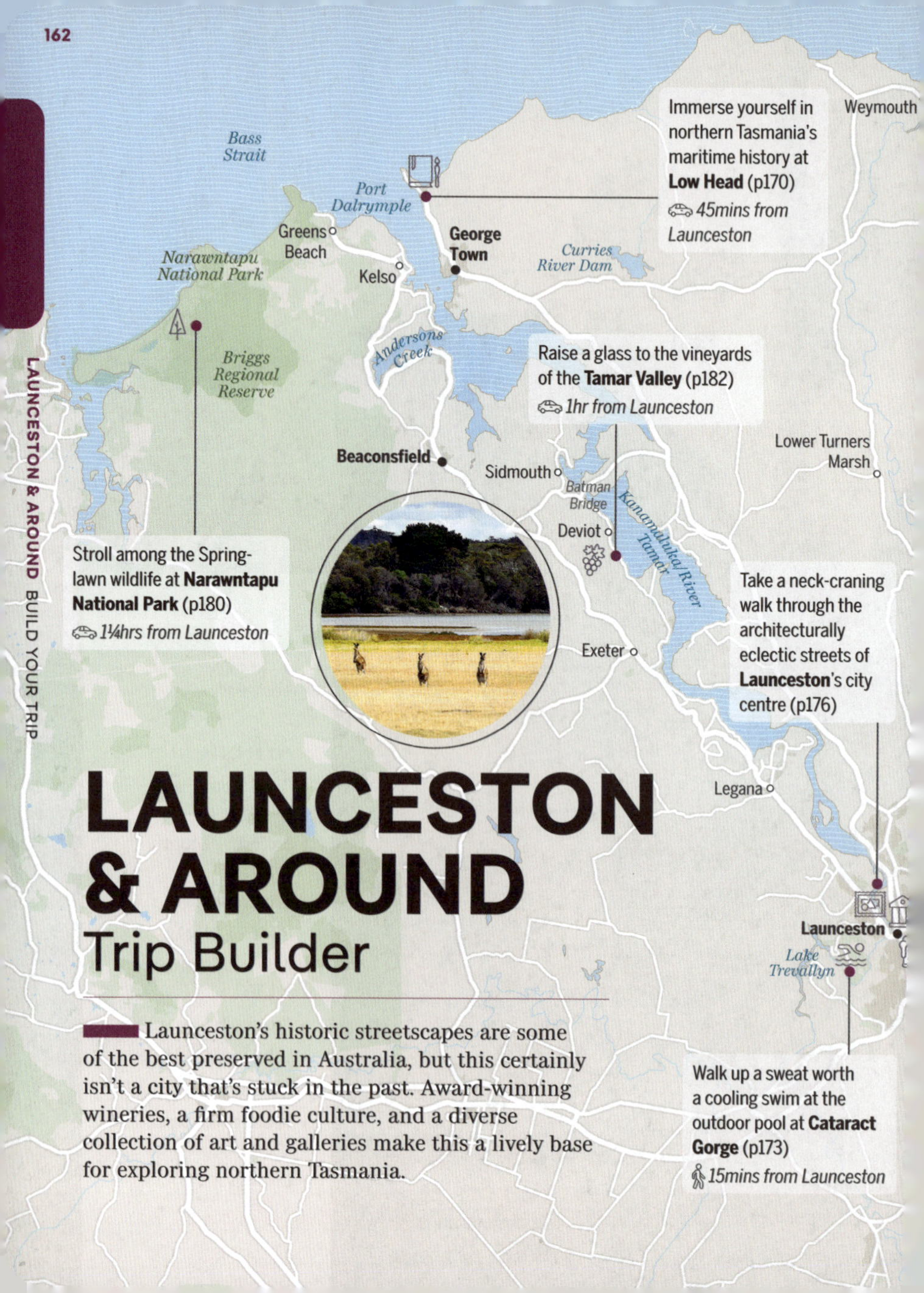

LAUNCESTON & AROUND

Trip Builder

Launceston's historic streetscapes are some of the best preserved in Australia, but this certainly isn't a city that's stuck in the past. Award-winning wineries, a firm foodie culture, and a diverse collection of art and galleries make this a lively base for exploring northern Tasmania.

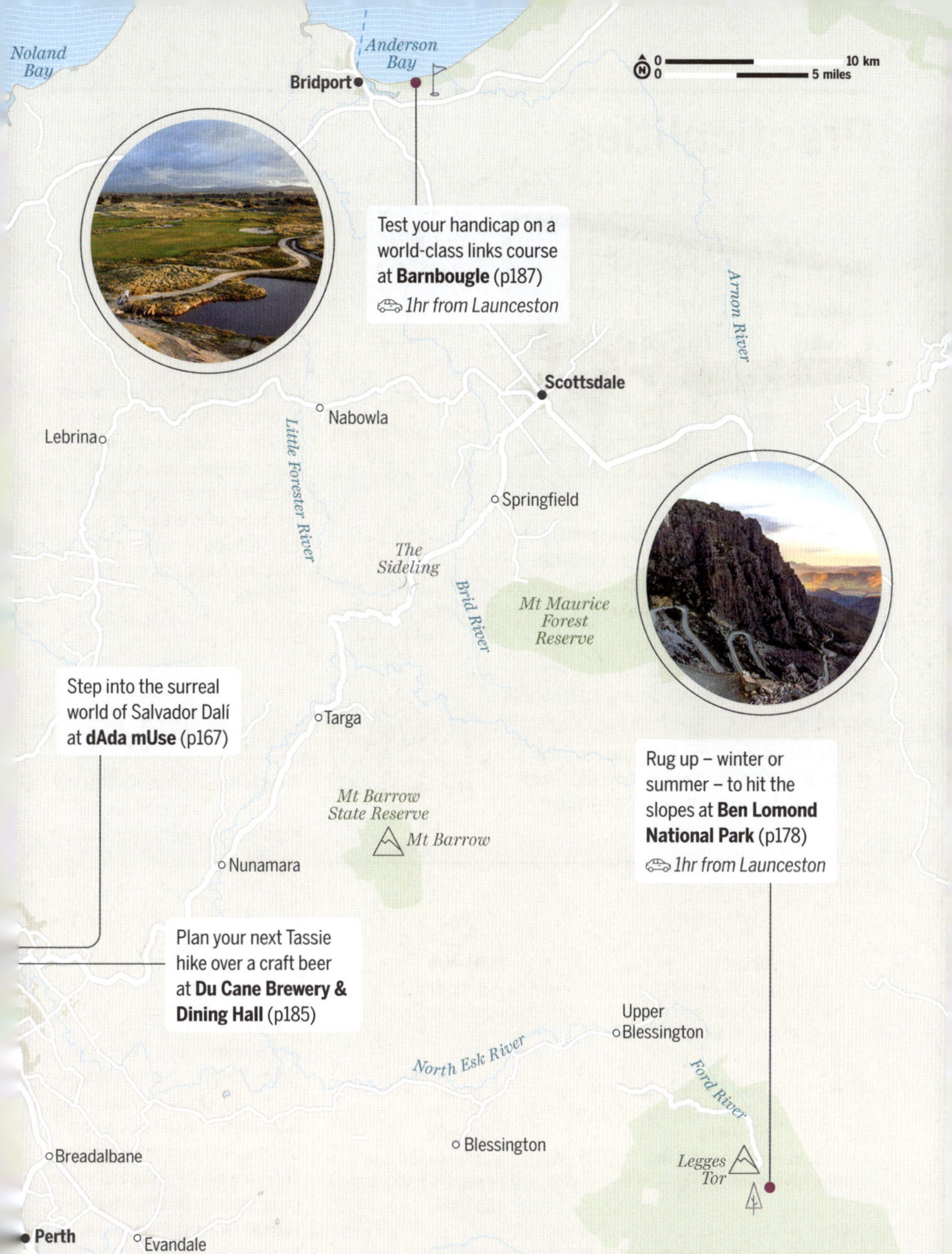

CLOCKWISE FROM LEFT: CAPE COCONUT/SHUTTERSTOCK, INESA HILL/SHUTTERSTOCK, LIAM PREECE/SHUTTERSTOCK. PREVIOUS SPREAD: NESS VANDERBURGH FOR LONELY PLANET

Practicalities

SHUANG LI/SHUTTERSTOCK

ARRIVING

Launceston Airport Located 15km south of the city centre. Jetstar, Virgin and Qantas operate flights here from mainland capital cities. Car hire is available at the airport; book ahead.

Taxi Around $45 to central Launceston. Wild Island Adventures operates a shuttle service from the city ($39/49 from/to airport) for one to four passengers.

Ferry Bring your own car or campervan from the mainland; the *Spirit of Tasmania* sails from Geelong to Devonport, 1¼ hours' drive from Launceston.

HOW MUCH FOR A

Schooner of craft beer $10

Cellar-door wine tasting $15

Full-day ski hire $65

GETTING AROUND

Car & taxi Northern Tasmania is a compact region where you're unlikely to need to travel more than a couple of hours in any direction. Hiring a car provides the freedom to explore at your leisure. If you're not keen to drive, taxis and rideshares are readily available.

Bicycle If you can deal with a few hills, cycling is an increasingly popular way of getting around. Bike hire is available.

Bus & tours Within Launceston, Metro operates the main bus services. For regional services, check with Kinetic, Tassielink, Calow's Coaches and Manion's Coaches. There are plenty of bus tours from Launceston to nearby attractions such as Tamar Valley wineries.

WHEN TO GO

DEC–FEB
Warm months, perfect for summer festivals and days among vineyards

MAR–MAY
Mild days, much cooler at night; good walking weather

JUN–AUG
Cold, often foggy in the mornings; snow on the peaks

SEP–NOV
Warming up; great time to enjoy Launceston's parks and gardens

TOP: KEIICHIHIKI/GETTY IMAGES
BOTTOM: JNESS VANDERBURGH FOR LONELY PLANET

EATING & DRINKING

Restaurant menus in and around Launceston are brimming with seasonal, regional produce – and in a small community where everyone pretty much knows everyone, you'll often be treated to behind-the-scenes stories of the growers and farmers who helped make your meal possible. There's also a big focus on small-scale distilling, craft beer and wine, with a wealth of wine bars, brewpubs and waterfront cocktail bars across the city.

Best sparkling wine House of Arras (p182)

Must-try fresh seafood George Town Seafoods (p189)

CONNECT & FIND YOUR WAY

Mobile phone There's good mobile-phone reception in Launceston, but as you travel out of the city it can become less reliable.

Wi-fi There are many free wi-fi spots around northern Tasmania, with each location providing 30 minutes of free wi-fi per device each day. Locations and access details can be found at digital.tas.gov.au/free-wifi.

WHERE TO STAY

Whether you're looking for a city break, a coastal retreat or a heritage cottage, there are plenty of accommodation options in and around Launceston to suit every traveller.

Town/City	Pros/Cons
Launceston	Compact city with a lively food and culture scene.
Derby	World-class mountain-bike trails, with accommodation geared to suit riders.
Longford	Stay in World Heritage–listed cottages at Woolmers and Brickendon estates.
Westbury	To-the-manor-born stays among the hawthorn-hedged countryside.
George Town	Riverside settlement well located for vineyards and maritime history.
Bridport	Traditional Tasmanian shack town; it's all about the beach or golf.

HARVEST MARKET

Prepare picnic provisions, and meet the makers behind the region's fresh produce, at the Saturday-morning Harvest Market Launceston (p168).

MONEY

Launceston's free Tiger Bus was discontinued in 2025, so the only way to save money on local transport is to walk – luckily, the city centre is largely flat and riverside trails connect the CBD to Cataract Gorge.

33 Art at its HEART

GALLERIES | DALÍ | LANDSCAPE ART PRIZE

Hobart may have hogged the art headlines since the celebrated arrival of MONA, but meanwhile Launceston has quietly gone about forging its own art reputation. Tasmania's second city is home to Australia's largest regional gallery and the world's biggest collection of Salvador Dalí drawings, while the country's richest prize for landscape painting is handed out in nearby Evandale.

HAIREENA/SHUTTERSTOCK

How to

Getting around If you're coming for the Glover Prize exhibition, Evandale is just 5km from Launceston Airport, making it a good start or finish point to a visit.

When to go Check the 'What's on' page on QVMAG's website (qvmag.tas.gov.au/Whats-on) for exhibition dates and information. Glover Prize entries are displayed for a week in March in the Falls Park Pavilion in Evandale.

KARIN WHEELER/SHUTTERSTOCK

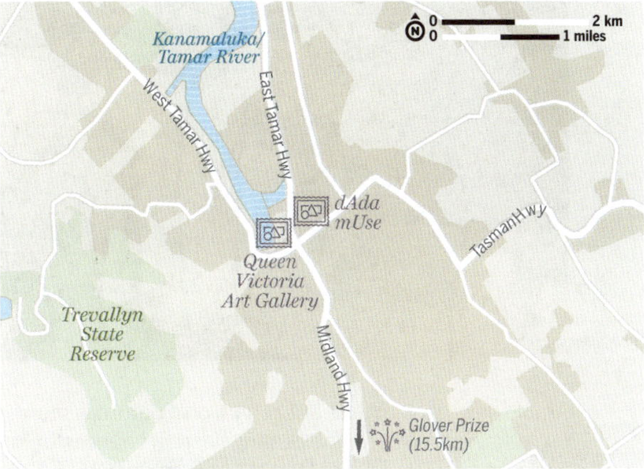

City Canvases

Launceston's Queen Victoria Museum and Gallery (QVMAG) is divided into two campuses, with the **Queen Victoria Art Gallery** in QVMAG's original 1891 building in Royal Park. Colonial paintings, including works by John Glover, the so-called 'father of Australian landscapes', are the pride of the art collection, but equally compelling is the First Tasmanians Gallery, featuring shelters, tools and the likes of kelp water carriers and beautiful rice-shell and maireener-shell necklaces created by Tasmanian Aboriginal artists. There's also a small-scale bark canoe built by the late palawa artist Rex Greeno.

An unexpected counterpoint to these colonial-era canvases is the collection at **dAda mUse**. Acquired over 35 years by a Launceston eye surgeon, this world-class collection of Salvador Dalí drawings totals around 1500 artworks, a rotating portion of which is on display across the two levels of the 1842 Johnstone and Wilmot building. If you're here on a Saturday morning, book in for a guided tour of the collection.

Glover Glory

Pretty Evandale, 20km south of Launceston, plays host each March to the acquisitive **Glover Prize**, Australia's most prestigious landscape-art prize. See the winner, the People's Choice winner, the Children's Choice winner and a suite of other entrants in early March inside the Falls Park Pavilion. If you happen to arrive a couple of weeks early, Evandale's streets also host the National Penny Farthing Championships.

Top left Queen Victoria Museum and Gallery (QVMAG) **Bottom left** Festivale

Festival Fun

Launceston and the towns around like nothing more than a good festival. Time your visit for one of the following.

Festivale Annual three-day celebration of food, beer, wine, spirits and cider, showcasing the best of Tasmanian produce. Takes place in City Park every January/February.

Junction Arts Festival Contemporary music, art and performances, centred around Princes Sq across two September weekends.

Tamar Valley Folk Festival Annual George Town event featuring music sessions, concerts, children's activities, poetry and dance. Held in January.

Tassie Scallop Fiesta Scallops are at their best in winter, and they're best celebrated (and devoured) at this Bridport celebration of fishing and seafood, held in August.

Good Mood Food

THE EMERGING ENERGY OF LAUNCESTON'S FOOD SCENE

With a 145-year-old brewery and a cityscape dotted with heritage flour mills, food has always been an integral part of Launceston's identity. Today, the brewery offers tours and tastings, while the mills have been turned into hotels and restaurants that proudly serve up local produce to contemporary visitors.

Left Elgaar Farm cheese, Harvest Market Launceston **Centre** Mushrooms, Harvest Market Launceston **Right** Stillwater (p188)

NESS VANDERBURGH FOR LONELY PLANET

Amble down to Cimitiere St car park on a Saturday morning, and you'll discover the beating heart of Launceston's lively food scene. Harvest Market Launceston hosts up to 50 stallholders each week – some permanent, others seasonal – the stands of which groan under the weight of fresh, local produce. From cheese to cherries, oysters to lamb and sourdough bread to sparkling wines, if you can't find it here, it's not worth eating.

Over the last decade, Tasmania's reputation for top-notch food and drink has exploded, but much of the focus has been on the state's south. It's only in the last few years that a national and international realisation has slowly emerged: the farms, vineyards and orchards in northern Tasmania are pretty special too.

City of Gastronomy

There have been some advantages to being overlooked by food writers and gourmands. If Hobart has been feeling the pressure of the spotlight, Launnie has been having fun working in the shadows. It has been a place for chefs and artisanal producers to play around, take risks and develop a vibrant culinary identity that is unique to the region.

One of the leading influencers in Launceston's food scene is Kim Seagram, whose culinary resumé is longer than the gin list in most Tasmanian bars. The Canadian-born restaurateur helped found the Harvest Market in 2011, was a founder of acclaimed restaurant Stillwater (p188) and is now chair of FermenTas, an organisation that has a world-first incubator for fermented food and beverage products – an 1800-sq-metre factory space called fermentHQ – 10km outside of Launceston. Kim also led

NESS VANDERBURGH FOR LONELY PLANET

NESS VANDERBURGH FOR LONELY PLANET

the charge for Launceston to be recognised as a City of Gastronomy; an effort that was rewarded in 2021 when UNESCO awarded the designation under its Creative Cities Network.

'The temperate climate and fertile soils of the region are the riches of the local community, nourishing a multitude of generations,' says Kim. 'Farming and making continues to drive the region, economically and socially.'

Spoilt for Choice

As a City of Gastronomy, Launceston has set itself a high bar for quality of produce and dining. The City of Gastronomy designation means the city must think creatively about challenges such as food security, environmental sustainability and nutrition, reflected in the creation of sites such as fermentHQ.

> It has been a place for chefs and artisanal producers to play around, take risks and develop a vibrant culinary identity that is unique to the region.

What does all this mean for the average visitor? It means that when it comes to eating out in the city, you'll be spoiled for choice. Regardless of your budget or dietary restrictions, you're likely to leave with a new favourite dish from a new favourite restaurant. That could be a hearty wagyu steak from the Black Cow Bistro, or a charcoal-grilled toastie from LeKoh (p188). It could even be a paper bag full of fresh, plump cherries from the Harvest Market – whatever the answer, you'll have great fun finding out.

Tasting Trail

While the bulk of the Tasmania Tasting Trail (p230) is clustered in the state's northwest, its tentacles stretch as far east as Launceston's outskirts. From the city, it's an easy day out to find all things hazelnuts at Hagley-based Hazelbrae and to delve into Tasmania's juggernaut whisky industry at nearby Western Tiers Distillery, run by Mark Kolodziej and Tim Freeman, who, in 2021, went from building distillation equipment for other producers to becoming distillers themselves.

Other Tasting Trail stops in the near vicinity include Bush Inn Brewhouse, Red Brick Road Ciderworks and Distillery, and Dixie Blue Gelato Cafe, all in Deloraine.

34 Saltwater STORIES

LIGHTHOUSE | MUSEUM | PENGUINS

Since Matthew Flinders and George Bass nosed their way through Bass Strait in 1798, Tasmania's north coast has had a rich and fascinating maritime history. From Australia's oldest pilot station to a foghorn that can be heard more than 30km away and several maritime museums packed with artefacts, there are countless opportunities to explore the stories from Tassie's seafaring past.

How to

Getting here George Town is around 40 minutes' drive northwest of Launceston on the East Tamar Hwy. Low Head is 5km further north.

When to go Low Head's bellowing foghorn sounds every Sunday at noon. Stick around because the little penguins shuffle ashore just below at dusk.

Need to know The Bass and Flinders Maritime Museum is staffed by volunteers, so call ahead to check that it's open.

George Town is Australia's third-oldest European settlement, behind only Sydney and Hobart, and it's the keeper of the early tales of local exploration at the **Bass and Flinders Maritime Museum**. A full-sized replica of the *Norfolk*, the sloop in which Matthew Flinders and George Bass circumnavigated Tasmania in 1798 to ascertain if it was an island, is the prized display – climb aboard for a look.

At nearby Low Head, you'll find even more maritime history to explore. It's only a short drive from George Town, but if you're feeling active, perhaps take the time to walk or cycle the 6km **Kanamaluka Trail** along the coastline.

This pretty peninsula is home to Australia's oldest pilot station, dating from 1805 and still active today. The pilot-station precinct contains the **Low Head Pilot Station Maritime Museum**, with 13 rooms of maritime memorabilia, from artefacts

MIRIAM NEWITT/SHUTTERSTOCK

salvaged from shipwrecks to a deep-sea diving suit weighing more than 70kg. Kids will love sending messages in morse code and discovering the locally made wooden surfboard that looks more like an ironing board.

At the road's end, a few hundred metres ahead, you'll find the **Low Head Lighthouse**, which offers sweeping views over the treacherous mouth of Kanamaluka/Tamar River. The famous foghorn hollers so loudly that it apparently used to confuse local cows. The Light Keepers House and several pilot-station buildings have been converted into heritage accommodation.

Happy Feet

Tasmania is home to a multitude of colonies of little penguins – at just 30cm in height, they're the world's smallest penguin and the only species to breed in Australia.

Little penguins build burrows along the coastline and return to them each night after spending the day feeding at sea. **Low Head Penguin Tours** operates environmentally sensitive guided tours each night at the mouth of Kanamaluka/Tamar River in Low Head, offering you the opportunity to watch these pretty little birds come ashore and waddle up the beach.

Book online and bring warm clothing. Cameras are allowed but no flash photography.

Above Low Head Lighthouse

35 Urban ESCAPES

CITY PARKS | TRAILS | WALKING TOUR

Launceston is Tasmania's second-largest city and has all the attractions you'd expect – food, culture and beautifully preserved heritage buildings. It also boasts a large number of parks and reserves, including a spectacular river gorge just a short walk from the city centre.

KIRSTEN WALLA/GETTY IMAGES

How to

Getting around Cataract Gorge and City Park are both on the edge of Launceston's CBD, making them easy to reach on foot. The Launceston Urban Fringe Trail (LUFT) has numerous access points around the edges of the city, but you're never more than 14km from the city centre.

When to go All these outdoor spaces are fully accessible throughout the year.

Need to know Download GPX maps of the LUFT route at ascentfitness.com.au/luft-routes-page.

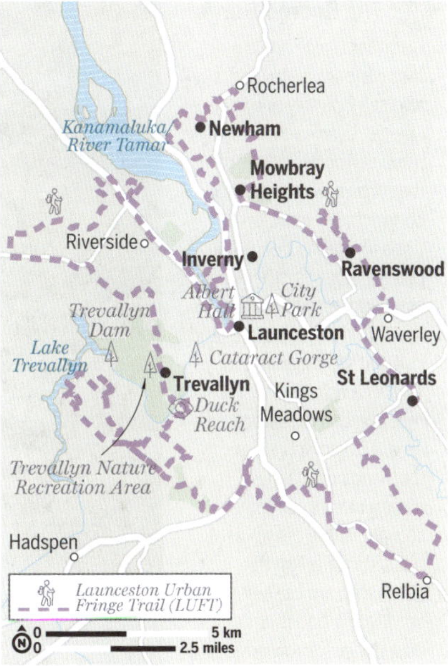

Cataract Gorge

Cataract Gorge Reserve is a stunning gorge and basin, just a 15-minute walk from central Launceston and cut by the longest river in Tasmania, the South Esk. A popular location for locals and visitors alike, it's home to walking tracks, an outdoor swimming pool, the world's longest single-span chairlift and numerous outlooks with spectacular views.

The **pool** is set amid the lawns of the First Basin, the gorge's central feature. On the shady north side, you'll discover a **Victorian garden** bursting with ferns and flowers. The peacocks are hard to miss, but look out for wallabies too. A 2km walk upstream is **Duck Reach**, a hydro-powered electricity station that kept Launceston's lights on from 1895 to 1955.

Adjacent to Cataract Gorge, you'll find the **Trevallyn Nature Recreation Area**, where the

Top left Kanamaluka/Tamar River and Cataract Gorge mouth **Bottom left** Cataract Gorge flowers

South Esk River winds through bushland on its way to the gorge. There are walking tracks and mountain-bike trails that cut through dry open grassland and forest, along with opportunities for rock climbing, horse riding, swimming and canoeing. **Trevallyn Dam** is a popular location for picnics and swims.

For a full day of exploration on foot, you can cross from Cataract Gorge into Trevallyn Nature Recreation Area (and eventually the dam) by crossing the South Esk River by the Duck Reach power station and ascending on a trail out of the gorge and into Trevallyn. The views by Deadmans Hollow in Third Basin are particularly good.

City Park

You've likely heard a lot about native Tasmanian wildlife, but did you also know there's a group of **macaques** that live in the middle of Launceston? A gift from Ikeda, Launnie's Japanese sister city, the lively monkeys seem to have had no trouble acclimatising to the cool climate.

The Sacred Gorge

Cataract Gorge holds a direct connection to land, sky and sea Country and is very special, even sacred, for Tasmanian Aboriginal people. It acts as a porthole that connects the rock formations formed in deep time by earthquakes, through ice ages and ancient history, to its contemporary usage and cultural significance today. The area was an important meeting and ceremony area, with an abundance of food and cultural resources. It even has its own mini climate. There are ancient trees surrounding the gorge that are the living archival embodiment of the experiences, knowledge and observation of our recent and ancestral past.

By Dean Greeno, *a trawlwoolway pakana artist and researcher*

Walking Tours

Launceston Walking Tours offers guided tours of Launceston's city centre and Cataract Gorge. Owner Geoff McLean, a Tasmanian Aboriginal historian, will lead you through the city streets, passing Gothic churches, Brutalist buildings and other architectural fancies, sharing his boundless knowledge of the city's history, culture and iconic local characters.

City Park itself dates back to the 1820s, when it was established by the local horticultural society. It's a great place to sit and enjoy a picnic lunch before walking around the well-kept gardens and admiring the plants in the airy **conservatory**.

Albert Hall, fresh off a $20-million redevelopment, is a Victorian-era hall with an elegant ornamental facade that sits in the northwest corner of City Park. Its Brindley pipe organ was made from local timbers, including Huon pine, and is lined with kangaroo skin.

Launceston Urban Fringe Trail (LUFT)

LUFT was conceived and designed by Dr John Ralph, Launnie local and founder of the personal training company Ascent Fitness. It's a 110km trail that winds around the outer edges of Launceston. Utilising existing cycle and pedestrian paths, it leads walkers through a variety of environments – from riverbanks to lakes, forests and suburban neighbourhoods. It's a wonderful way to explore parts of Launceston that most visitors wouldn't reach otherwise. The highest point of the LUFT, just 223m above sea level, is on the Powerline Track in the Trevallyn Nature Recreation Area, and most of the route is accessible for bikes and wheelchairs.

Left Cataract Gorge (p173) **Top right** Albert Hall. **Bottom right** City Park

36 Building BLOCKS

ARCHITECTURE | WALKING | HISTORY

Launceston's cityscape is a mosaic of architectural styles, which makes it a fabulous city to wander. Turn any corner and the colonial mills and warehouses find curious companions in the likes of Brutalist behemoths, Gothic churches and even an art deco lift.

NESS VANDERBURGH FOR LONELY PLANET

Trip notes

Getting around Launceston city's centre is fairly compact, with just a 10- to 15-minute walk between each of these stops. It's an easy one-day itinerary.

Need to know As you explore the city, look for painted traffic-control boxes on street corners. Inspired by the botanical illustrations of Margaret Stones, the works by local artists are part of the Electric Botany art trail. A trail map is available at qvmag.tas.gov.au.

Lord Scabar

Pay close attention to the finer details of Launceston's buildings and you might start to notice stencils of black cats along with tiny, doll-house-like windows and doors. These are the work of Lord Scabar, Launceston's anonymous answer to the likes of street artist Banksy. Keep alert – they pop up in random places.

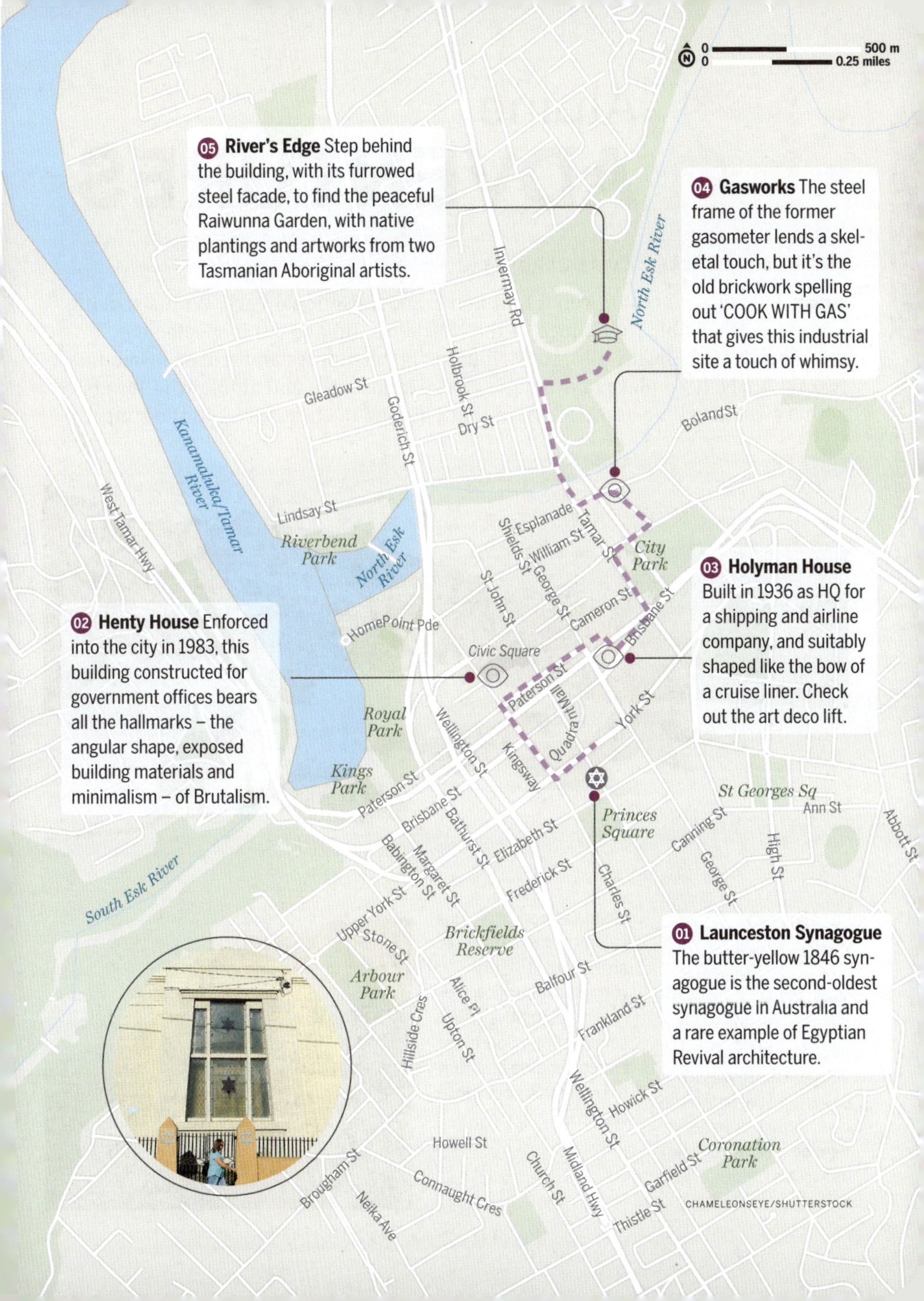

CHAMELEONSEYE/SHUTTERSTOCK

01 Launceston Synagogue The butter-yellow 1846 synagogue is the second-oldest synagogue in Australia and a rare example of Egyptian Revival architecture.

02 Henty House Enforced into the city in 1983, this building constructed for government offices bears all the hallmarks – the angular shape, exposed building materials and minimalism – of Brutalism.

03 Holyman House Built in 1936 as HQ for a shipping and airline company, and suitably shaped like the bow of a cruise liner. Check out the art deco lift.

04 Gasworks The steel frame of the former gasometer lends a skeletal touch, but it's the old brickwork spelling out 'COOK WITH GAS' that gives this industrial site a touch of whimsy.

05 River's Edge Step behind the building, with its furrowed steel facade, to find the peaceful Raiwunna Garden, with native plantings and artworks from two Tasmanian Aboriginal artists.

37 Alpine ADVENTURES

SNOW | BUSHWALKS | WINTER SPORTS

East of Launceston you'll find Ben Lomond National Park. With a striking plateau that's visible from much of the Northern Midlands, this spectacular destination offers bushwalks, rock-climbing opportunities and one of Tasmania's two ski fields. It's a place of dramatic glacial landscapes and alpine wildflowers, with a switchbacking approach road that's among the best drives in the state.

FILEDIMAGE/SHUTTERSTOCK

How to

Getting here Ben Lomond is around an hour east of Launceston. It's 18km from the park boundary to the Alpine Village – the road is unsealed and the final climb curls through a series of tight hairpin turns known as Jacob's Ladder.

Need to know From June to September all vehicles are required to carry correctly fitted snow chains. Alternatively, Ben Lomond Snow Sports operates a shuttle bus from the mountain's bottom car park.

M3GAWATTS/SHUTTERSTOCK

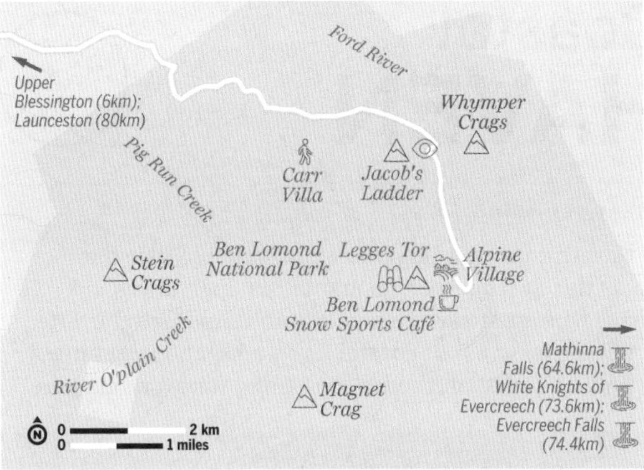

Tasmania has many hair-raising roads, and **Jacob's Ladder** may be the most daunting and delightful of all – there's a reason for that 30km/h speed limit. But once you navigate the steeply ascending hairpin bends, which carve their way between dramatic dolerite cliffs, there are rewards aplenty waiting at the summit. At its top, pull over at the **Watchtower lookout** and give yourself a pat on the back for a job well done. After that, pick your pleasure.

Fun in the Sun

In summer, a range of walks offer access to Ben Lomond's beautiful alpine landscape. The 10km, three-hour-return **Carr Villa to Alpine Village Track** ascends through boulder fields to Ben Lomond's open plateau and the summit of 1572m **Legges Tor**, the second-highest peak in Tasmania, before continuing to the Alpine Village. A shorter, easier way onto Legges Tor is along the easy-to-moderate **Summit Link Track** (1km return) from the Alpine Village.

Winter Wonderland

In winter, **Ben Lomond** is Tasmania's major centre for snow-sports enthusiasts, though even here snow isn't reliable, so check ahead. The Alpine Village sits at the foot of the ski slopes, offering lodge accommodation, lessons and equipment hire. Downhill skiing, snowboarding, cross-country skiing and even tobogganing are available when the conditions are right. If that sounds like too much hard work, just grab a hot chocolate or pizza at the **Ben Lomond Snow Sports cafe** and admire the snowy wonderland.

Top left Kangaroos, Ben Lomond
Bottom left Jacob's Ladder

Falling for Ben Lomond

Mountain slopes often mean waterfalls, and Ben Lomond's surrounds are no exception. On the mountain's eastern side, seek out **Mathinna Falls**, reached at the end of a 15-minute walk, where even just the accessible lowest tier of the four-level waterfall reaches a height of around 25m. Nearby **Evercreech Falls** are lower, but pour through rainforest and can be combined with a short walk to the grandly named **White Knights of Evercreech**, a stand of white gums growing to more than 90m in height – they're the tallest white gums in Australia.

38 Coastal HAVEN

WILDLIFE | BUSHWALKS | BEACHCOMBING

Wildlife viewing at Narawntapu National Park is so reliable that the park has long been known as the 'Serengeti of Tasmania'. Its open lawns, wetlands and woodland make this an attractive habitat for marsupials, birdlife and reptiles. With a short but enticing list of coastal day walks, and sweeping beaches where it's easy to find a quiet spot, there's something for everyone here.

LIAM PREECE/SHUTTERSTOCK

How to

Getting here Narawntapu stretches from Greens Beach in the east to Bakers Beach in the west. The main section of the park, at Springlawn, is a 1½-hour drive northwest of Launceston, while Green Beach at the eastern end can be reached in just under an hour.

Need to know A Tasmania Parks and Wildlife Service visitor centre at Springlawn has staff on hand to offer guidance on walks, wildlife and its three camping grounds.

FLORENCE-JOSEPH MCGINN/SHUTTERSTOCK

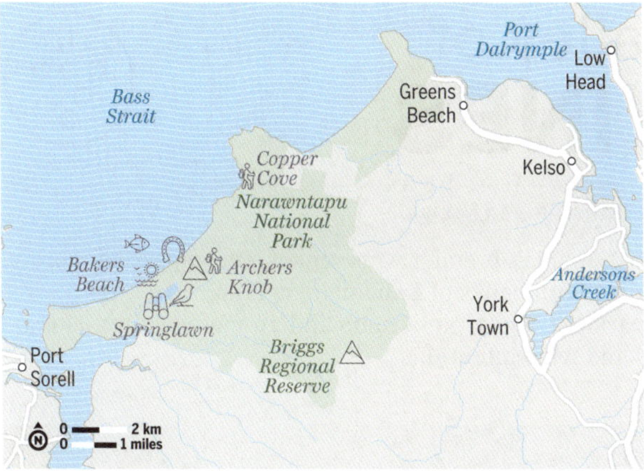

Wildlife Ways

Tasmania offers some of Australia's best wildlife watching. There are fewer introduced predators on the island state than on the mainland, and more than 40% of the state is protected as national park and other reserves.

Even among such credentialled counterparts, Narawntapu National Park stands tall as a wildlife destination. Each dawn and dusk, the marsupial lawns around **Springlawn** fill with a rich diversity of animals. Forester kangaroos, Bennett's wallabies and pademelons can be easily observed without needing to venture much further than the visitor centre at Springlawn. Wombats were once prolific here too. Decimated by a sarcoptic mange outbreak in the 2010s, these cute nuggets of fur have recently begun to return in small numbers, so keep an eye out.

Twitchers will enjoy the chance to see a wide variety of birds, especially around the lagoon at Springlawn, where you'll find a hide offering the literal bird's-eye view.

Coastal Walks

Using Springlawn as a springboard, you can find a range of walks along or just inland from Narawntapu's Bass Strait coastline. Do a two-hour circuit around the lagoon on the Springlawn Nature Walk, or set out for a full day along the coast on the 21km **Coastal Traverse**, which stretches the length of the park from Bakers Beach to Greens Beach. For an abbreviated version, head along Bakers Beach and cross a small headland into **Copper Cove**.

Top left Bakers Beach, Narawntapu National Park **Bottom left** White wallaby, Narawntapu National Park

Archers Knob

Narawntapu National Park is the quiet achiever of Tasmania's national parks. An abundance of native flora and fauna inhabits sprawling grasslands, a paperbark-enveloped wetland and lagoon, plus a stretch of seaside with some of the finest sand in the state. The family-friendly circuit walk (9km) to Archers Knob, returning along **Bakers Beach**, should not be missed. It takes in every element of the park, culminating in spectacular views of the northern coastline. Keep an eye out above for soaring white-bellied sea eagles and scour the beach for washed-up shark eggs! Definitely a favourite destination.

By Simon McInerney, *who runs Concierge Tasmania, @concierge.tasmania*

39 Valley of VINES

DRIVING ROUTE | CELLAR DOORS | RIVER VIEWS

The Tamar Valley is Tasmania's premier wine region, encompassing more than 30 vineyards spread over both banks of Kanamaluka/Tamar River. It's a region celebrated for its sparkling wines, pinot noirs and aromatic whites. Plot a road trip with water views and wine intentions.

MARCIN MADRY/SHUTTERSTOCK

Non-Alcoholic Attractions

There are plenty of alcohol-free attractions through the Tamar Valley to keep the designated driver happy. **Notley Fern Gorge** is a fern-filled wonderland and **Brady's Lookout** offers a commanding view over Kanamaluka/Tamar River. **Tamar Island Wetlands** has a bird-filled, over-water boardwalk out to Tamar Island in the middle of the river.

Trip notes

Getting around The West Tamar and East Tamar Hwys connect across the Batman Bridge, making for an easy driving loop. Or leave the car keys in your hotel room and book a day among the wineries with Tamar Valley Wine Tours.

Need to know On the eastern side of the river, the Pipers Brook and Legana areas produce some of the world's best sparkling wines, with the awards to back it up.

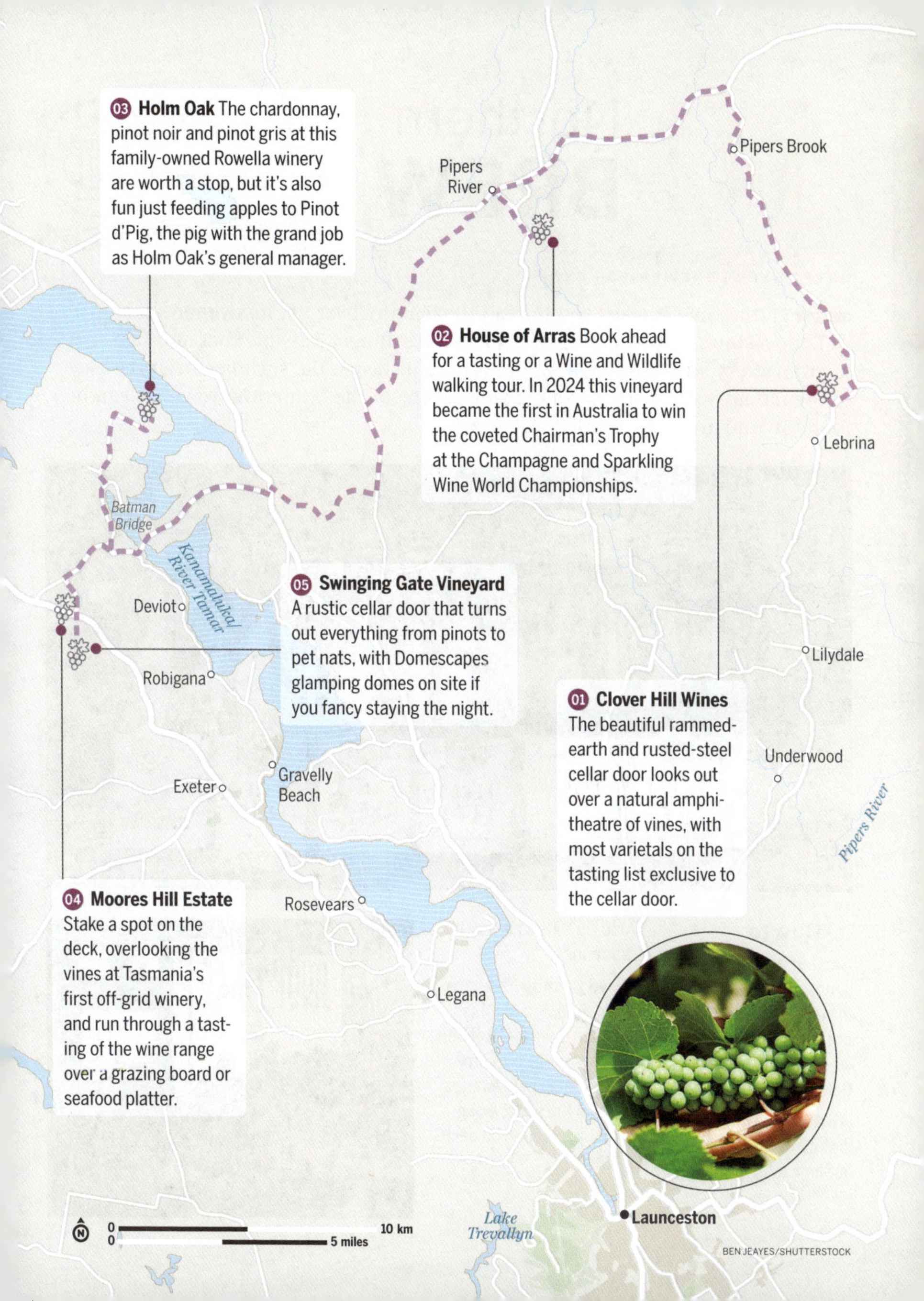

01 Clover Hill Wines The beautiful rammed-earth and rusted-steel cellar door looks out over a natural amphitheatre of vines, with most varietals on the tasting list exclusive to the cellar door.

02 House of Arras Book ahead for a tasting or a Wine and Wildlife walking tour. In 2024 this vineyard became the first in Australia to win the coveted Chairman's Trophy at the Champagne and Sparkling Wine World Championships.

03 Holm Oak The chardonnay, pinot noir and pinot gris at this family-owned Rowella winery are worth a stop, but it's also fun just feeding apples to Pinot d'Pig, the pig with the grand job as Holm Oak's general manager.

04 Moores Hill Estate Stake a spot on the deck, overlooking the vines at Tasmania's first off-grid winery, and run through a tasting of the wine range over a grazing board or seafood platter.

05 Swinging Gate Vineyard A rustic cellar door that turns out everything from pinots to pet nats, with Domescapes glamping domes on site if you fancy staying the night.

BEN JEAYES/SHUTTERSTOCK

40 Northern BREW

CRAFT BEER | BREWERIES | BARS

In the time it takes you to read the lengthy beer list in a venue such as Launceston's Saint John Craft Beer Bar, it's almost possible that another microbrewery will have opened somewhere in Tasmania, such has been the pace of the industry's spread across the state. Some of the best craft breweries can be found in and around Launceston.

VAN DIEMAN BREWING

How to

Getting around Saint John and Du Cane are in Launceston's CBD, but you'll need your own wheels to visit Miners Gold and Little Rivers.

When to go Outdoor tables come into their own at Saint John Craft Beer and Du Cane Brewery in summer.

Need to know Though a little outdated, the Tasmanian Beer Trail website (tasbeertrail.com) provides a map of breweries around the state, along with background on each of them.

NESS VANDERBURGH FOR LONELY PLANET

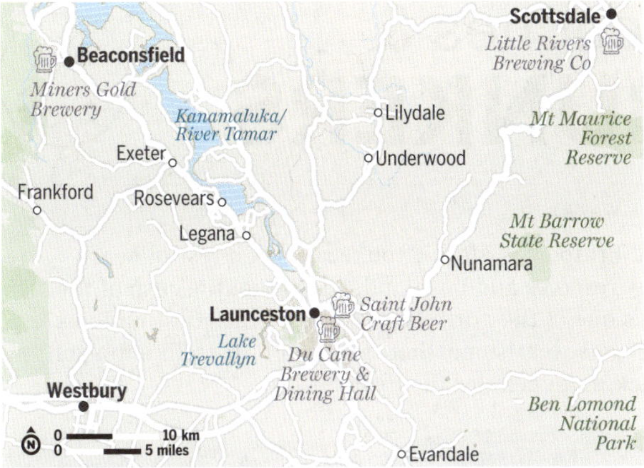

Top left Beers from Van Dieman Brewing **Bottom left** Saint John Craft Beer

Launceston Libations

Back when Tasmania was still a barren desert for craft beer, **Saint John Craft Beer** was the one frothy oasis. More than a decade on, it continues to pour international, Australian and Tasmanian craft beers from 18 taps (with a fridgeload of other brews).

Newer to the scene is cavernous **Du Cane Brewery & Dining Hall**, which is as much an ode to bushwalking as beer – its walls and space are filled with maps and other information on trails around Tasmania. Even the name Du Cane is taken from a mountain range in Cradle Mountain-Lake St Clair National Park (as is the Rendezvous at Pelion Gap IPA). Unsurprisingly, brewer Will Horan was once a guide on Tassie's walking trails.

A Short Hops Away

Head downstream along Kanamaluka/Tamar River to find **Miners Gold Brewery** in Beaconsfield, beside the town's former gold mine turned museum, with the bar and lounge inside what was originally the mine's chief engineer's residence. Owner Stu Grant is also the man behind Ocho Beer, which pours from Miners Gold's taps. **Little Rivers Brewing Co** is a mountain-bike-inspired craft brewery in Scottsdale, created by Chris Cairns, a one-time brewer at Queensland's Burleigh Brewing Co. Stop in for a tasting paddle and a pizza supplied on site by the local Two Sisters Patisserie and Providore.

Tassie's Best Brews

Spotty Dog Portland One of those beers you just can't get bored of. It's Saint John's everyday cool and crisp pale.

Morrison Irish Red Paul has been a friend of Saint John forever. His talent for traditional ales shines on this deep, dark and infinitely drinkable red with a huge malt hit.

Deep South Sharksjaw My favourite Tassie IPA. A great example of a modern Australian IPA, it's big and hoppy while still being balanced.

Moo Brew Stout Known as the 'Velvet Sledgehammer', for me this is a perfect stout. Luscious dark malty goodness.

■ **James Pearson**, *co-owner of Saint John Craft Beer in Launceston @saintjohncraftbeer*

41 Beaches & BUNKERS

BEACHES | GOLF | COASTAL WALKS

The seaside town of Bridport is ideal if you're seeking a restful beach holiday. Almost encased by reserves and bushland, and yet on the cusp of the Tamar Valley vineyards, it's one of the north coast's finest beach destinations. And when the beach towel gets wearisome, there's a trio of Australia's top golf courses and a walking track that encircles the town.

ANGIE SQUIRES/GETTY IMAGES

How to

Getting here Bridport is an hour's drive northeast of Launceston, via the East Tamar Hwy and Bridport Rd.

When to go Summer, but get in early because the best accommodation gets snapped up fast.

Need to know The CWA (Country Women's Association) holds the Bridport Village Market on the first Saturday of every month in the Community Hall. Pop along for more than 40 stalls, including some of the best homemade jams and cakes you'll find in the state.

RICHARD I'ANSON/GETTY IMAGES

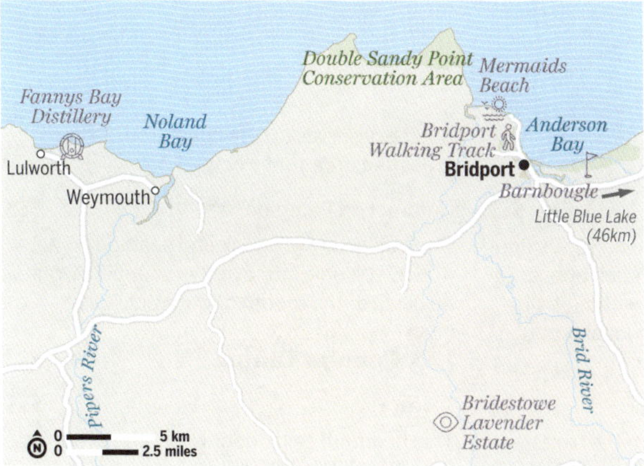

Top left Bridport **Bottom left** Bridestowe Lavender Estate

You could spend a happy week exploring the area around Bridport without even touching the car keys. There are safe, sheltered, family-friendly beaches, coastal reserves alive with birdlife, and walking tracks that offer easy access to forests, wildflowers and ocean views. No wonder this friendly little town is such a popular summer destination, with the permanent population of 1500 often tripling in the warmer months.

The **Bridport Walking Track** is a great place to start. An 11km circuit that leads through several distinct environments, the track is flat and is broken into four sections, if you fancy a shorter walk. The History Foreshore and Wildflower Reserve sections are the most enticing – the former takes in the standout beaches of **Mermaids Beach** and **Old Pier Beach**, where the remains of the namesake pier stretch long out to sea.

At the town's edge, **Barnbougle** hosts three world-class golf courses – **Dunes** was rated the fourth-best course in Australia in 2024, with neighbouring **Lost Farm** at seventh on the list – contoured across the dunes of Anderson Bay. The food, wine and accommodation are as good as the golf.

The tiny village of **Lulworth**, half an hour west of Bridport, has a beautiful wide beach and the unlikely treasure of **Fannys Bay Distillery**, a small, artisanal operation with a home-built still. Book ahead if you fancy a dram and a yarn.

Venture Out of Town

Tear yourself away from the sand and the greens and there are a couple of fine half-day trips in easy reach of Bridport. **Bridestowe Lavender Estate** is at its purple best in December and January, but the likes of lavender ice cream and lavender scones are on offer year-round.

Just as colourful is **Little Blue Lake**, Tasmania's brightest, bluest lake, filling a former mine across the base of Poonerluttener/Mt Cameron. Follow walking tracks around its edges, but leave the swimmers back in Bridport – its vivid colour is the result of high mineral levels from the mine.

Listings

BEST OF THE REST

City Eats

Stillwater $$$

Upmarket restaurant housed in an 1830s flour mill, with boutique accommodation above. Excellent service that's attentive without being obsequious, and a big focus on local produce. A real treat.

Mad Apple $$

This apple hasn't rolled far from the fruit tree, serving up veg and vegan breakfasts from banoffee crepes to open toasties and carrot porridge.

Stelo @ Pierre's $$$

With local produce prepared with Italian flair, longstanding Stelo – the city's first commercial espresso machine was unveiled here in 1956 – does very good things with pasta.

Alps & Amici $$

Bright, airy cafe attached to a gourmet food store selling fruit and veg, meat, dairy and deli items. Simple but tasty menu of soups, burgers and sandwiches, along with Launnie's best smoothies.

Havilah $$

Cosy wine bar also serving cocktails and a fun menu of small plates, charcuterie and cheese. Short but precise list of Tasmanian and European wines, including three of its own labels.

LeKoh $$

Fire up your day with a char-grilled toasted sandwich at this central cafe.

Black Cow Bistro $$$

Ready for the best beef of your visit? This welcoming fine-dining restaurant in a former butchery serves up the finest from Tassie's grass-fed, free-range cows.

Cataract on Paterson $$$

Cook up your own steak and seafood on a 400°C volcanic stone at this Launnie favourite close to the mouth of Cataract Gorge.

Country Dining

Clover Hill $$$

This beautiful cellar door is just the wrapping for a weekend multicourse, Japanese-style *omakase* (chef's choice) dining experience.

Josef Chromy $$$

Upmarket winery and restaurant 10 minutes' drive south of Launceston. Beautiful local produce cooked with care and delivered with fine vineyard views.

Lock Shop Cafe $$

Quality cafe fare in the most unusual of settings – a retro-furnished former petrol station attached to a safe-making business in Lilydale.

St Mark's Bridport $$

Let your mood guide you as to whether this venue, inside a former Bridport church, is a restaurant or a cocktail bar. Try the Bridport Distilling spirits.

Love Lucy Boots $$

Quirky Westbury cafe that doles out toasties and coffee by morning, but favours a long wine session on Sunday afternoons.

Truffle Farm $$$

Visit the home of Australia's first black truffles, near Deloraine, and join the truffle dogs on a hunt before enjoying a truffle tasting and

Tasmanian produce platter accompanied by local wines. Bookings essential.

Timbre Kitchen @ Velo $$$

Popular contemporary restaurant at Velo Wines on the Tamar's west bank. Menus change depending on what's in season (or the day) and are shared table banquets.

George Town Seafoods $

Eating the classic way – fish and chips (or the Tassie requisite, scallops) to enjoy at your favourite beach or park near the mouth of Kanamaluka/Tamar River.

NESS VANDERBURGH FOR LONELY PLANET

Timbre Kitchen @ Velo

Outdoor Adventures

Liffey Falls

Beautiful multi-tier waterfall 45 minutes' drive southwest of Launceston. Enjoy the walk to the falls through lush mossy forest across the slopes of the Great Western Tiers. Best in winter or early spring.

Floating Sauna Lake Derby

A wood-fired sauna atop a pontoon on Lake Derby. Bake yourself then plunge into the lake's frigid waters as mountain bikers swirl around you. Great post-ride therapy, or just a treat for anytime.

Launceston Kayak Tours

Locally owned business offering scenic tours of Launceston waterfront and Kanamaluka/Tamar River in single and double pedal-powered kayaks. No experience necessary, and a great option for families.

Penny Royal Adventures

This kids' favourite has rock climbing, zip lining, cliffside boardwalks and the chance to jump off the cliffs by the mouth of Cataract Gorge.

Mole Creek Caves

Spectacular caves in Mole Creek Karst National Park. Two caves are open to the public, with ranger-led tours – Marakoopa Cave is home to the largest public glow-worm display in Australia and a magnificent cavern known as the Great Cathedral.

Treetops Adventure Hollybank

A fun day out encompassing tree rope courses, mountain biking, Segway tours and a 400m-long zip line, all in the beautiful surroundings of blue gum forest 20 minutes' drive north of Launceston.

Special Stays

Domescapes in the Vines

Glamping among the vines at Swinging Gate Vineyard in the Tamar Valley. Spend the night in a bespoke geodesic dome, enjoying the starlit sky from the comfort of your king bed, with wine and a cheese platter thrown in.

Peppers Silo

This conversion of a 1950s grain silo provides great views over Launceston and Kanamaluka/Tamar River – try to nab a Gorge River room. Expect a gentle welcome from Archie, the hotel dog.

Quamby Estate

Live regally in this 1828 country homestead, with dinner in the formal dining room and perhaps a spot of golf on the estate's own course.

NORTHWEST & WEST COAST

HISTORY | WILDERNESS | ADVENTURE

RESEARCHED BY ANDREW BAIN

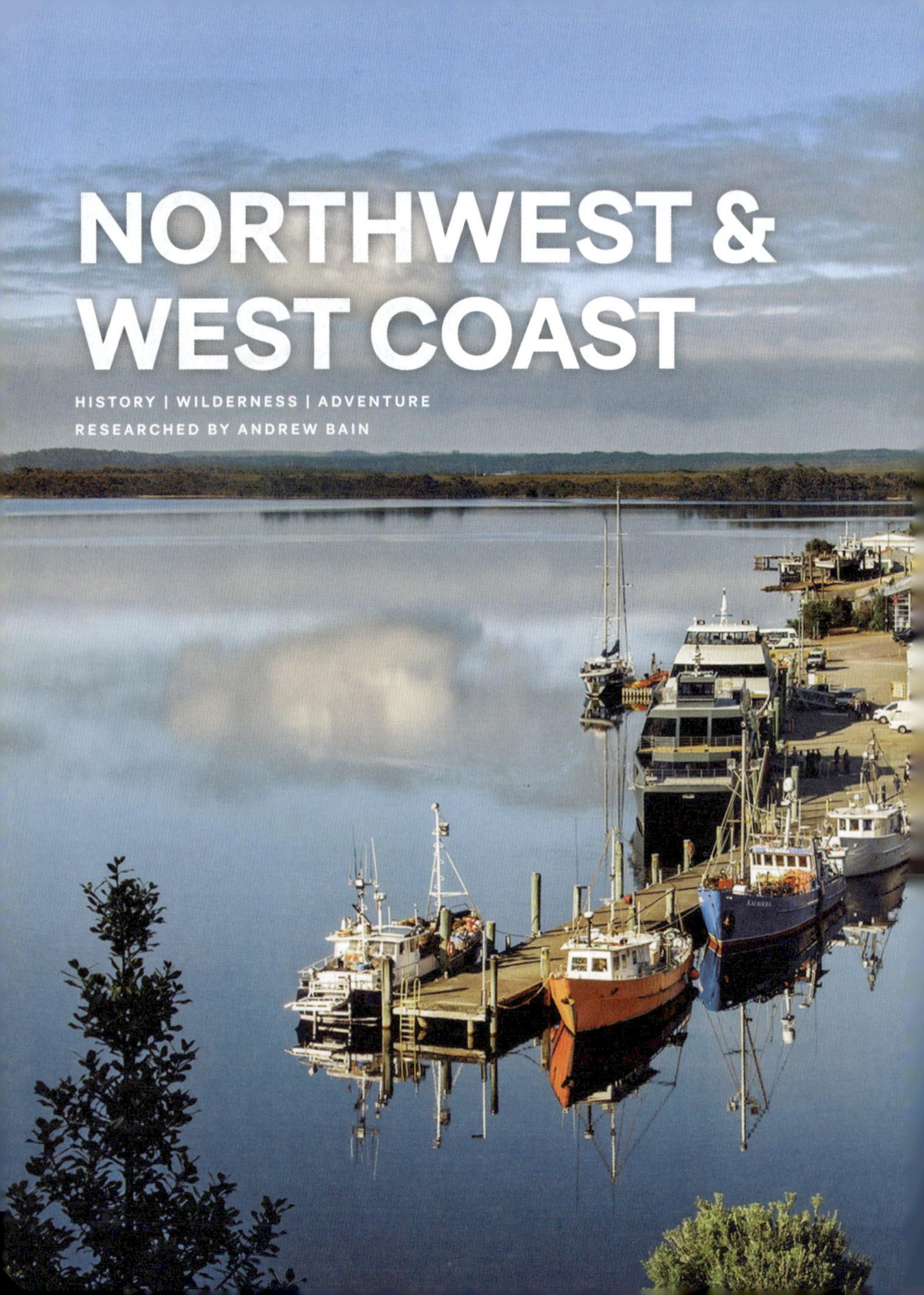

NORTHWEST & WEST COAST

Trip Builder

Experience a vast range of landscapes as you explore Tasmania's northwest and west coast, from towns huddled behind beaches, to forest-filled wilderness and the rolling farmland that makes this region a foodie's delight. Welcome to the literal wild west.

0 50 km
0 25 miles
Discover caves, coastal walks and Aboriginal heritage at Rocky Cape National Park (p197)
45mins from Burnie
Bass Strait
Wynyard
Burnie
Penguin
Ulverstone
Devonport
Plan for platypus on a stroll through the Tasmanian Arboretum (p210)
20mins from Devonport
Bridport
Scottsdale
Gunns Plain
Leven Canyon Regional Reserve
Leven Canyon
Sheffield
Mt Roland
Launceston
Deloraine
Westbury
Visit Tasmania's biggest and brightest outdoor art gallery in Sheffield (p212)
30mins from Devonport
Perth
Longford
Hop between stops along the flavoursome Tasmania Tasting Trail (p230)
Start in Devonport
Tullah
Rosebery
Cradle Mountain-Lake St Clair National Park
Mt Jerusalem
Yingina/Great Lake
Feel the misty spray of a waterfall after rain at Nelson Falls (p232)
30mins from Queenstown
Leeawuleena/Lake St Clair
Queenstown
Ross
Lake Burbury
West Coast Range Regional Reserve
Lake King William
Steam through the west coast's mining heritage on the West Coast Wilderness Railway (p228)
Start in Queenstown or Strahan
Bothwell
Gordon River
Franklin-Gordon Wild Rivers National Park
Ouse
Melton Mowbray
Kempton
Black Bluff
Lake Gordon
Mt Field National Park
Southwest Conservation Area
Strathgordon
Lake Pedder
Hobart

Practicalities

JAX10289/SHUTTERSTOCK

ARRIVING

Airports Devonport and Burnie (its airport is actually located in Wynyard) are serviced by Qantas and Rex flights from Melbourne. Both airports offer easy access to all areas of the northwest. Car rental is available, but book ahead.

Car To bring your own car or campervan, the *Spirit of Tasmania* ferry sails from Geelong to Devonport.

HOW MUCH FOR A

Curried scallop pie $10

Bottle of Tasmanian gin $75

Gordon River cruise $155

WHEN TO GO

DEC–FEB
Sunny and warm; perfect for beaches, bushwalks and boat rides

MAR–MAY
Mild days with cooler evenings and a lull ahead of the winter winds

JUN–AUG
Chilly and wet; the season for waterfalls and snowcapped vistas

SEP–NOV
Fresh, bright and breezy; it's tulip time on Table Cape

GETTING AROUND

Car This region is an ideal self-drive destination. Some roads are narrow and unsealed and you'll be sharing them with native wildlife, so take it easy, especially around dawn and dusk. Drive according to conditions – roads can get slippery in the colder months.

Bicycle The east coast might be where it's at for most cycle tourers, but there's less traffic and vaster spaces in the west. To put it bluntly, though, it's bloody hilly out this side.

Bus While a car is recommended to explore these regions, buses from Hobart and Launceston service Devonport and Burnie, with Kinetic buses further connecting Burnie to Stanley, Strahan and Queenstown. There's also an infrequent Hobart–Queenstown bus.

EATING & DRINKING

Driving through the lush green farmland of Tasmania's northwest provides a tantalising sense of the edible delights that await. Fresh vegetables, creamy dairy, sustainably raised pork and beef, wine, spirits and sweet treats are all on the menu. There's a dedicated Tasmania Tasting Trail (p230) if you want to build an itinerary around your taste buds.

Best produce stop King Island Dairy (p225)

Must-try seafood chowder Hursey Seafoods (p234)

TOP: VANDELAY INDUSTRIES/SHUTTERSTOCK
BOTTOM: SOUTHERN LIGHTSCAPES-AUSTRALIA/
GETTY IMAGES

WHERE TO STAY

Unique overnight stays await. Luxury wilderness lodges, free campsites and everything in between.

Town	Pros/Cons
Strahan	Pretty fishing village surrounded by ocean and rainforest. Nearby Lettes Bay is the ultimate away-from-it-all stay.
Queenstown	Burgeoning arts community and MTB hub, with solid rather than swish accommodation options.
Stanley	Historic town full of small shops and galleries, with the region's plushest digs.
Devonport	A starting point and springboard to the northwest for disembarking ferry travellers.
Smithton	Pole position for entering the Takayna/Tarkine wilderness and well located for surfing at Marrawah.
Burnie	Central to everything, making this lively and creative city a good base.

CONNECT & FIND YOUR WAY

Mobile phones There's limited or no mobile-phone reception at many locations on the west coast and far northwest.

Maps This is no place to be caught out without signal and access to maps. Download any maps before setting out from Stanley, Smithton, Strahan or Queenstown.

Wi-fi A map of free wi-fi locations and access details can be found at digital.tas.gov.au/free-wifi.

DRIVE SAFELY

The west and northwest are especially prone to changeable road conditions in the cooler seasons. Road closures and weather alerts can be found at alert.tas.gov.au.

MONEY

ATMs might be limited to the larger towns. Bring a combination of cards and cash so you don't end up doing the dishes to pay for your dinner.

42 Capes & CANYONS

HIKING | WILDLIFE | VIEWS

The incredible scenery of northwest Tasmania has long been a magnet for hikers. One of the joys of walking in this part of the state is that it doesn't need to be an epic undertaking. There are short trails that allow access to rich cultural heritage, unusual geological formations, and spectacular flora and fauna – all walkable in a couple of hours.

TRABANTOS/SHUTTERSTOCK

How to

When to go Before you head out and about, even on a short walk, check the weather. It can quickly change from sunshine to snow at any time of year. Make sure you're prepared with warm, waterproof clothing.

Need to know Visit the Tasmania Fire Service website (fire.tas.gov.au) for the latest information on bushfires. Managed burning to reduce fuel load takes place in spring and autumn and may also affect your plans.

RYAN HOI/SHUTTERSTOCK

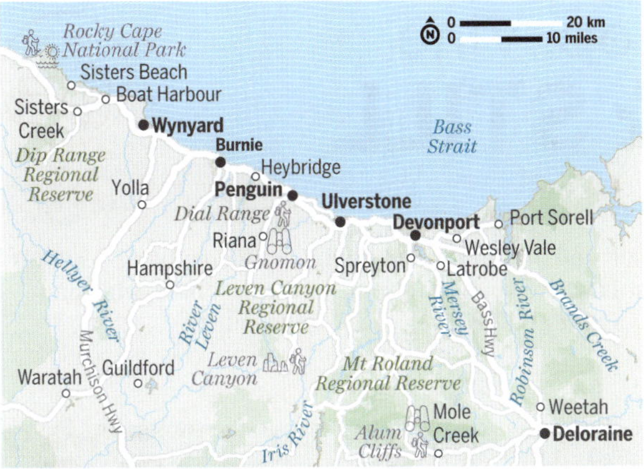

Along the Coast

There are walks ranging from 20 minutes to four hours at **Rocky Cape National Park**, offering the chance to see striking rock formations, secluded beaches, caves, and rich bird and plant life. The 15-minute return walk to North Cave provides a glimpse into the Tasmanian Aboriginal heritage of the cape, while the walk to Anniversary Bay, passing through Banksia Grove, is a good option if you want to break things up with a swim.

Running in a low line south from Penguin is the **Dial Range**. Walking tracks ascend to four peaks – Gnomon, Montgomery, Dial and Duncan – ranging from one hour to five hours in length, and all with good views along the range and the north coast.

Hinterland Hikes

It only takes a 45-minute loop walk to experience the unexpected wilderness of **Leven Canyon**. Cruickshanks is the most spectacular of two lookouts atop the canyon cliffs, with its platform hanging 275m above the gorge, looking down onto the wild Leven River and across to hulking Black Bluff, where the river begins its journey. If you'd rather skip the 697 stairs between the two, return from Cruickshanks by the same route instead of doing the circuit.

An equally deep view awaits at the **Alum Cliffs** outside of Mole Creek. Ascending through forest, the 45-minute return walk suddenly emerges atop the toothy cliffs, 200m above the frothy rapids of the Mersey River.

Top left Rocky Cape National Park
Bottom left Leven Canyon

Aboriginal Experiences

Rocky Cape is a special place. Originally called Pinmatik, the local area was home to the Tommeginer people who lived across the coastline, taking advantage of the resource-rich waters that provided food and materials for surviving the harsh local environment. It's an ancient landscape like much of the northwest coast – the land windswept, the trees and tussocks warped and twisted by the sheer force of nature. Walk any of the tracks and you'll find hidden rock shelters where my Old People would have taken refuge. Look and observe but don't take anything with you other than the memories you make.

By Caleb Nicholls-Mansell, a Tasmanian Aboriginal artist and Creative Director of Blackspace Creative @caleb_visualartist @blackspace.creative

43 Hop, Vine & STILL

CRAFT BEER | SPIRITS | WINE

Clean air, rich red soil and a community bursting with creativity – is it any wonder that the northwest is where you'll find some of the best beer, wine and spirits on the island? Take a tour and discover your own favourite.

PENGUIN BEER CO

Trip notes

Getting around You'll need your own vehicle to weave between this maze of producers.

Good to know Get the lowdown on the region's wineries at winetasmania.com.au/wine-trails/north-west-trail; for distilleries, head to taswhiskyandspiritstrail.com.au.

Top tip You could easily visit all five drink stops in a day, though they can be spread over a couple of days with an overnighter around Devonport if you want a more relaxed pace and a clear head in the morning.

One-of-a-Kind Varietals

The northwest wine industry might be small – five vineyards make up the North West Wine Trail – but you'll find a couple of varietals along the way that lend it a distinctive edge. **Meander Valley Vineyard** produces Australia's only baco noir, while **La Villa Wines** grows what's believed to be the world's southernmost nebbiolo and savagnin vines.

05 Hellyers Road Distillery Curiously, Australia's largest distillery was started by local dairy farmers. Go behind the scenes on a guided tour, and take the opportunity to pour and purchase your own bottle.

Southern Wild Distillery

02 Settle into a tasting or a cocktail made from Southern Wild's own Dasher + Fisher spirits in the heart of Devonport. The copper still was made by Southern Wild's distiller.

04 Penguin Beer Co This small-batch craft brewer has staked the only truly waterfront location in Penguin. The taps pour a good range of its beers, and the food menu includes burgers, quesadillas and tacos.

Bass Strait

Burnie

Heybridge

Penguin

Blythe River Conservation Area

Mt Dial Nature Recreation Area

Ulverstone

Riana

River Forth

Devonport

Egg Island

Port Sorell

Wesley Vale

Spreyton

Mersey River

Latrobe

03 Spreyton Cider Family-run orchard that has been growing apples and pears since 1908. Watch the factory bottling line as you sip on the award-winning ciders or dine in the restaurant. Regular live music.

01 Ghost Rock Wines A modern cellar door with views across its vines and rolling countryside to Bass Strait. Tastings include five of its 19 wines, and the Eatery has a seasonally changing menu of predominantly local produce.

Leven Canyon Regional Reserve

Mt Roland Regional Reserve

0 20 km

0 10 miles

FROM TOP: NORMAN POGSON/ALAMY, ANDREW BAIN/ALAMY

44 Reflections on A RIVER

RIVER CRUISE | RAINFOREST | CONVICT ISLAND

Look south from Strahan across Macquarie Harbour and pretty much all you see – and far beyond – is World Heritage-listed wilderness. Take a boat cruise across the harbour and up the Gordon River and you'll find yourself immersed in this wilderness, with a dash of convict history rolled in.

DAMITHA PEIRIS/SHUTTERSTOCK

How to

Getting here World Heritage Cruises and Gordon River Cruises both run daily tours along the river, departing from Strahan at 9am and 8.30am respectively. The arm-powered approach is on a seven-day kayaking tour of Macquarie Harbour and the Gordon River with Roaring 40s Kayaking.

When to go Boat tours run daily year-round. Strong winds and rain are common on the west coast at any time of year, so bring appropriate warm and waterproof clothing.

DALLAS AND JOHN HEATON/GETTY IMAGES

Cruising the River

Before beelining for the Gordon River, the two boat tours take a peep at **Hells Gates**, the treacherous, narrow opening to the ocean from Macquarie Harbour, given its name by despondent convicts. **Cape Sorell Lighthouse**, just outside the mouth of the harbour, is Australia's second-tallest lighthouse (40m).

Crossing the harbour, which is six times the size of Sydney Harbour, you'll cruise upstream on the **Gordon River**, where the reflections of riverside rainforest on the tannin-darkened waters are typically mirror-perfect. On a still day, it can feel almost as if the world has stopped breathing – this is very much the day to make sure your camera batteries are fully charged.

The boats head as far upstream as **Heritage Landing**, where a 400m-long boardwalk

JACQUI MARTIN/SHUTTERSTOCK

Stormbreaker

If the Gordon River captures your imagination, why not stay the night on the river? Based out of Strahan, the 20m *Stormbreaker* ketch runs overnight trips to the Gordon River, spending the night moored at Heritage Landing. Some trips continue upstream to Sir John Falls, picking up rafters at the end of Franklin River trips.

Top left Strahan foreshore **Top right** Gordon River Cruises **Bottom left** Gordon River

loops through the forest, passing a clearing that was created when a 2000-year-old Huon pine crashed down, flattening the forest around it.

Hell on Earth

As the boats return from the river, they make a stop at **Sarah Island**, a pebble of land with a big reputation for inhumanity. Tasmania's oldest convict settlement was established here in 1821 and was regarded as one of its most brutal – it was the 'Hell' in Hells Gates. Convicts were sent here to fell Huon pines, which were (and still are) revered for their timber, which was especially suited to shipbuilding. The original plan to ship the raw pine to Hobart was thwarted by the fierce west-coast conditions, so instead the convicts ended up building ships. In its day, it was the most productive shipyard in Australia.

The ruins of the convict settlement remain on the island, and boats are met by actor-

The Cruel Island

Most historians agree that Sarah Island was the most dreaded and brutal of penal settlements. Often when I'm on the island, we end up getting wet, but at the end of the day, I know that I can dry off when I get home. I always picture the convicts, who were given two sets of clothes a year. They were often waist- or shoulder-deep in freezing water, and they'd get back to the penitentiary at night and have to decide whether they wanted to take their damp clothes off and sleep naked in the freezing cold, or whether to spend the entire night in their completely damp clothes.

By Josh Selby, *a Sarah Island tour guide with the Round Earth Company roundearth.com.au*

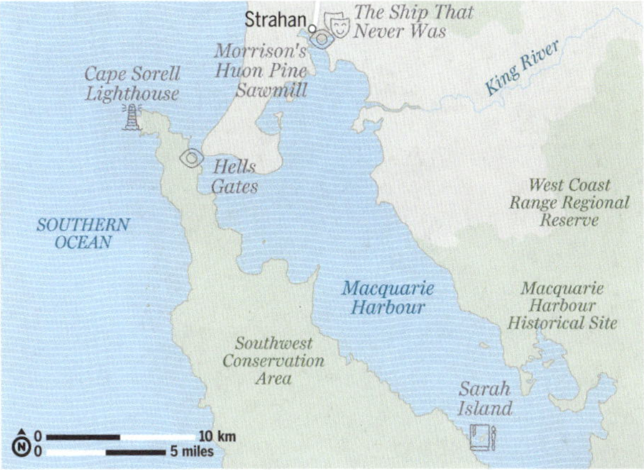

guides from the Round Earth Company for an entertaining tour of the island and its history.

Back on Land

The star of the arboreal show along the banks of the Gordon River (and in Sarah Island's history) is unquestionably the Huon pine, one of the world's longest-living tree species, growing for up to 3000 years. On the boats' return to Strahan (typically around 3pm), dockside **Morrison's Huon Pine Sawmill** runs free milling demonstrations – it's now illegal to harvest Huon pines and all logs here have been ethically salvaged after washing down rivers.

Complete the Sarah Island story in the evening by catching a performance of **The Ship That Never Was** at the Richard Davey amphitheatre in Strahan. Australia's longest-running play, it's an engaging and dramatic retelling of the last escape from Sarah Island in 1834, when a convict-built ship was hijacked by 10 convict shipwrights. Your guides on Sarah Island might well pop up again as actors in the play. Performances take place daily, and bookings are essential.

Left Sarah Island **Below** Milling demonstration, Morrison's Huon Pine Sawmill

FROM LEFT: TOM JASTRAM/SHUTTERSTOCK, ANDREW BAIN/LONELY PLANET

45 Terrific TAKAYNA

RAINFOREST | NATURE | WALKING

Tasmania holds Australia's largest expanse of temperate rainforest – Takayna/Tarkine. Bursting with natural treasures, from wild rivers to luminous sinkholes, endangered wildlife and rugged coastline, the region can be experienced through walks, drives and river cruises.

TRABANTOS/SHUTTERSTOCK

How to

Getting around To fully explore the richness of Takayna/Tarkine, you'll need to take your time, but a good starting place is the Tarkine Drive, a 60km route on sealed roads that allows easy access to the dramatic natural landscapes of the reserve's northern fringe. Details at discoverthetarkine.com.au.

When to go Summer is more likely to be dry and mild, but wet winters have their own charm – rainforest in the rain.

BRUCE GRAHAM/SHUTTERSTOCK

Forest Walks

Takayna/Tarkine is stitched with walking trails, from ascents of peaks such as Mt Donaldson to forest-floor rambles beside rivers as dark as stout.

For a flat and easy walk through cool myrtle rainforest, try **Trowutta Arch**. Just 30 minutes' return, the trail leads to an archway created by a cave collapse and a sinkhole filled with vibrant-green water.

Dip Falls and **Big Tree** are two short walks that are very easy to combine. At two-tiered Dip Falls, there's an elevated platform looking onto the distinctive hexagonal columns that form the falls' cliffs. Just a few metres down the road, you can also walk to the Big Tree, a magnificent 400-year-old stringybark with a trunk girth of 17m.

TRABANTOS/SHUTTERSTOCK

Responsible Tourism

Takayna/Tarkine is named after the tarkiner – Tasmanian Aboriginal people who have called the area home for 30,000 years. It remains a place of deep cultural significance and visitors should tread softly and respectfully. If you encounter a midden, rock carving or settlement site, do not touch or disturb it.

Top left Arthur River (p206) **Top right** Dip Falls **Left** Trowutta Arch.

River Runs

At Takayna/Tarkine's southern edge, Corinna was once a thriving gold-mining town, and now an opportunity to connect with nature in pristine surroundings. From here, the Huon-pine-built **MV Arcadia II** runs daily sailings down the glass-smooth, rainforest-crowded waters of the Pieman River to the contrastingly wild shores of Pieman Heads.

Corinna also hires out kayaks, which can be paddled downstream to a surreal set of wooden steps leading into the rainforest and on to **Lovers Falls**. Nearby, by the confluence with Savage River, you can paddle over the top of Australia's furthest-inland shipwreck.

In the region's north, enjoy a cruise along the **Arthur River**, where the lush riverside forest of myrtle, sassafras and tree ferns creates perfect reflections in the tannin-stained water. As you head further into the wilderness, lose yourself in the sound of birdsong – white-bellied sea eagles perch in the trees and

Among the Ferns & Falls

After four years working at Corinna Wilderness Village, the Tarkine has become more than a workplace to me – it feels like an old friend. I still remember one crisp and misty morning at Lovers Falls when the forest seemed to breathe as the sun slowly filtered through the canopy of tree ferns, rays reflecting off the mist. A fairy wren landed on my shoulder to say hello, curious and unafraid, completely unbothered by my presence, as if I belonged there as much as it did. Moments like this stay with me. The Tarkine has a quiet, grounding magic, and every day I spend here deepens my connection to this wild and beautiful place.

■ **By Kirsi Simpanen,** *who works in guest relations at Corinna Wilderness Village corinna.com.au*

Left Superb fairy wren **Below** 'Edge of the World', Gardiner Point

azure kingfishers can be spotted darting along the banks.

Coastal Pursuits

With dense forest on one side, and wild ocean on the other, the settlement of Arthur River is a great base for exploring Takayna/Tarkine's coastline and waterways.

At **Gardiner Point**, adjacent to the mouth of the Arthur River, you'll find a plaque marking the 'Edge of the World'. There's no land between here and Argentina – nothing to stand in the way of the wind or the waves – which might be why the shore is covered in driftwood the size of tree trunks. South of here, in **Sundown Point State Reserve**, a short coastal walk from Laraturunawn/Sundown Point leads to ancient Aboriginal petroglyphs by the mouth of a creek.

Experienced surfers are drawn to the challenging conditions at **Marrawah**, while the road into nearby **Preminghana Indigenous Protected Area** ends at a lookout platform peering over the wild coast and as far north as the Woolnorth wind farm – the air here has been decreed to be the cleanest on Earth, so fill your lungs. A trail from the lookout weaves down to a long, wave-pounded beach at the foot of low Mt Cameron West.

FROM LEFT: PHOTOTRIP/GETTY IMAGES, VISUAL COLLECTIVE/SHUTTERSTOCK

Tasmania's Spirited Revival

INNOVATION AND AWARDS IN THE ISLAND'S DISTILLERIES

In 1839, frustrated at the rampant drunkenness of Hobart, Governor John Franklin banned the distilling of spirits in Tasmania. It wasn't until 1992 that a local surveyor, Bill Lark, lobbied to overturn the law. Finally, Tasmanian distillers could take advantage of the state's climate, native ingredients and clean water – to great effect.

Left Lark Distillery (p47) **Centre** Gin and tonic **Right** Sullivans Cove Distillery (p47)

FILEDIMAGE/SHUTTERSTOCK

When Lark was granted Tasmania's first distilling licence in 150 years, he couldn't have known that he was kickstarting something so special. In the almost 35 years since he began making whisky in a 5L copper still bought for $65, more than 70 distilleries have arisen across the state.

The environmental conditions in Tasmania are perfect for whisky production. The state has an abundance of clean water, rich barley fields and a moderate climate that's ideal for ageing whisky barrels. It even has peat bogs.

But it also needed somebody like Bill Lark, who has affectionately been dubbed the 'Godfather of Australian Whisky'. So many of Tasmania's distillers have been mentored by the generous Lark, including Matt and Sarah Packwood-Hollings of Alchymia Distillery on Table Cape.

'When we first met Bill, he said, "If you want to ask anything, I will help as long as you promise that if you then have the knowledge and someone asks you a question, you'll help them"', says Sarah. 'Bill has driven a culture within Tasmanian whisky that, as many together, we become a destination, whereas singularly we're only one distillery on our own. He's really keen that everybody makes the best whisky possible, rather than just churning out stuff that's sellable.'

It's an ethos that has resonated to global effect, with Tasmanian whisky now considered among the finest in the world, with a swathe of gongs to back it up.

Sarah and Matt's own place in the Tasmanian whisky scene began in 2016, when they ditched corporate careers on the mainland to ponder the purchase of a food-based

ATSUSHI HIRAO/SHUTTERSTOCK

ADAM GIBSON/SULLIVANS COVE

business. They settled on distilling after Sarah bought Matt a whisky-making course as a birthday gift.

'On day one, we were down in Hobart with Captain Bligh's (brewery), doing the first part of the whisky-making process, which is where you make your mash,' Sarah recalls. 'We looked across the mash at each other, and we both had big silly grins on our faces and realised that we'd found what we were going to do.'

'He's really keen that everybody makes the best whisky possible, rather than just churning out stuff that's sellable.'

Alchymia has established itself as a destination distillery, with bottles selling only through its cellar door on Table Cape. The entire process for its single malt, single cask whisky is done on site, from the grist to bottling, and should you book a tour, you're absorbed into the daily routine, guided through whatever tasks are on the roster that day. It's also the only distillery in Australia where, if you purchase a private cask of whisky, you're invited to take part in its making. And, like so many Tasmanian distilleries, Alchymia's sense of place is evident in its whisky.

'We get a sea mist that rolls off Bass Strait – we're within 100m of the ocean – probably once every two weeks,' says Sarah. 'So we're going to put a cage on the outside of the bond store and mature one of the casks outside to see whether we can get any of that sea-mist influence into the final flavour of the whisky.'

Get in the Spirit

Whisky is Tasmania's pin-up spirit, but the state's distillers are an experimental bunch, creating a range of wild and wonderful sips.

Hartshorn Distillery produces a vodka and a gin made from sheep's whey – in 2018 the former was named the world's best vodka.

Gins are about as widespread as whiskies, and often flavoured with native botanicals such as pepperberry and kunzea. New Norfolk's **7K Distillery** is even producing the 'world's hottest gin', made with Carolina reaper chillies.

Keep an eye out also for **Hellfire Bluff Distillery**'s Potato Vodka, made with its own spuds; **Bakehouse Distillery**'s Evoke, the world's only spirit made with sassafras; and **Willie Smith**'s Apple Brandy.

46 Monotreme MANIA

PLATYPUS | WALKS | RIVERS

Wombats are cute, echidnas are prickly goodness and wallabies – well, they're pretty much everywhere in Tasmania; but there's something very special about the rarity of a platypus sighting. And there's nowhere on the planet that offers better prospects than northwest Tasmania.

PHOTOTRIP/GETTY IMAGES

Trip notes

Getting around The platypus waterways covered here are well spread out and largely in remote, out-of-the-way places, so you'll need a vehicle to access them.

Need to know Though most sites can be accessed at any time, the Tasmanian Arboretum has set opening hours – 9am to 8pm during daylight savings (early October to early April), and until 5pm outside of that period.

Platypus Viewing Tips

The best viewing times are around dawn and dusk.

Scan flat stretches of water, looking for concentric circles or ripples of water created by the movement of the platypus.

Be very quiet – platypus are shy creatures.

Look for the animal's back and top of its head rising just above the surface of the water.

01 The Australian Platypus Monitoring Network describes Founders Lake in the **Tasmanian Arboretum** as 'the most productive single site (in Australia) to see a platypus' – we saw four in just five minutes one evening.

02 Home to mountain bikers and platypus spotters, **Warrawee Forest Reserve** borders a sheltered stretch of the Mersey River suitably known as the Platypus Pool.

03 **Fern Glade Reserve** at Burnie's edge was primarily established to protect its waterways' platypus, which are readily seen along the 500m fern-shaded Fern Glade track and its lookout platform.

04 The **Mole Creek Hotel** might have a minor obsession with thylacines, but step out back and it's platypus you might see in tiny Limestone Creek running through its backyard.

05 Pause by the footbridge over the Liffey River at **Oura Oura** – once the home of former Greens leader Bob Brown, now a reserve – and you might well get a platypus appearance.

FROM LEFT: PAWAN KAWAN/SHUTTERSTOCK, LUKAS_VEJRIK/SHUTTERSTOCK

47 Outdoor GALLERY

ART | MURALS | FESTIVAL

A hub for fine arts and studio-galleries, the small town of Sheffield is a living canvas of outdoor murals. There are more than 200 murals decorating walls around the town, depicting the history, culture and natural attractions of the area.

Trip notes

Getting around Sheffield is 26km south of Devonport. Most of the murals can be seen on a walk around the town, but some require a short drive. Find full details and a map at sheffieldtasmania.com.au.

When to go Visit in November to see the annual International Mural Fest, when artists compete in a public 'paint off' in Mural Park, each one completing a mural based around a theme.

The Canadian Club

In the mid-1980s, Sheffield was a struggling rural town looking for inspiration. When two residents saw a documentary about murals in the Canadian town of Chemainus, an idea was seeded. A mural was commissioned by artist John Lendis and a 40-year (and counting) mural obsession began.

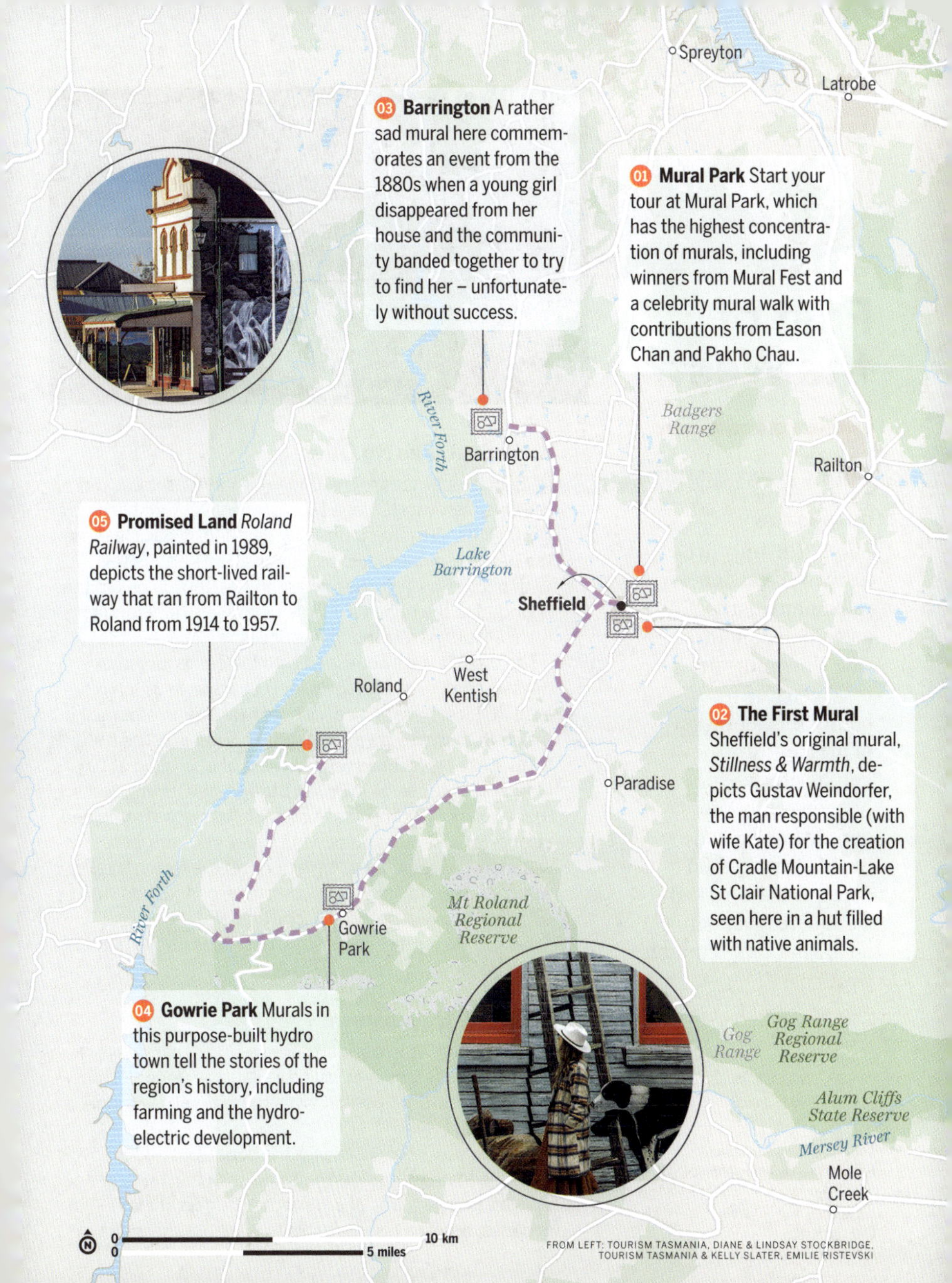

01 Mural Park Start your tour at Mural Park, which has the highest concentration of murals, including winners from Mural Fest and a celebrity mural walk with contributions from Eason Chan and Pakho Chau.

02 The First Mural Sheffield's original mural, *Stillness & Warmth*, depicts Gustav Weindorfer, the man responsible (with wife Kate) for the creation of Cradle Mountain-Lake St Clair National Park, seen here in a hut filled with native animals.

03 Barrington A rather sad mural here commemorates an event from the 1880s when a young girl disappeared from her house and the community banded together to try to find her – unfortunately without success.

04 Gowrie Park Murals in this purpose-built hydro town tell the stories of the region's history, including farming and the hydro-electric development.

05 Promised Land *Roland Railway*, painted in 1989, depicts the short-lived railway that ran from Railton to Roland from 1914 to 1957.

FROM LEFT: TOURISM TASMANIA, DIANE & LINDSAY STOCKBRIDGE, TOURISM TASMANIA & KELLY SLATER, EMILIE RISTEVSKI

Fest of the West

FROM COPPER MINING TO CULTURE IN QUEENSTOWN

Surely the only arts festival in existence to be named after a geological fault, The Unconformity is Queenstown's biennial celebration of arts, culture and heritage. Authentically raw and deeply rooted in this very special place, it has sparked a creative awakening on Tasmania's remote west coast.

KEELAN O'HEHIR

Left *Flux* by Liquid Architecture and Unconscious Collective **Middle** QVOD. AMARE exhibition by Rory Wray-McCann **Right** Screening of *The Falls*, directed by Halcyon MacLeod

A Festival Like No Other

In its first incarnation, The Unconformity was known as the Queenstown Heritage and Arts Festival. Established in 2010 in response to community demand, it was clear from the beginning this would be a festival unlike any other. With a focus on site-specific art and performances that responded to the region's unique history and environment, the festival was a resounding success.

The 2012 festival coincided with the centenary of a devastating fire at the North Mt Lyell mine, in which more than 40 local miners died, with festival events embracing rather than shying away from the anniversary. The third festival (2014) focused on 100 years of operation at Lake Margaret Hydroelectric Power Station, and it was clear that audience enthusiasm for a biennial festival remained strong. However, the core team, many of whom were volunteers, were keen to consider how the festival could mature – maintaining that strong local connection while simultaneously growing in scope and ambition.

It was time for the Queenstown Heritage and Arts Festival to become The Unconformity.

Uniquely Queenstown

An unconformity is a buried surface that separates rock masses of different ages, and the Haulage Unconformity – the geological outcrop that gives the festival its name – is found at Mt Lyell.

It is, in a way, responsible for the boom-bust-boom cycle that Queenstown has long endured, with mining riches that left behind a trail of environmental degradation – for decades, barely a tree was able to grow on Queenstown's

JESSE HUNNIFORD

JACK ROBERT-TISSOT

moonscape slopes. The Mt Lyell Mine closed in 2014, and at the following Unconformity festival in 2016, the opening event was The Rumble: a large-scale sound installation that included a procession of mining machinery and trucks along Main St. What's become best about the arts festival is that it doesn't take place in white-cube galleries – Queenstown doesn't have any – but in venues such as a limestone quarry, a steam train and a mine shaft. Self-guided art trails and mural tours lead down backstreets and alleyways, and local footballers get themselves bloodied and bruised with a match on the town's infamous gravel oval.

> It was clear from the beginning this would be a festival unlike any other.

Artistic Growth

The result of all this visionary effort is that Queenstown's celebration of arts is no longer restricted to a weekend of events every two years. The town has arisen as an unlikely centre of the arts, drawing prominent Tasmanian artists such as Raymond Arnold and Helen Demczuk to set up home here. With this upsurge of creative energy has come a range of galleries, such as Empire Art Box tucked into the grand Empire Hotel, Q-West, Soggy Brolly, WAS (Western Art Space) and the bright PressWEST, adorned with a green mural and a cartoonish thylacine – the distinctive work of Tassie artist Tom O'Hern.

Soggy Brolly

On Queenie's main street, push open the door of Soggy Brolly. This art and graphic-design studio is imaginative and delightful, much like owner Lea Walpole. Lea grew up in the town and today celebrates its artists, each drawn by the landscape in curiously beautiful ways. Exhibitions change regularly and you might even meet the artist or maker. Stick around town for the evening to catch the 5pm (weekdays) screening of the 2002 documentary film *Franklin*, about the fight to save the Franklin River from dams, at the art deco Paragon Theatre (c 1933). When the theatre opened, 1150 locals flocked to see the first film.

48 Nuts about STANLEY

HIKES | HERITAGE STREETSCAPE | PENGUINS

Tasmania has no lack of likeable seaside towns, and yet Stanley remains a perennial crowd favourite. Is it The Nut, the steep-sided volcanic plug that towers above town? Is it the colourful heritage buildings huddled at its base? The penguins that march ashore each evening? The colourful fishing fleet? Or is it the combination that creates Stanley's distinctive magic?

SHUANG LI/SHUTTERSTOCK

How to

Getting here Stanley is an hour's drive west from Burnie, or 1½ hours from Devonport if you're hurrying here from the ferry.

Need to know There's a visitor centre in the heart of town, though it's unstaffed. Let yourself in and flick through the available brochures.

Top tip If you're going to take The Nut's chairlift just one way, make it the descent back into town, when it delivers the best views.

PETR PODROUZEK/SHUTTERSTOCK

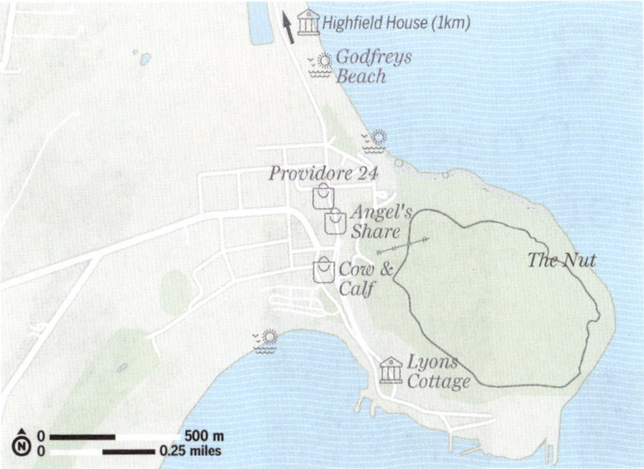

Mixed Nuts

There's no mistaking **The Nut**, the compact 143m hill – essentially a plateau ringed with cliffs – that rears out of Bass Strait and looms over the town. There are two ways to its top: a charmingly antiquated chairlift and a short but surprisingly steep sealed path – it's about a 20-minute climb. Once on the plateau, a 2km walking track circles the summit, pausing at four lookouts with different angles on the world.

Town Time

At sea level, Stanley is custom-made to be wandered. Skirt the base of The Nut, passing **Lyons Cottage** – the birthplace of Joseph Lyons, the only Australian Prime Minister to come from Tasmania – and you'll eventually come to the fishing port with its bright-red boats. Take a shop-hop along the chocolate-box cottages of Church St and you'll find the **Cow & Calf** photographic gallery, a bounty of Tassie produce at **Providore 24** and perhaps time for a tipple at **Angel's Share**, with tastings and sales of whiskies from more than two dozen Tasmanian distilleries.

Make time in the evening for penguins, watching them pass under your feet from a boardwalk at the southern end of **Godfreys Beach** as they come ashore to their burrows each evening. They're not immune to wandering beyond, into the town's streets, so keep an eye out for unexpected birds after dark.

Top left The Nut and Stanley
Bottom left Church St shops

Royal Charter

Looking down on Stanley from the ridge behind is **Highfield House**, built in 1835 for the chief agent of the Van Diemen's Land Company. This company operated a farm that extended almost all the way across the northwest, from Kennaook/Cape Grim almost to Burnie, and was established by a rare royal charter from King George IV. The property, now known as Woolnorth, has shrunk into Tasmania's northwest corner, though it remains the largest farm in the state, while Highfield House is open for self-guided visits and perhaps the classic view of Stanley and The Nut.

PLANTS
of the West Coast & Northwest

01

02

03

04

05

01 Deciduous beech (Nothofagus gunnii or fagus)
Tasmania's only winter deciduous species; in autumn, people flock to see its stunning display of golden leaves.

02 Huon pine
Once heavily logged for boat building, you can still find stands along west-coast rivers. Can grow to be 3000 years old.

03 King Billy pine
Often rather gnarly and twisted looking, these conifers grow up to 1800 years of age in alpine areas and the west-coast rainforest.

04 Tasmanian waratah
A much-loved icon of Tasmania's forests that flowers from spring to summer. Most are bright red but you might spot a yellow one.

05 Buttongrass
Expansive buttongrass moorlands are common through the west of the state. They love fire and come back strongly after a burn.

06 Myrtle beech orchid
Small orchid that grows in the leaf litter and on fallen myrtle logs in wet forests and rainforests,

08

06

07

09

10

mainly along the west coast.

07 Tasmanian leatherwood
One of the main trees you'll find growing in temperate rainforest. Highly prized by beekeepers for the distinctive honey it produces.

08 Pandani
The world's tallest heath plant has a Dr Seuss-ian appearance. Growing up to 12m in height, it's found in alpine areas and wet forest mountains.

09 Snowberry
Found in wet forests and alpine areas, you'll recognise this photogenic plant by its glossy leaves and clusters of plump white berries.

10 Richea scoparia
Known to many as 'bushman's curse' for its sharp, prickly foliage, this endemic plant also flowers brilliantly, brightening alpine and subalpine areas, where it's abundant.

01 HARRY FOSTER/SHUTTERSTOCK, **02** STEVE LOVEGROVE/SHUTTERSTOCK, **03** STEVE LOVEGROVE/SHUTTERSTOCK, **04** LCAT PRODUCTIONS/SHUTTERSTOCK, **05** K.POCK PICS/SHUTTERSTOCK **06** DAVE WATTS/ALAMY STOCK PHOTO, **07** LUKE OBRIEN PHOTOGRAPHY/GETTY IMAGES, **08** ACROPOLYPSEPHOTOGRAPHY/SHUTTERSTOCK, **09** CRBELLETTE/SHUTTERSTOCK, **10** MICHAEL DOWLING/GETTY IMAGES

49 On the EDGE

BEACH | DUNES | SUNSETS

There are beaches and then there's Ocean Beach. A short drive from Strahan, this stretch of dune-backed sand runs 40km north from Macquarie, heading all the way to Trial Harbour. It's exhilarating to stand and look towards the horizon, knowing the next landfall isn't until South America. Expect wild weather, big waves and beautiful west-coast sunsets.

How to

Getting here Ocean Beach is 6km west of Strahan and accessible on an unsealed road. Henty Dunes are 14km north of Strahan on the road to Zeehan.

Need to know This is not the place to test out your swimming skills. The surf can be ferocious – Australia's largest wave (20m!) was recorded near Ocean Beach – so it's definitely water that's best admired from a distance.

Beach Views

The west coast is best known for great expanses of lush green rainforest, but there's a desert of sorts amid all those ancient trees. Windswept, wave-battered **Ocean Beach** forms a salt-licked 40km line along the coast behind Strahan. It's hard to imagine a better way to experience the true nature of this region than a long walk on the empty expanse of hard-packed sand, with the sound of pounding surf ringing in your ears. You can also walk to the beach, following the wide and easy Ocean Beach Trail for 2km through coastal scrub to a wild patch of the beach.

Ocean Beach provides an amazing outlook to **Hells Gates**, the narrow and notoriously dangerous entrance to Macquarie Harbour. It's also a great place to watch the sunset.

Top right Hells Gates lighthouse
Bottom right Henty Dunes

STEVE TODD/SHUTTERSTOCK

STEVE LOVEGROVE/SHUTTERSTOCK

Wild Walk

Things get even wilder around Ocean Beach at night. Evening walking tours with Strahan-based **Whitmore's Wild** head through the coastal bush behind the beach, finally emerging onto its sands in search of local wildlife. The two-hour tours are family-friendly and it's a treasure hunt of sorts for tracks, scat, burrows and, of course, sightings of west-coast wildlife, all set to the booming soundtrack of the Ocean Beach surf.

Guides carry spotlights with red filters, but it's worth bringing your own torch to light the track as you walk.

All up, you'll walk around 3.4km and hopefully sight the likes of possums, micro-bats and local frogs.

Dune Discovery

If a beach walk – even an Ocean Beach walk – feels too tame, head slightly further north to **Henty Dunes**. Reaching heights of 30m, these giant sand dunes extend for 15km along the coast behind Ocean Beach. Keep an eye out for all kinds of animal tracks in the sand as you explore. You can hire a toboggan from Gordon River Cruises if you want to whizz down the dunes at top speed...but don't forget you'll need to haul it back up the soft sands under your own power.

50 Coastal CRAWL

ROAD TRIP | FOOD | TULIPS

Spend a day or two on coast-hugging roads between Devonport and Boat Harbour Beach for a real treat. On the right, beautiful views of Bass Strait. On the left, rich red soil and fertile farmland. Leave plenty of time for beach walks and snack stops.

TOM JASTRAM/SHUTTERSTOCK

Trip notes

Getting around It's 90km along the coastal roads from Devonport to Boat Harbour Beach, a 1½-hour drive if you do it non-stop. But allow time for surprises and detours.

When to go If you want to take advantage of tulip time at Table Cape, aim to make this drive in October. The tulip farm is open from late September to late October, with flowering usually at its best in the first half of October.

Fossil Bluff

Hunt for dinosaurs – okay, the smaller fossilised imprints of prehistoric marine creatures – in the cliffs and rocks at Fossil Bluff on Wynyard's outskirts. At low tide, you can walk all the way along the rock platforms that line the base of the bluff.

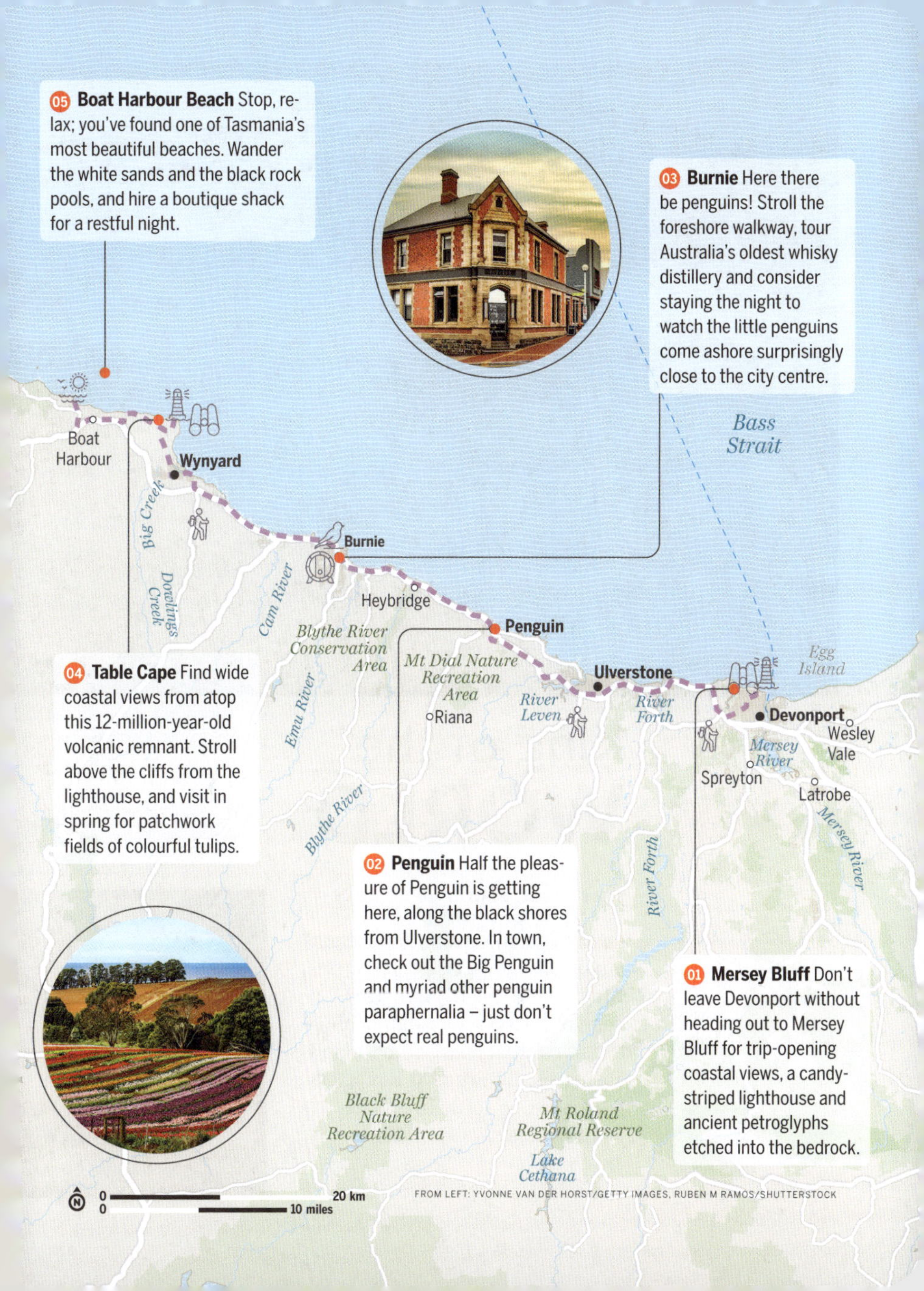

05 Boat Harbour Beach Stop, relax; you've found one of Tasmania's most beautiful beaches. Wander the white sands and the black rock pools, and hire a boutique shack for a restful night.

03 Burnie Here there be penguins! Stroll the foreshore walkway, tour Australia's oldest whisky distillery and consider staying the night to watch the little penguins come ashore surprisingly close to the city centre.

04 Table Cape Find wide coastal views from atop this 12-million-year-old volcanic remnant. Stroll above the cliffs from the lighthouse, and visit in spring for patchwork fields of colourful tulips.

02 Penguin Half the pleasure of Penguin is getting here, along the black shores from Ulverstone. In town, check out the Big Penguin and myriad other penguin paraphernalia – just don't expect real penguins.

01 Mersey Bluff Don't leave Devonport without heading out to Mersey Bluff for trip-opening coastal views, a candy-striped lighthouse and ancient petroglyphs etched into the bedrock.

FROM LEFT: YVONNE VAN DER HORST/GETTY IMAGES, RUBEN M RAMOS/SHUTTERSTOCK

51 King of the WORLD

SEAFOOD | ISLAND LIFE | GOLF

Famed for its produce and a pair of world-class golf courses, King Island is anchored at the edge of Bass Strait, 80km from the northwest coast of mainland Tasmania. Life runs at a relaxed pace here, so settle in and get comfortable.

PHILLIP WITTKE/SHUTTERSTOCK

How to

Getting here Flights to King Island are available from Melbourne, Launceston and Burnie. There's no public transport on the island, so you'll need to arrange car hire. Book in advance (kingislandcarrental.com.au) to ensure availability.

When to go The weather on King Island varies dramatically, but the warmest and driest months tend to be from December through to March, when average highs are around 20°C. July and August are usually coolest and wet.

Island Larder

Long headlining King Island's gourmet goodness is **King Island Dairy**, turning out award-winning cheeses. Call in at its Cheese Shop, attached to the dairy, for free tastings of six cheeses, which can be enjoyed with a Tassie beer, cider or wine.

Fancy a pint in a paddock? Stop in at **King Island Brewhouse**, among farmland between the island's two main towns, Currie and Grassy. Its taproom pours six brews.

Distilleries are twofold: contact **King Island Distillery** owner Heidi Weitjens for a nose through the shed that is the island's original distillery; while **King Island Distillery Bass Strait** runs King Island's coolest bar...inside the airport.

Top left Stokes Point (p227)
Bottom left Cheese at King Island Dairy

Tee Time

Dramatic coastal scenery and rolling sand dunes are the perfect combination for links golf, and King Island punches well above its weight on the fairways and greens. The windswept (read, challenging) **Cape Wickham** course, at the foot of Cape Wickham lighthouse in the rugged north, was named Australia's top golf course in 2025 by Golf Australia, with the more southerly **Ocean Dunes** at No 5 on the list. There's also a fabulous nine-hole course in the main township of Currie.

Out & About

King Island's natural beauty is at its most pronounced around cliff-lined **Seal Rocks**. A lookout platform peers along the line of cliffs and the Southern Ocean that assaults them. From the lookout, a 1½-hour (return) walking trail called Copperhead meanders north along the top of the cliffs. Be sure to head

Get Wrecked

There's a reason King Island is home to the largest lighthouse in the southern hemisphere – ships (around 140 of them) slammed into the island's reefs and shores with too regular frequency. This horrible history is recognised along the island's Maritime Trail, featuring more than a dozen stops. Prime among them are the remains of a Murray River paddle steamer amid the waves at Yellow Rock Beach (it was wrecked while being delivered across Bass Strait), and a sobering memorial to the *Cataraqui*, Australia's worst maritime disaster, when 400 people drowned after the ship was wrecked on a reef south of Currie.

Pick up a trail brochure at the airport.

The Restaurant with No Food

The most intriguing dining destination on this island of gourmet repute is the **Currie Boathouse**, aka the Restaurant with No Food. The colourful boathouse on the shore of Currie Harbour is stocked with cutlery, crockery, stove, BBQ and myriad quirks, but you need to bring your own food for DIY dining.

ANDREW BAIN/LONELY PLANET

to the end of the trail for exhibit A on island humour. Along the same road, pull up at the **Calcified Forest**, where a short walking trail heads into an open patch of sand covered in the so-called 'forest' – remnants of sand that cemented themselves around tree roots 7000 years ago.

Surfers in the know revere **Martha Lavinia Beach** in the island's north, once named among the world's 10 best waves and a favourite with Kelly Slater and his surfing buddy, Pearl Jam's Eddie Vedder. Pay further surfing homage at **Stokes Point**, the island's southern tip. You might not want to put a board in here, but it was the site of the world's first tow-in surfing competition.

Not far from Martha Lavinia, you can stand in the shadow of **Cape Wickham Lighthouse**, the tallest lighthouse in the southern hemisphere at 48m. You can't enter this lighthouse, but you can take a tour of **Currie Lighthouse**, which was built in 1879, 18 years after Cape Wickham. Make the dizzying ascent of the 93 steps of the spiral staircase inside the prefabricated metal structure for a view down into Currie Harbour and beyond.

NEAR & FAR LEFT: SOUTHERN LIGHTSCAPES-AUSTRALIA/GETTY IMAGES

Left Cape Wickham Lighthouse
Top right Currie Boathouse **Bottom right** Martha Lavinia Beach

52 Making TRACKS

RAILWAY | HERITAGE | WILDERNESS

The inland towns of the west – Queenstown, Tullah, Rosebery and Zeehan – hold layers of rich mining heritage. The intense contrast between the lush forests that blanket the coast and the barren moonscape around Queenstown testifies to the environmental destruction of the early mines. Learn more about the region's history on a reconstructed railway route or at a local museum.

STEVE LOVEGROVE/SHUTTERSTOCK

How to

Getting here The West Coast Wilderness Railway offers a range of full- and half-day tours, most starting in Queenstown, with one route from Strahan. Make sure you double check your starting point to avoid missing your departure.

When to go Summer is more likely to provide a warm, calm day for your tour. Winter can be charming in its own way, with fog blanketing the forest, but dress appropriately.

SLOVEGROVE/GETTY IMAGES

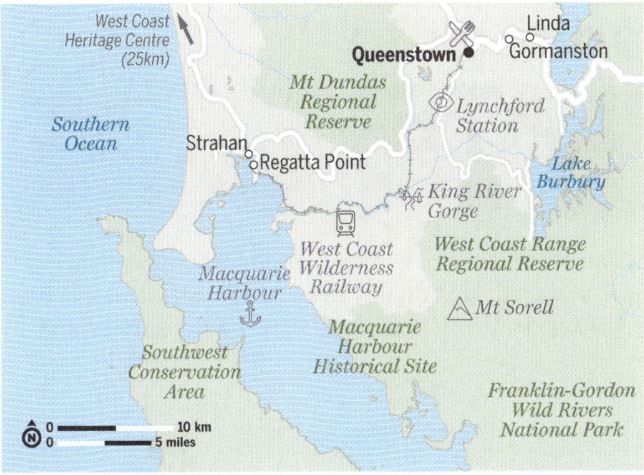

Top West Coast Wilderness Railway
Bottom Main street, Zeehan

Ride the Rails

The **West Coast Wilderness Railway** is a chance to step back in time and follow sections of a 35km track between Queenstown and Strahan – a reconstruction of the route used from the late 1890s onwards by the Mt Lyell Mining and Railway Company.

Routes change according to works along the line, but at the time of writing the **Rinadeena, Rack & Rainforest** and the **Lynchford Express** were operating out of Queenstown's old-world station. The former is a three-hour trip through beautiful rainforest to the King River Gorge. You'll climb one of the steepest tracks in the southern hemisphere to Rinadeena Saddle, using a unique rack and pinion system, and have the opportunity to pan for gold at Lynchford Station.

The **Teepookana & the King** departure from Strahan crosses an iron bridge, shipped to Tasmania in pieces from England, into once-thriving Teepookana and travelling on to Lower Landing Station, where you can head out for a walk.

Mining Heritage

If you're keen to dig deeper into the area's mining history, don't miss Zeehan's **West Coast Heritage Centre**, where the exhibits include minerals and rocks of every size, shape and colour in the collection of the original Zeehan School of Mines and Metallurgy. Kids of all ages will love the chance to experience what an underground mine was like in the replica crocoite cavern.

60 Great Short Walks

For a compiled (and subjective) list of the best day walks on the west coast and across the state, check out the 60 Great Short Walks put together by Tasmania Parks & Wildlife Service. The selection offers a readily accessible portfolio of walks, from river rambles to peak pushes.

Walks around the west coast include Kelly Basin, the Huon Pine Walk at Corinna, and Nelson Falls.

Find the full list, and details of each walk, at parks.tas.gov.au/things-to-do/60-great-short-walks, or scout out a hard copy at national park and other Tasmanian visitor centres.

53 Paddock to PLATE

FOOD | FARM GATES | TASTING TOUR

The northwest enjoys an abundance of artisanal producers offering an astonishing selection of local, seasonal, sustainably grown food. Stretching across the region is the Tasmania Tasting Trail, offering more than 40 stops. Here are some starting points.

WILLIAM EDGE/SHUTTERSTOCK

Trip notes

Getting around The Tasting Trail stretches right across the northwest, from Hagley in the east to Smithton in the west, a distance of around 200km.

When to go Summer is best for a food-focused itinerary, but consider also visiting in April when TrailGraze, a weekend festival of food, prises open the farm gates.

Need to know Find a full list of Tasting Trail producers, and a map, at tasting trail.com.au.

The Secret is in the Soil

Take a look at the rich-red colouring of the northwest's soil and you'll quickly appreciate the health and vitality of the land – how could you not grow great produce here? The soil comes from the weathering of basalt from eruptions of volcanoes such as those at Table Cape and The Nut.

01 Anvers Tasmania
Chocolate factory in Latrobe with a viewing area, small museum, tasting centre and cafe, and Australia's only access to Fortunato No 4, a Peruvian cacao bean thought to be extinct until its rediscovery in 2009.

02 Turners Beach Berry Patch
Summer berry picking is as Tasmanian as devils. Stop at this family-run farm to pick your own berries in season, or simply enjoy a wood-fired pizza and berry ice cream in the cafe.

03 Melita Honey Farm
Leatherwood honey is one of the tastes of the state, and you can watch the busy bees inside a glass hive, as well as shop for almost 50 honey varieties.

04 Truffle Farm
Scratch up a black truffle on a hunt with the truffle dogs almost year-round, followed by a truffle pizza or truffle toastie.

05 41° South Tasmania
Ethical inland salmon and ginseng producer. Walk through the property and its filtering wetland and grab a salmony lunch at Georgie's Cafe.

54 Chasing WATERFALLS

WALKING | SCENERY | WATERFALLS

The west coast is Tasmania's wettest region – Strahan lands a damp 1.5m of rain a year – but visiting the soggy side of the state has its benefits, too. Waterfalls, including the highest one in the state, tend to be much more powerful and dramatic on this side of the island.

Favourite Falls

A great walk to take in three waterfalls is the **Castra Circuit** near Nietta. It's a five-minute walk to Silver Falls, and your next stop is Castra Falls, which is a bit more difficult to get to – you've got to use fixed rope to get you down because it's steep. Then loop around to Step Falls, which flows over picturesque rock columns.

By Craig Doumouras, *the author of Waterfalls of Tasmania waterfallsoftasmania.com.au*

Trip notes

Getting around The waterfalls are concentrated around Rosebery, Queenstown and Strahan. Don't rush to see them all in one day. Instead, consider combining Nelson Falls and Horsetail Falls into one excursion, Montezuma Falls and Stitt Falls into a second, and Hogarth Falls a third.

Need to know West-coast weather is a changeable beast – even on an expected sunny day, take warm, waterproof clothing.

04 Montezuma Falls Follow a former logging tramway near Rosebery to reach Tassie's highest waterfall. It's a beautiful 11.5km-return walk or bike ride. The suspension bridge at the trail's end provides an airy look onto the waterfall.

03 Stitt Falls It couldn't be easier to see Stitt Falls. Just a five-minute walk from the road, in the heart of Rosebery, is a purpose-built lookout where you can view the falls side-on.

02 Horsetail Falls Reach this seasonal 50m waterfall, best in winter and spring, by following a level boardwalk that traverses the slopes of Mt Owen. Lovely mountain views even when the falls are dry.

05 Hogarth Falls From Strahan's People's Park, follow fern-lined, platypus-inhabited Botanical Creek to the base of the falls – be alert to the slippery rocks at the base of the stairs down to the falls.

01 Nelson Falls An easy stroll from the Lyell Hwy, this 20-minute-return nature trail heads through thick, mossy forest to the fanning falls that are spectacular after heavy rain.

FROM LEFT: STEVE TODD/SHUTTERSTOCK, SPINNING DUCK/SHUTTERSTOCK

Listings

BEST OF THE REST

West Coast Welcome

Empire Hotel $$

This 1901 Queenstown institution – the Grand Old Lady of the West – has a lovely traditional dining room, open fire, heritage-listed staircase and a menu of traditional Tassie pub grub.

Coffee Shack $

Cute little tin shack across from Strahan's main wharf serving coffee, homestyle baking and small bites. Indoor and outdoor seating, with blankets provided for cooler days (aka most days).

Orange Pete's $

Come for a coffee or toastie, but get lost in the orange decor at this Queenstown cafe and the orange suits of the very characterful Pete.

Tracks Cafe $$

Railway-station cafe at the Queenstown departure point for West Coast Wilderness Railway trips. Good for pre-rail breakfast or a post-rail celebration over its own brew, the Mt Lyell Mongrel Lager.

Pitstop Café $

Only in Zeehan would you find a locally made log cabin converted into a retro cafe with motor memorabilia on display. Service is friendly and the homemade sausage rolls are a winner.

Risby Cove $$$

Views across the cove to Strahan's wharf complement the short menu of local fish, beef and house-made gnocchi.

Northwest Nibbles

Pam's Bottles & Cups $$

Pink-walled and mirror-balled decor sets the tone in this laneway Devonport cocktail bar with a finely honed wine list and great seasonal restaurant bites.

Laneway $$

Devonport's cool kids gather over breakfast at this stellar cafe in, you guessed it, a laneway.

Hursey Seafoods $$

Look beyond the warehouse-like exterior – with its own fishing fleet moored metres away, you know things are fresh at this Stanley restaurant with dining upstairs and takeaways downstairs.

Foreshore $$

Local favourite on the Burnie beachfront serving up quality Tasmanian seafood alongside burgers, breakfasts, a decent wine list and Bass Strait views.

T's $$

Paddock-to-plate Chinese, in Sheffield, with heritage-breed meats direct from the owner's farm, all cheerfully served by Bella the robot waiter.

Mrs Jones $$$

Restaurant above the Devonport surf club with huge floor-to-ceiling windows offering spectacular views of Bass Strait. Contemporary menu with a focus on seasonal, sustainable produce.

The Vault $$

Heritage-listed bank building by the Inglis River in Wynyard that has been repurposed into a cafe and wine bar. Outdoor seating with a view, and Tassie's coolest wall of books inside.

Oleada $$$

Tiny, cosy and pasted in maps, friendly Oleada in Currie delivers Italian-accented dining brimming with island produce, beers and spirits.

VDL Creamery $

Cafe and ice-cream factory in Elizabeth Town that produces more than 20 flavours of ice cream and gelato using fresh Tasmanian ingredients such as leatherwood honey, pepperberry and whisky.

Bruce's Cafe $$

Casual Wynyard beachside eatery with a simple but flavour-filled menu. There's a kids' play area and plenty of homemade desserts.

The Chapel $$

A longtime Burnie favourite, this licensed cafe occupies a former city church, pouring a different form of spirits and serving up Burnie's best breakfasts.

Bar, Bar

Stanley Wine Bar

This wine bar's street cred is unquestionable – it was awarded Best Tasmanian Small Bar Wine List in 2025 – but you might even want to come just for the cabinet-of-curiosities interior (think steampunk meets farmhouse).

Penguin Beer Co

This welcoming brew-bar pours its own creations while holding place as the only true waterfront venue in Penguin.

Empress Craft Beer

Pouring 14 taps of craft beers hand-selected from near and far – Ulverstone to the world – inside a Devonport shopping centre.

Moonscape

Cafe meets wine bar meets beer garden – make whatever you like of this likeable Queenstown venue.

PENGUIN BEER CO

Penguin Beer Co

Arts & Heritage

QBank Gallery

Old Queenstown bank building with a studio space for artists-in-residence and an accompanying gallery where the artists exhibit.

Wee Georgie Wood Steam Railway

A 1924 narrow-gauge steam locomotive that runs 20-minute rides through the centre of Tullah, from a time when the railway was the only way into the town. Great fun for kids and lovers of nostalgia.

Gaiety Theatre

Visit Zeehan's West Coast Heritage Centre to step into this 1898 theatre and watch surviving snippets of the world's first feature film, *The Story of the Kelly Gang* (1907), or the B&W silent *Jewelled Nights* (1926).

Galley Museum

Volunteer-managed collection sprawling through 30 rooms of the former Imperial Hotel in Queenstown. Exhibits include a massive mineral collection and reminders of Queenstown's 1912 mine disaster that killed 42 men.

Spray Tunnel

A 100m-long abandoned railway tunnel near Zeehan originally connected to a silver mine.

Wander through in the dark to spy its glow-worm colony.

Burnie Art Deco Trail

Burnie's industrial boom in the 1930s coincided with the growing popularity of art deco architecture. A self-guided trail (tashistory.com/burnie-art-deco-walk) leads to 25 of the best examples.

Devonport Regional Gallery

Vibrant contemporary arts centre with three gallery spaces, housed in the paranaple arts centre. Hosts work by local artists and touring exhibitions, and presents the biennial Tidal festival.

Bass Strait Maritime Museum

Devonport museum devoted to local maritime history, including shipwrecks, industry and the First Mariners Sea Country People display, looking at Tasmania's Aboriginal seafarers and canoe-building traditions. Try the SS *Woniora* simulator to see how you do at the helm of a steamship.

Get Active

Mt Owen Mountain Biking

Running like scribbles through Queenstown's denuded landscape are the testing trails on the slopes of Mt Owen. Easier runs are on the lower slopes, with the tough stuff up top.

Rafting the Franklin River

One of the world's great rafting adventures, running the mythologised Franklin in an off-grid, eight- to 10-day adventure through the heart of Tasmania's Wilderness World Heritage area. Guided trips are run by several professional companies.

Arthur River Canoe & Boat Hire

Paddle up the Arthur River for a Takayna/Tarkine picnic, or set out on a two- or four-day self-guided wilderness paddle down the river.

Meander Wilderness Experiences

Carry a Lilo-like 'sled' to the bank of the Meander River, then plunge into its rapids and pilot yourself downstream on this gentle guided tour at the edge of the World Heritage area.

Scenic Spots

Lake Mackintosh

A beautiful lake near Tullah managed by Hydro Tasmania, stocked with trout and surrounded by myrtle, sassafras and eucalypt forest. There are walking tracks around the lake and plenty of picnic spots.

Donaghys Hill

Easy 2.2km-return walk to a lookout point with wide views of the Franklin River and Frenchmans Cap. The gradual uphill track passes through cool temperate rainforest, mosses and lichen.

Franklin Nature Trail

Scenic short walk (1km return), partly on boardwalk, through mossy rainforest to the bank of Tasmania's most celebrated river. A great place to stop and stretch your legs on the drive between Queenstown and Derwent Bridge.

Mt Murchison

One of Tassie's best day walks for experienced hikers. Expect rock scrambling and steep sections on your way to the summit of the highest peak in the West Coast Range. Well worth it for the wilderness panoramas.

Mt Roland

If Cradle Mountain has a competitor for the title of most prominent peak in the region, it's craggy Mt Roland. The four- to six-hour return walk begins at Gowrie Park.

Spion Kop Lookout

Short but steep 300m walkway on the eastern edge of Queenstown. Named after a Boer

War battle, the walk is paved and includes several mining exhibits and interpretation boards along the way.

Mole Creek Karst National Park

Among the 500-plus caves that puncture this karst landscape, two are open for ranger-led guided tours. The larger of the pair, Marakoopa, has glow worms for bright company.

Mt Farrell

The moderately challenging walk up this rugged trail (4.3km each way) rewards hikers with spectacular 360-degree views of orange-hued buttongrass slopes, mountain peaks and crystal-clear lakes.

Shop Till You Drop

Lake Leather

Tasmanian institution supplying fine leather goods and accessories. Started as a market stall, but its third shop opened on the Esplanade in Strahan in 2022.

Leven Antiques Centre & Fern Oasis

Friendly antique centre in Ulverstone catering for all budgets. Ceramics, silver, jewellery and collectibles are beautifully arranged and browsers are welcome. You can even pick up a fern to go with your purchase.

Cow & Calf Gallery

The gallery of local photographer David Murphy is like a sightseeing journey of its own, with beautiful images from Murphy and more.

Wattlebird Yarn

Studio shop in Latrobe selling hand-dyed Australian merino sock-weight yarn. The beautiful colours have to be seen to be believed.

Missing Tiger

Small, independently run Queenstown bookshop with a wide range of secondhand titles, novels by Tasmanian authors, and history books about the west coast. It's a real community hub and often exhibits work by local artists.

Providore 24

Stanley's speciality food shop showcasing premium Tasmanian produce. Gather fresh deli foods, sweet treats and beverages to take on a picnic or to stave off hunger on hikes and drives.

Huon Pine Shop & Gallery

Attached to Morrison's Huon Pine Sawmill, selling all things Huon pine, from bags of wood shavings to dining tables worth tens of thousands of dollars. Check the mill shelves for shapely offcuts if you fancy making something of your own.

Unusual Stays

Coastal Pods Wynyard

River's-edge shipping containers cobbled together like Jenga pieces. The tiny reading rooms are worth the money alone, and you need only step out your door to find waterside fish and chips.

Compass Hut

Three self-contained, off-grid tiny houses balanced on the slopes of a farm 10 minutes' drive from Devonport. Supremely peaceful, with sheep as your noisiest neighbours.

Mt Gnomon Farm

In the shadow of the Dial Range, five geodesic domes circled around the heritage-breed farm's sundial-inspired veggie garden. Choose your dome according to its perspective: ocean, mountain, sunset.

Practicalities

Opposite: Pademelons, Flinders Island (p156)

EASY STEPS FROM THE AIRPORT TO THE CITY CENTRE

Hobart is the principal port of arrival for most visitors. The airport is 18km east of the city centre, and is a single terminal – though decreed an international airport, its only international flights are to New Zealand, so almost every visitor arrives on domestic flights from the Australian mainland. You can also fly into Launceston, Devonport and Burnie, while the* Spirit of Tasmania *vehicle ferry connects Devonport to Geelong (Victoria).

AT THE AIRPORT

JAX10289/GETTY IMAGES

SIM CARDS
SIM cards aren't available at the airport (since almost every visitor is coming from another Australian state). If you do need a SIM card, head into the city centre, where there are plenty of stores selling them.

CURRENCY EXCHANGE
Facilities are non-existent at the airport, due to the fact that almost every flight is domestic. Change at least some money ahead of arrival, and then head into a bank or moneychanger in the city centre if you need more cash.

FREE WI-FI Wi-fi is available throughout the terminal, including the taxi and SkyBus terminal. Look for the Hobart Airport Free Wi-Fi network.

ATMS These are in the arrivals hall (beside the Saffire lounge) and in the departures lounge (near the Tasmania & Beyond store).

CHARGING STATIONS These facilities aren't available, but the benches beside the central bar in the departures lounge have power sockets.

BIOSECURITY That cute pooch greeting you as you step off the plane into the airport terminal isn't there for the pats and admiration. Sniffer dogs are present because of Tasmania's strict island biosecurity measures – no fresh fruit, vegetables, fish or honey are allowed to be brought into the state. Bin them before you board your flight.

GETTING TO THE CITY CENTRE

SKYBUS Shuttle buses meet every flight and stop at six locations in the city, including the MONA ferry and four CBD hotels. Pick-up is across the forecourt outside the airport terminal doors, and tickets can be purchased online *(skybus.com.au)* or from ticket machines by the baggage carousels.

UBER
Pick-up (and drop-off) is almost immediately across the road from the taxi rank, directly across the forecourt from the terminal.

BUSES
Metro public buses don't run to the airport; the closest they get is Seven Mile Beach.

TAXI Taxis pick up from directly opposite the terminal doors – cross the forecourt and road, and step directly into a car. A taxi into the city centre will cost around $55 and take about 25 minutes.

DISCOUNTS If you plan to get around Hobart by bus, pick up a Metro Greencard (metrotas.com.au) for ease and a 20% discount on fares. There is no other form of public transport in the city (or state), with no passenger train services operating.

OTHER POINTS OF ENTRY

Launceston Airport is 13km south of the city centre, near Evandale, and has flights to and from Melbourne, Sydney, Brisbane and Adelaide. Wild Island Adventures runs an airport-shuttle service between the airport and the city, dropping passengers at any hotel, motel or hostel in the city centre.

Devonport Airport has flights to/from Melbourne, and is 10km east of the city centre. Call the Devonport Shuttle Service for pickups.

Burnie Airport is in the town of Wynyard, 20km west of Burnie. It has flights to/from Melbourne (as well as to King Island). There's no shuttle service to the airport, but there is a Metro bus stop in Dodgin St, 300m from the terminal.

Car ferries to Devonport dock in East Devonport, on the Mersey River's eastern bank. Ferries sail to and from Geelong (one hour's drive west of Melbourne). There are day and night sailings, and the ships tend to book up well ahead, especially in summer, so plan accordingly. The sailing takes around 10 hours.

TRANSPORT TIPS TO HELP YOU GET AROUND

The only way to really get under Tasmania's skin is to have your own wheels. Reaching anywhere away from the main cities is a mission in anything but your own vehicle, which also allows you to stop and savour those roadside walks and attractions that are so abundant in Tasmania. Getting to places on Tasmania's wiggly roads takes longer than you expect.

CAR & CAMPERVAN HIRE

Rental companies have desks in Hobart and Launceston airports, and the island is ideal for a campervan lap. The temptation can be to rush to complete the lap, but expect reasons to stop around any bend.

ROADKILL

You can't fail to notice the volume of roadkill across Tasmania's roads – hundreds of thousands of animals are killed every year. Try to avoid driving at dawn or dusk, when wildlife activity can be frenetic.

HOW MUCH FOR...

Car rental per day from $150

Petrol approx $1.80/litre

Bus from Hobart to Launceston $17

FERRIES Bruny Island is a 20-minute ferry ride from Kettering and Maria Island is 30 minutes by ferry from Triabunna. If travelling up the west coast between Zeehan and Smithton, the Pieman River at Corinna is crossed on the Fatman barge.

BUSES Bus services in Tasmania are patchy and infrequent. Kinetic runs the major service between Hobart, Launceston, Devonport, Burnie and Smithton (and places between), while Tassielink can get you from Hobart to the east coast, Tasman Peninsula and Huon Valley, and along the west coast from Burnie.

DRIVING ESSENTIALS

KEEP LEFT

Drive on the left; the steering wheel is on the right.

100

The speed limit in built-up areas is 50km/h. On the highway it's 100km/h or 110km/h.

Blood alcohol limit is 0.05%.

21

Drivers must typically be 21 years or older to rent a car.

Those road signs that appear to show a giant kangaroo overturning a car? They're simply warning of the presence of wallabies. Phew.

PLANES Intercity passenger flights don't exist in Tasmania, but King Island is serviced from Launceston and Burnie, and Flinders Island can be reached from Launceston and Bridport (as well as an uncomfortable weekly ferry service from Bridport), while it's a week of wilderness walking or a Par Avion flight to remote Melaleuca, the start or finish of the South Coast Track.

BIKE TOURING Tasmania's compact shape has made it a favourite with cycle tourers flying into Launceston or Hobart and pedalling the east (particularly) or west coast, or riding the full lap. The west coast is the hilly coast, while the east coast is flatter and sits in a rain shadow, making for typically sunny and dry cycling. Long Haul Tasmania hires bikes that can be picked up/dropped off in Hobart and Launceston.

TRAINS Tasmania has no passenger rail services, but you can experience the rail life on a few surviving tourist railways – the West Coast Wilderness Railway (p228) between Queenstown and Strahan, the Don River Railway near Devonport, and the Wee Georgie Wood Steam Railway (p235) in Tullah.

4WD TRACKS The bulk of Tassie's 4WD-ing is on the west coast. Before hitting the tracks, read the Parks and Wildlife Service's 'Off Road Vehicles' page for route ideas and its code-of-conduct notes.

KNOW YOUR CARBON FOOTPRINT A domestic flight from Melbourne to Hobart will emit around 200kg of carbon dioxide per passenger, while a flight from Sydney to Hobart will emit around 270kg of carbon dioxide.

There are a number of carbon calculators online. Try co2.myclimate.org.

ROAD DISTANCE CHART (KM)

	St Helens	Burnie	Coles Bay	Cradle Mountain	Devonport	Hobart	Stanley	Launceston	Port Arthur
Burnie	290								
Coles Bay	115	300							
Cradle Mountain	285	100	293						
Devonport	250	45	255	77					
Hobart	252	325	195	320	280				
Stanley	370	80	375	175	125	403			
Launceston	165	145	175	140	100	202	215		
Port Arthur	260	380	200	375	335	95	450	255	
Strahan	415	180	425	137	223	301	240	270	375

SAFE TRAVEL

Tasmania is one of the world's safest destinations, with low crime rates and little history of natural disasters beyond bushfires. Narrow roads surrounded by gobsmacking scenery could be the greatest risk you'll encounter, though the surprisingly remote wilderness demands preparation and respect.

BUSHFIRES Tasmania carries a very real threat of fires, and the state carries a heavy fuel load. The Tasmania Fire Service (fire.tas.gov.au) posts fire alerts and daily fire weather forecasts. Local ABC radio stations broadcast detailed fire information during bushfires.

SNAKES There's surety in the knowledge that all three of Tasmania's snake species are venomous – you simply don't go near any snakes here, if you can help it. Learn ahead how to apply a pressure immobilisation bandage. If bitten, immobilise the person and call 000. Snake bites from all three species are treated with the same anti-venom.

JACK JUMPERS It might come as a surprise to learn that Tasmania's most dangerous animal is an ant, with more deaths from jack-jumper stings than from sharks or snakes. Watch for their pincers and aggressive, stilted movements as they protect their nests. Up to 3% of the population is allergic to their venom, which can cause anaphylaxis.

DRINKING WATER Tap water is safe to drink across the state. Water from wilderness rivers often appears brown – this is tannin staining from the vegetation and is safe (and tasteless) to drink.

COJOCEARO/SHUTTERSTOCK

ORSO BIANCO/SHUTTERSTOCK

SAFETY ON THE TRAIL If you're heading into the bush, Personal Locator Beacons (PLBs or EPIRBs) can be hired from Service Tasmania centres in Hobart, Launceston, Devonport and Burnie. Demand is high – book well ahead. Carry a map, compass and first-aid kit.

INSURANCE
Things go wrong, even in Tasmania, so be sure to have a good travel-insurance policy, taking particular note as to whether it excludes designated 'dangerous activities', which sometimes even means bushwalking.

OUT OF RANGE
Outside of cities and towns, mobile-phone coverage is patchy at best. Don't rely on your phone for emergency communication – always let someone know of your plans if you're heading to a remote location.

QUICK TIPS TO HELP YOU MANAGE YOUR MONEY

CREDIT CARDS Cash is the unloved cousin of the all-conquering credit card in Tasmania these days – some venues are fully cashless. Mastercard and Visa are the most widely accepted, welcomed by everyone from car-rental agencies to hotels, restaurants and market stalls. If cash is needed, credit cards can be used to get cash advances from many ATMs.

CURRENCY

Australian dollar

HOW MUCH FOR A...

Flat white $6

Shot of whisky from $18

Dinner for two $100

PAYING THE BILL

Restaurants vary in policy around whether to pay the bill at the table or head to the counter to pay. In cafes, you almost universally pay at the counter.

TIPPING

About as rare as Tasmanian tigers – ie non-existent – though it's not uncommon to round up the fare in a taxi, or add 10% to a restaurant bill if the service is good.

MONEY CHANGERS

Tasmania has very few money-changing services outside of banks – hunt around in the cities and you will find an occasional one aimed at international students.

BARGAINING

You'll likely get blank stares if you try to haggle for an item, even at markets. The price tag is typically the price tag.

FOOD, FUEL, FLIP! Tasmania has traditionally been Australia's poorest state, but that hasn't stopped food and fuel prices from skyrocketing. Grocery prices are higher than in most other states, and petrol is among the country's most expensive, though the daily fluctuations you see in petrol prices in other states are mostly absent here.

BUDGETING With Tasmania's penchant for high-quality food, craft beer, whisky and wine (Tasmanian wines sell at the high end of the market), it pays to have a budget that flexes. However, the state's mass of wilderness and national parks makes it easy to have frugal days out (beyond the pricey park passes). Once inside a park, the only currency you pay in is trail snacks and boot leather. The cost of tours can quickly add up, but few attractions demand ransoms for entry.

DISCOUNTS & SAVINGS Tasmania has no discount cards aimed at travellers, but most sights offer reduced-rate entry to seniors, young children and families.

RESPONSIBLE TRAVEL

Tips to leave a lighter footprint, support local and have a positive impact on local communities.

ON THE ROAD

Calculate your carbon by emissions using any number of online carbon calculators. Try carbon positiveaustralia.org.au.

Hire an electric vehicle at car-rental agencies in Tasmania, including locally owned Drive Car Hire, which typically now have electric and hybrid vehicles for hire in Hobart and Launceston.

E-scooters were introduced to Hobart and Launceston in late 2021 – look for the purple scooters – making for an emissions-free way to hop between city sights.

Bike hire is available in the two major cities. Try Hobart Bike Hire and Roll Cycles (Hobart and Launceston).

Phytophthora (root rot) is a plant pathogen that gets into the roots of trees and eventually kills them. Help stop the spread by cleaning your shoes or boots after walks, and using the dedicated cleaning stations along many of the state's walking tracks.

Drones are not permitted in national parks.

GIVE BACK

Purchase a Parks Pass before visiting any national park – the money goes back into the parks system.

Tasmanian Land Conservancy is a not-for-profit organisation raising funds to purchase and protect private land in Tasmania. Donations can be made through its website.

Wildcare Tasmania is a volunteer organisation with more than 60 groups working in natural and cultural protection across the state.

Looking to help out while in Tasmania? Get in touch with Volunteering Tasmania (volunteeringtas.org.au).

Look for companies running tours associated with the Green Guardians program, which incorporate small-scale conservation projects (removing weeds along rivers, shorebird surveys etc) into trips.

TAYLOR WILSON SMITH/SHUTTERSTOCK

SUPPORT LOCAL

Seek out local produce at markets and the state's rich selection of local grocers.

Buy gifts and souvenirs from businesses that support local artists and makers, such as Design Tasmania (pictured below) and Spacebar Gallery.

Keep Tassie Wild donates half of all profits from sales of its popular T-shirts, patches and caps to Tasmanian environmental organisations.

NESS VANDERBURGH FOR LONELY PLANET

DOS & DON'TS

Don't feed wildlife – processed food can cause a condition called 'lumpy jaw' that kills animals.

Do look for local Aboriginal experiences, which have begun to emerge in recent years, providing a new perspective on history, culture and country.

Don't have campfires in national parks. They're permitted only in Narawntapu National Park and at Fortescue Bay in Tasman National Park.

LEAVE A SMALL FOOTPRINT

Follow the seven Leave No Trace principles when bushwalking and camping (parks.tas.gov.au/explore-our-parks/know-before-you-go/leave-no-trace).

Stick to tracks when bushwalking and 4WDing. Read the Parks and Wildlife Service's 'Off Road Vehicles' page for the code of conduct for 4WDs.

Take the Maria Island Pledge before heading to Maria Island (eastcoasttasmania.com/maria-island-pledge).

Pitch your tent at least 50m from any waterway or lake, and don't use soap anywhere near the water.

RESOURCES

passes.parks.tas.gov.au

wildcaretas.org.au

tasclimatecollective.org

bobbrown.org.au

parks.tas.gov.au/explore-our-parks/know-before-you-go/leave-no-trace

CLIMATE CHANGE & TRAVEL It's impossible to ignore the impact we have when travelling, and the importance of making changes where we can. Lonely Planet urges all travellers to engage with their travel carbon footprint. There are many carbon calculators online that allow travellers to estimate the carbon emissions generated by their journey; try resurgence.org/carbon-calculator. Many airlines and booking sites offer travellers the option of offsetting the impact of greenhouse gas emissions by contributing to climate-friendly initiatives around the world. We continue to offset the carbon footprint of all Lonely Planet staff travel, while recognising this is a mitigation more than a solution.

UNIQUE & LOCAL WAYS TO STAY

Tasmania is the kind of place where you can find million-dollar views for a few dollars, or a couple of thousand. Options range from campsites hidden behind empty beaches to the full-luxe primp and pamper of a world-class luxury lodge. A beachside shack will immerse you in the local way of holiday life.

HOW MUCH FOR A NIGHT IN...

National park campsite free–$13

Glamping from $290

Saffire Freycinet luxury lodge $3100

KAREL STIPEK/GETTY IMAGES

CAMPING Pick almost any favourite natural location – Freycinet, Cradle Mountain, Takayna/Tarkine, the Southwest – and there's a camping ground to put you within it. Apart from the most popular camping grounds, such as Richardsons Beach (Freycinet) and Fortescue Bay (Turrakana/Tasman Peninsula), national park campsites are typically first-come, first-served. Caravan parks are plentiful; find a full directory at caravanparks tasmania.com.

GLAMPING The glamping phenomenon has well and truly landed in Tasmania, where there are opportunities to flash up the camping experience at places such as Larapuna/Bay of Fires, the Tamar Valley, Sisters Beach, the Derwent Valley, Richmond and Port Arthur. Expect everything from king-size beds to outdoor baths, fire pits and resident wildlife.

RAY WARREN CREATIVE/ALAMY

LUXURY RETREATS As Tasmania's high-end tourist market has grown over recent years, so too have the off-the-scale luxe possibilities. Saffire Freycinet has led the charge, and you can stay atop the waters of Lake St Clair at Pumphouse Point, have a personal butler on the Hobart waterfront at MACq 01, rule the forest in a private tower at The Keep, go castaway on a private island on Picnic Island, or step into heritage luxury at the likes of Quamby Estate. The options are only limited by your budget.

CHAMELEONSEYE/SHUTTERSTOCK

TASSIE SHACKS

The humble (and often not so humble) beachfront shack is an enduring Tasmanian family institution. In places such as Freycinet Peninsula and the west coast, they have become as much a part of the landscape as they are a place to stay, presenting a chance to experience a slice of local holiday life.

Prices range from as low as $100 a night for a basic, original shack to $700 for plush modern takes on the genre at the likes of Captains Rest (Strahan) and Sea Stacks (Bicheno).

East Coast

Shacks line this holiday coast, with their epicentre at Coles Bay on Freycinet Peninsula, a longtime Tasmanian weekend favourite – the shacks at the Fisheries, a community now enclosed by Freycinet National Park, sprang up in the 1920s. Look to local holiday-home rental services such as freycinetrentals.com and freycinetholidayhouses.com.au.

West Coast

Get a taste of old-school shack existence at a string of tiny coastal settlements, including Trial Harbour, Granville Harbour, Couta Rocks and Nelson Bay. The shacks at Lettes Bay, just outside of Strahan, were built for employees of the Mt Lyell Mining and Railway Company early last century. Today, a number of them have been converted into chic seaside shacks for rent. Look for Captains Rest, Bushy Summers and Salt Box Hideaway.

BOOKING Book well in advance in peak tourist seasons, which in Tasmania are largely through the summer school holidays (about a week before Christmas to early February) and around Easter. Tasmanians love a long-weekend getaway – keep an eye on public-holiday dates because there are a couple that are unique to the state (and even different ones in different parts of the island). Big-ticket events such as Dark Mofo also put a strain on occupancy.

Discover Tasmania (discovertasmania.com) Tasmania's official tourism website features almost all of the state's accommodation offerings, with links to operators' websites for bookings.

Tasmania Luxury Accommodation (tasmanialuxuryaccommodation.com.au) The island's high-end world of resorts, boutique hotels, luxury B&Bs and swish shacks.

Green Getaways Australia (greengetawaysaustralia.com.au) Concise listings of environmentally aware accommodation, with around 16 Tasmanian properties.

Airbnb (airbnb.com.au) Global homestay accommodation provider with more than 1000 options across Tasmania.

CITY HOTELS

A rash of hotel openings have transformed the offerings across Hobart and Launceston in recent years. The city centres are filling with chain names, while boutique offerings are adding charm to the urban experience.

ESSENTIAL NUTS & BOLTS

SMOKING
Smoking is banned in indoor public spaces, and also in vehicles carrying children under the age of 18.

TOILETS
Find public toilets across the state on the National Public Toilet Map (toiletmap.gov.au). They are universally free to use in Tasmania.

PUBLIC HOLIDAYS Public holidays specific to Tasmania are Hobart Regatta Day (February; southern Tasmania), Launceston Cup (February; Launceston), Recreation Day (November; northern Tasmania) and local Royal Show days.

FAST FACTS

Time Zone
GMT+10

Country Code
03

Electricity
220V/50Hz

GOOD TO KNOW

Etiquette on escalators and stairs: stand on the left, walk on the right.

It's illegal to possess an open container of alcohol in a public street. Drinking in parks or on beaches is allowed where council by-laws permit.

The legal drinking age in Tasmania is 18.

To contact local police for a non-emergency situation, call 131 444.

Find complete topographic mapping of the state at maps.thelist.tas.gov.au.

ACCESSIBLE TRAVEL

Facilities for wheelchairs are improving in accommodation, but there are still many older establishments where upgrades haven't been implemented.

All-terrain TrailRider wheelchairs are available for free at Cradle Mountain and Freycinet and Mt Field national parks, and also via the Hobart City Council. Book through the park visitor centres.

Find the City of Hobart Mobility Map through the Hobart City Council website (hobartcity.com.au).

Access-friendly walking tracks include Russell Falls (Mt Field National Park), Tamar Island (Launceston), Nelson Falls (Franklin-Gordon Wild Rivers National Park), Tahune AirWalk, Cape Tourville (Freycinet National Park), Fern Glade (Burnie) and the Goblin Forest Walk (near Derby).

Check out Parks and Wildlife Services 'Access friendly' page for information about accessibility in national parks.

Motorised wheelchairs and scooters are permitted within national parks and reserves.

The Wheelie Good Guide (wheeliegoodguide.com.au) is an invaluable resource for travellers, with accessibility details on accommodation, attractions, parks and reserves (outside of national parks), events and transport.

City bus timetables in Hobart, Launceston and Burnie display a wheelchair icon to indicate wheelchair-accessible bus services.

TELEPHONES
There are about 450 (free) public telephones left in Tasmania, some in places that struggle for mobile-phone reception.

DINNER ETIQUETTE
If you're invited to someone's house for dinner, bring a bottle of wine or some beers.

WORK
Seasonal fruit-picking work can typically be found in the Huon and Tamar valleys from December to April.

BIOSECURITY To protect Tasmania's 'disease-free' agricultural status, fresh fruit, vegetables and plants cannot be brought into the state. Visitors must discard all such items prior to their arrival. There are sniffer dogs at the airports, and quarantine inspection posts at the Devonport ferry terminal.

FAMILY TRAVEL

Wildlife is more readily seen in Tasmanian national parks than in most other parts of the country, making it easy to keep kids happy in parks and reserves.

Children are permitted to travel without car seats in taxis in Tasmania, but taxi companies can organise them if requested.

Children aged six and under often get free admission into attractions, with kids aged seven to 17 at discounted rates.

Distances between towns and attractions are short, making for stress-free family travel.

WILD NAMES If you're here to see wildlife, you'll need to learn a few local abbreviations and nicknames. If you hear 'OBP', it's the endangered orange-bellied parrot; Tasmanian devils are simply 'devils'; and the Tasmanian native hen, which darts about madly, is better known as the 'turbo chook'.

YELLOWSARAH/GETTY IMAGES

LGBTIQ+ TRAVELLERS

In 1997 Tasmania became the last Australian state to decriminalise homosexuality, and LGBTIQ-rights groups now consider homosexual and heterosexual people to have greater equality under the law in Tasmania than they do in most other Australian states.

Most urban bars and venues are open-minded.

TasPride (taspride.com) is a statewide support group and a good source of upcoming events, including February's annual TasPride Festival.

Working It Out (workingitout.org.au) is another Tasmanian support and education service, with a list of local events on its homepage.

Index

000 Map pages

D

E

F

G

H

000 Map pages

000 Map pages

'Hitting the west coast during heavy rain to find Nelson, Horsetail and Montezuma falls pumping unseasonally with water.'

ANDREW BAIN

'Paying $31 for a half-dozen fresh Pacific oysters in Adelaide, then $9 en route to Turrakana/Tasman Peninsula a week later. Priceless!'

CHARLES RAWLINGS-WAY

THIS BOOK

The 2nd edition of Lonely Planet's Tasmania guidebook was written and researched by Andrew Bain and Charles Rawlings-Way. Previous edition writers include Ruth Dawkins and Rani Milne. This guidebook was produced by the following:

Destination Editor
Jessica Lockhart

Production Editor
Kathryn Rowan

Cartographer
Valentina Kremenchutskaya

Image Researcher
Katherine Marsh

Coordinating Editor
Mani Ramaswamy

Assisting Editors
Alice Barnes-Brown, Ailbhe MacMahon, Charlotte Orr

Cover Researcher
Sam Ubinas